After Patriarchy

FAITH MEETS FAITH

An Orbis Series in Interreligious Dialogue

Paul F. Knitter, General Editor

In our contemporary world, the many religions and spiritualities stand in need of greater intercommunication and cooperation. More than ever before, they must speak to, learn from, and work with each other, in order to maintain their own identity and vitality and so to contribute to fashioning a better world.

FAITH MEETS FAITH seeks to promote interreligious dialogue by providing an open forum for the exchanges between and among followers of different religious paths. While the series wants to encourage creative and bold responses to the new questions of pluralism confronting religious persons today, it also recognizes the present plurality of perspectives concerning the methods and content of interreligious dialogue.

This series, therefore, does not want to endorse any one school of thought. By making available to both the scholarly community and the general public works that represent a variety of religious and methodological viewpoints, FAITH MEETS FAITH hopes to foster and focus the emerging encounter among the religions of the world.

Already published:

Toward a Universal Theology of Religion, Leonard Swidler, Editor
The Myth of Christian Uniqueness, John Hick and Paul F. Knitter, Editors
An Asian Theology of Liberation, Aloysius Pieris, S.J.
The Dialogical Imperative, David Lochhead
Love Meets Wisdom, Aloysius Pieris, S.J.
Many Paths, Eugene Hillman, C.S.Sp.
The Silence of God, Raimundo Panikkar
The Challenge of the Scriptures, Groupe de Recherches
    Islamo-Chrétien
The Meaning of Christ, John P. Keenan
Hindu-Christian Dialogue, Harold Coward, Editor
The Emptying God, John B. Cobb, Jr. and Christopher Ives, Editors
Christianity through Non-Christian Eyes, Paul J. Griffiths, Editor
Christian Uniqueness Reconsidered, Gavid D'Costa, Editor
Women Speaking, Women Listening, Maura O'Neill
Bursting the Bonds?, Leonard Swidler, Lewis John Eron, Lester Dean, and
    Gerard Sloyan
One Christ—Many Religions, Stanley J. Samartha
The New Universalism, David J. Krieger
Jesus Christ at the Encounter of World Religions, Jacques Dupuis, S.J.

FAITH MEETS FAITH SERIES

After Patriarchy

Feminist Transformations
of the World Religions

Edited by
Paula M. Cooey
William R. Eakin
Jay B. McDaniel

ORBIS BOOKS

Maryknoll, New York 10545

The Catholic Foreign Mission Society of America (Maryknoll) recruits and trains people for overseas missionary service. Through Orbis Books, Maryknoll aims to foster the international dialogue that is essential to mission. The books published, however, reflect the opinions of their authors and are not meant to represent the official position of the society.

Permission is gratefully acknowledged to Harper & Row publishers for reprinting "Transforming the Nature of Community," from *Standing Again at Sinai* by Judith Plaskow, © 1990 by Judith Plaskow

Library of Congress Cataloging-in-Publication Data

After patriarchy : feminist transformations of the world religions /
    edited by Paula M. Cooey, William R. Eakin, Jay B. McDaniel.
        p.   cm.
    ISBN 0-88344-749-5 (hard) ISBN 0-88344-748-7 (pbk.)
    1. Religions—Controversial literature.   2. Women and religion.
    3. Patriarchy—Religious aspects—Controversial literature.
    I. Cooey, Paula M. 1945-   .   II. Eakin, William R.   III. McDaniel,
    Jay B. (Jay Byrd), 1949-   .
    BL85.A44   1991
    291'.082—dc20   91-3287
                                                            CIP

To our children, present and future

To Benjamin Charles Cooey-Nichols
Benjamin Wade Eakin
Dylan Christopher Eakin
Hannah Erin Eakin
John Byrd McDaniel, IV
and Matthew Himmel McDaniel

Contents

INTRODUCTION   ix
Paula M. Cooey, William R. Eakin, Jay B. McDaniel

1. BLACK WOMEN'S SURROGACY EXPERIENCE AND THE CHRISTIAN
   NOTION OF REDEMPTION   1
   Delores S. Williams

2. KALI, THE SAVIOR   15
   Lina Gupta

3. MUSLIM WOMEN AND POST-PATRIARCHAL ISLAM   39
   Riffat Hassan

4. BUDDHISM AFTER PATRIARCHY?   65
   Rita M. Gross

5. TRANSFORMING THE NATURE OF COMMUNITY   87
   Toward a Feminist People of Israel
   Judith Plaskow

6. THE REDEMPTION OF THE BODY   106
   Post-Patriarchal Reconstruction of Inherited Christian
   Doctrine
   Paula M. Cooey

7. IMAGES OF THE FEMININE IN APACHE RELIGIOUS TRADITION   131
   Ines Talamantez

8. THE SPIRITUAL, POLITICAL JOURNEY OF A FEMINIST FREETHINKER   146
   Emily Culpepper

CONTRIBUTORS   167

Introduction

PAULA M. COOEY, WILLIAM R. EAKIN, JAY B. McDANIEL

"*After* patriarchy?" exclaimed one student who heard the title of this work. "Do you really think that any of the world religions can evolve *beyond* patriarchy? Don't you realize that the world religions are *inherently* patriarchal and that we must reject them *all*?"

Each of us, the three editors of this book, has been asked these questions before; we have asked them ourselves. We are teachers of religious studies in various contexts, and the questions emerge amid class discussions. In our classes and in other contexts, most of our students study the world religions, at least enough to recognize, usually to their chagrin, that almost all the religions are male-dominated. Some of them then hope that this male-domination is not essential to the religions. They hope that the religions — at least those with which they identify and sympathize — can somehow meet social and spiritual needs by transcending patriarchy. Others deem the religions hopelessly patriarchal, incapable of being appropriated either by women or by men who truly seek to move beyond patriarchy.

When we, as teachers, ask these questions, we are by no means certain of answers. But we do recognize the need for a resource, an anthology, to which students and teachers alike can turn for a sample of opinions. The needed anthology must feature feminist thinkers from *within* the various world religions who make the case that their religions *can* contribute to a post-patriarchal world. Yet it needs also to feature the dissenting view as well, the view that, at best, the religions can be but compost for post-patriarchal consciousness. We have compiled these essays to form that anthology.

As it turns out, the exponents of the various religions we have selected (and our selection of religions is not exhaustive) respond to student concerns in different ways. Some, like Lina Gupta (Hinduism) and Riffat Hassan (Islam), seek the reappropriation of what they believe to be the liberating and even essential elements of their traditions, elements in scriptures or tradition that have been suppressed, forgotten, or erased by patriarchal power relations and theory. Some, like Judith Plaskow (Judaism),

Rita Gross (Buddhism), and Paula Cooey (Christianity), emphasize reconstruction, rethinking, and reformulating the aspects of their traditions that have legitimated and encouraged oppression.

In all of the essays, however, there is an element of what must *not* be included in a post-patriarchal vision. For example, Delores Williams (Christianity) warns that any religious tradition must allow women of color, in her case African-American, to speak for themselves. In her essay she shows how the surrogacy experience of African-American women makes explicit the need for women of color to have their own voices. And in all of the essays we find proposals for ideas, images, and rituals that might help move religions beyond patriarchy. Ines Talamantez (Native American) recommends the adoption of something like a North American Indian ritualistic paradigm for nurturing women in ways many traditions have found all too foreign.

The authors just mentioned share the view that there is some hope for one or several of the world religions. In our view, if this hope can be realized, it must involve critique, reconstruction, and active engagement with other traditions. Wherever we stand, we must learn to listen, that is, to internalize insights from a Hindu-feminist reconstruction of Kali, from a Christian-feminist reinterpretation of the meaning of Christ, from a Buddhist-feminist reappropriation of the ideal of community.

A note on the order of the essays is appropriate. We begin this collection with an essay by Delores Williams because, while still operating within a given tradition, her work is most *explicitly* critical of what has come before. We then move to the work of Lina Gupta and Riffat Hassan, who exemplify most clearly attempts to reappropriate what have been integral parts of their traditions, taking the image of Kali and the Qur'an, respectively, as potential resources for critiquing patriarchy and affirming post-patriarchal vision. Then Rita M. Gross and Judith Plaskow, while remaining within their traditions and drawing liberating elements from their faiths, most clearly *reconstruct* their traditions, in many ways arguing for conditions that may very well be requisite for the continuing vitality of their faiths.

We next include an essay by Paula Cooey—a second essay in post-patriarchal Christianity—because it emphasizes and makes clear, more than any other in the book, that while a post-patriarchal vision must be one that is concerned with the well-being of women, it must also be an inclusive one concerned with the well-being of those others who have also been oppressed by patriarchy. Our post-patriarchal vision must include a concern for oppressed peoples, animal life, and the earth itself.

Finally, Ines Talamantez and Emily Culpepper propose alternatives and attitudes they feel are appropriate for post-patriarchal thought and practice irrespective of the traditions from which we come. Talamantez proposes a paradigm of nurturance and empowerment from her own tradition; Culpepper encourages a creativity not bound by any tradition.

It is our hope that as you read these essays an "interfaith dialogue" will occur in your own mind. You will place yourself in the situation of the feminist Hindu, feminist Christian, the feminist Buddhist; you will compare and contrast their journeys with your own; and you will grow in the process. We also hope that you will imaginatively place yourself in the position of the dissenter. As Culpepper makes clear, growth entails an openness to the possibility of shedding those things we hold most dear, a cutting into compost of the visions, images, and ideas of our traditions. It entails the kind of diligent questioning and re-questioning that characterizes Culpepper's essay. Culpepper argues that a project of critique and reconstruction can be nothing but a reformation, not a true transformation. For those who have been reared in a world religion, she recommends the organic shedding of that past. In her own experience, at least, she has had to view her Christian heritage as a kind of compost, a decayed organism that, though important, must be transcended.

This is a necessarily incomplete anthology because it is a finite collection of individual voices from a small number of religious backgrounds. Not all religious and conceptual perspectives can be represented. Many have been unfortunately left out, including some which have proved important in the transformation and growth of feminist thought (including much of the thought represented here). Wicce is an example. For many feminists it is a creative, liberating, and empowering alternative to the world religions. We have not included Wicce in this anthology precisely because Wicce is essentially woman-defined, and not therefore in need of the kinds of transformation explored in this volume. This distinguishes Wicce, for example, from Apache traditions (see the essay by Talamantez) which, though in certain important respects non-patriarchal, are nevertheless not exclusively woman-defined.

DEFINITIONS

However you evaluate these various attempts to appropriate, transform, or transcend world religions, some working definitions are in order to help get us started.

Patriarchy can be defined in various ways. We use the word to refer to the social organization of a culture into systems that are hierarchical and male-dominated in terms of value and power. Though slightly more fluid than the image of a pyramid suggests, patriarchy nevertheless resembles a pyramid in that an extremely small minority of people hold the greatest power over the remaining majority. The pyramid or system as a whole includes members ranked in power according to class, race, ethnicity, and creed, in terms of the interests and norms established and maintained by the minority in power. Both access to material goods and cultural capital depend in large part on one's particular rank and the extent to which ranking itself is fluid or rigid. (*Cultural capital* refers to the power, value, and authority—if not money—one gains in return for intellectual or artistic achievement according to patriarchal canons of taste.)

As the word *patriarchy* denotes, the fathers rule the system. Just as *arche* or "rule" assumes difference in rank; so, *pater* or "father" presupposes male supremacy. The chief characteristic all ranks hold in common, irrespective of all other differences, is that within the designation of class, ethnicity, or creed a woman's status, power, and authority, indeed her identity as a woman, derive from her affiliation with a man of the same rank according to whether he is her father or husband. The derivative character of woman's power, status, and authority as it influences identity usually means that her value—whether positive or negative—is secondary, subordinated to that of a man within the same rank, even though she may be ranked as superior or inferior relative to other ranks within the system. The substance of her role in society will ordinarily be determined according to a division of labor broken down along the lines of sexual difference, justified biologically. The society or culture will seek further to cultivate certain traits in each sex amenable to fulfilling the division of tasks. On the whole, regardless of culture or rank, the tasks allotted to men will be more highly valued and rewarded in terms of both economic and cultural capital than those tasks allotted to women. In this sense patriarchal culture is characteristically "androcentric"; that is, the dominant norms and values center on male perceptions, interpretations, experience, needs, and interests.

ASPIRATIONS

Our hope is that *patriarchy* and *androcentrism* as just defined can become compost for a post-patriarchal age. Whether or not the world religions we have selected for this anthology can contribute to that age is a question we leave open. Whatever you decide, one thing is clear. A post-patriarchal age, even if an ideal only to be approximated, is worthy of commitment by men as well as by women. That is why two among us are men.

A post-patriarchal age is one in which women and men find possibilities for the fullness of life, not through rule over one another, but rather through freedom and mutuality, trust and ecstasy. The mutuality at issue is not between people alone, but between people and other creatures, between people and the earth. It is the fullness of *all* life—not human life alone, much less male life alone—toward which so many rightly aspire.

At this stage in the journey toward a post-patriarchal age, one of the most important things we can do is to listen: men to hear women on their terms, not on male-defined terms; women to hear each other on their own terms. Such listening has its own kind of liberation, a freedom from the presumption that men are the center around which all important insight revolves. Indeed, listening can be a spiritual discipline in its own right, and a much-needed one at that.

We hope this book will be read by men, but we also trust it will be read by women. Men have spoken too much, too exclusively, and for too long. Now is the time for women's voices to be heard, strongly and loudly.

After Patriarchy

1

Black Women's Surrogacy Experience and the Christian Notion of Redemption

DELORES S. WILLIAMS

Often, African-American women in church and society have character-ized their oppression as unique. Some black female scholars define this uniqueness on the basis of the interfacing of racial, class, and gender oppression in the experience of black women. However, this interfacing of oppressions is not unique to black women's experience. Jewish, Hispanic, Asian, and other women of color in America can also experience this real-ity. My exploration of black women's sources has revealed a heretofore undetected structure of domination that has been operative in African-American women's lives since slavery. This structure of domination is sur-rogacy, and it gives black women's oppression its unique character—and raises challenging questions about the way redemption is imaged in a Chris-tian context.

TWO FACES OF SURROGACY

On the basis of African-American women's sources it is possible to iden-tify two kinds of surrogacy that have given rise to the unique character of black women's oppression. They are *coerced surrogacy* and *voluntary surro-gacy*. Coerced surrogacy, belonging to the pre–Civil War period, was a forced condition in which people and systems more powerful than black women and black people forced black women to function in roles that ordinarily would have been filled by someone else. For example, black female slaves were forced to substitute for the slave owner's wife in nur-turing roles involving white children. Black women were forced to take the

1

place of men in work roles that, according to the larger society's understanding of male and female roles, belonged to men. Frederick Law Olmstead, a Northern architect writing in the nineteenth century, said he "stood for a long time watching slave women repair a road on a South Carolina Plantation" (quoted in White, 41). During the antebellum period this coerced surrogacy was legally supported in the ownership rights by which slave masters controlled their property, for example, black women. Slave women could not exercise the choice of refusing the surrogacy role.

After emancipation the coercion associated with antebellum surrogacy was replaced by social pressures that influenced black women to continue to fill some surrogacy roles. But surrogacy in the antebellum period differed from surrogacy in the postbellum period. The difference was that black women, after emancipation, could exercise the choice of refusing the surrogate role. Because of this element of choice, postbellum surrogacy can be referred to as voluntary surrogacy, even though social pressures influenced the choices black women made as they adjusted to life in a "free" world.

A closer look at these two modes of surrogacy in the two different periods (antebellum and postbellum) provides an in-depth view of the differences between the two modes.

COERCED SURROGACY AND ANTEBELLUM REALITIES

In the period before the Civil War coerced surrogacy roles involving black women were in the areas of nurturance, field labor, and sexuality.

The mammy role was the direct result of the demands slavocracy made upon black women's nurturing capacities. Standing in the place of the slave owner's wife, mammy nurtured the entire white family. A long and respected tradition among many southern whites, mammy was an empowered (but not autonomous) house slave who was given considerable authority by her owners. According to the existing scattered reports of mammies and how the tradition operated, we know many southerners thought "mammy could do anything, and do it better than anyone else. Because of her expertise in all domestic matters, she was the premier house servant and all others were her subordinates" (White, 47). According to White, Eliza Riply, a southern white woman who received nurture from a mammy, remembers her as

a "supernumerary" who, after the children grew up . . . managed the whole big and mixed household. In her [Eliza Riply's] father's house, everyone was made to understand that . . . all applications were to go through Mammy Charlotte. Nobody thought to go to the judge or his wife for anything (White, 47).

The testimony of ex-slaves themselves also attests to the value and power of mammies in the slaveholders' household. Drucella Martin remembers "that her mother was in full charge of the house and all marse children" (White, 47). Katherine Epps of Alabama said that her mother "worked in the Big House, 'aspinnin and 'anussin de white chillun" (White, 47). Epps also claimed that the slave owner's wife was so fond of her mother "that when she learned . . . the overseer had whipped the woman whom everyone called 'Mammy,' she dismissed him and gave him until sundown to remove himself and his family from the plantation" (White, 47).

Mammy was not always so well-treated, however. Frederick Douglass tells of his grandmother, who was mammy to a white family. When she became too old and frail to work, "they took her to the woods, built her a little hut with a mud chimney, and left her there to support and care for herself." As Douglass put it, "they turned her out to die" (White, 56). And there is the awful fate of one mammy told by ex-slave Jacob Stroyer. This mammy was named Aunt Betty. "She nursed her master through infancy, lived to see him become a drunk, and then became his victim when," during one of his drunken rampages, he took his shotgun and killed her" (White, 55). Nevertheless, the mammy role was probably the most powerful and authoritative one slave women could fill. Though slave women in their coerced roles as mammies were often abused, they were also empowered.[1]

This was not the case for slave women laboring beyond the "big house," that is, the slave owner's dwelling. In the area of field labor, black women were forced into work usually associated with male roles.[2] Feminist scholar Bell Hooks claims that on large plantations "Women plowed, planted . . . harvested crops. On some plantations black women worked longer hours in the fields than black men" (Hooks, 23). What this amounted to, in terms of coerced surrogacy, was black female energy substituting for male energy. This resulted in what Hooks refers to as the masculinization of the black female (Hooks, 22).

In their autobiographies some ex-slave women describe the masculine work roles black women were forced to fill. Bethany Veney tells of helping her cruel slave owner haul logs, drive out hogs, and set posts into the ground for fences (Veney, 12-13). Louisa Picquet told of slave women who drove ox wagons, tended mills, and plowed just like men (Picquet, 17). Another ex-slave Mary Prince tells of a slave woman who drove cattle, tended sheep and did general farming work in the fields (Prince, 6).

Unlike the mammy role of the female house slave, the masculinized roles of the female field slave did not empower black women in the slave structure to the extent that mammies were empowered. In the fields the greatest amount of power a slave could hold was in the position of slave driver or overseer. Usually, only males could ascend to these roles. Thus the driver was a male slave. Though a few black males served as overseers, this role was usually filled by white men of lower social class than the slave owner. Females who filled the masculinized roles in the fields were less respected than mammies and drivers. Field women were not often given recognition for their service, seldom realized the endearment of the white folks as did some of the mammies, got worse food and clothing, and often received more brutal punishment. These masculinized female field slaves were thought to be of a lower class than the female house slaves, who usually did "women's work" consisting of cleaning, spinning, cooking, sewing, and tending to the children.

More than in the areas of nurturance and field labor, coerced surrogacy in the area of sexuality was threatening to slave women's self-esteem and sense of self-worth. This is the area in which slave women were forced to stand in the place of white women to provide sexual pleasure for white male slave owners. The Victorian ideal of true womanhood (for Anglo-American women) supported a consciousness which, in the area of sexual relations, imagined sex between free white men and their wives to be for the purpose of procreation rather than for pleasure. Many white males turned to slave women for sexual pleasure and forced these women to fulfill needs which, according to racist ideology concerning male-female relations, should have been fulfilled by white women.

In her narrative *Incidents in the Life of a Slave Girl*, Linda Brent presents a vivid description of her slave owner Dr. Flint, who tried to force her into one of these illicit female slave/slave master sexual liaisons. Brent escaped his advances by fleeing from his house and hiding for seven years in a crawl space in the roof of her grandmother's home (Brent, 6-36). The octoroon slave woman Louisa Picquet was not as fortunate as Linda Brent. Louisa was purchased by a Mr. Williams when she was about fourteen years old. He forced her into sexual relations with him. From these relations four children issued (Picquet, 18-21). Another slave woman, Cynthia, was purchased by a slave trader who told her she would either accompany him home and become his "housekeeper" or he would sell her as a field worker to one of the worst plantations on the Mississippi River. Cynthia thus became the slave trader's mistress and housekeeper (Brown, 194-95).

There was in the antebellum South a kind of institutionalizing of female slave/slave master sexual liaisons that was maintained through the "fancy trade." This was a special kind of slave trading involving the sale of what were thought to be beautiful black women for the exclusive purpose of becoming mistresses of wealthy slave owners. Though New Orleans seems to have been the center of this trade, it also flourished in Charleston and Columbia, South Carolina; St. Louis, Missouri; and Lexington and Richmond, Virginia (White, 37-38). The famous octoroon balls that occurred in New Orleans allowed rich white men to meet and purchase these black women, who became their mistresses and often bore children by these slave owners.

Beyond this special kind of arrangement, slave owners also frequented the slave quarters and established sexual relations with any female slave they chose. The slave woman in either kind of arrangement had no power to refuse this coerced surrogacy in which she stood in the place of the white woman. Sometimes these slave women hoped for (and were promised) their freedom through sexual liaisons with the slave master. But more often than not their expectations were futile, and they were "sold off to plantations where . . . [they] shared the misery of all slaves" (White, 15).

All three forms of coerced surrogacy illustrate a unique kind of oppression only black women experienced in the slavocracy. Only black women were mammies. Only black women were permanently assigned to field labor. Only black women permanently lost control of their bodies to the lust of white men. During slavery, black women were bound to a system that had respect for neither their bodies, their dignity, their labor, nor their motherhood except as it was put to the service of securing the well-being of ruling class white families. In North America fierce and violent struggle had to afflict the entire nation before southern slave women could experience a measure of relief from coerced surrogacy roles.

VOLUNTARY SURROGACY AND POSTBELLUM REALITIES

When the American Civil War ended and the master-slave relation was officially terminated in the South, black people tried to determine for whom or what black women *would not* stand in place. They were especially anxious to relieve black women from those coerced surrogacy roles related to field work and to black women's sexuality involving black female/white male sexual liaisons. Ex-slave women themselves are reported to have said "they never mean to do any outdoor work, that white men support their wives and the [black women] mean that their husbands shall support them" (Giddings, 62). Black men were just as anxious for black women to quit the fields. According to historians Carter G. Woodson and Lorenzo Greene, "The Negro male when he worked for wages . . . tended to imitate the whites by keeping his wife and daughters at home" (Woodson and Greene, 31).

Of even greater concern to black males and females were their efforts to terminate the forced sexual relations between black women and white men that existed during slavery. Inasmuch as marriage between African-American women and men became legal after freedom and droves of black women and men came to official locations to be married (Giddings, 57-58), sexual liaisons between white men and black women could be curtailed, although white men (without regard for black marriage) still took advantage of some black women. Bell Hooks points out that after black reconstruction (1867-77) "black women were often . . . [pressured] into sexual liaisons with white employers who would threaten to fire them unless they capitulated to sexual demands" (Hooks, 37).

Nevertheless, there was not nearly as much sexual activity between black women and white men after slavery because black women themselves could refuse to substitute for white women in providing sexual pleasure for white males. Nancy White, a contemporary black female domestic worker, testified about refusing this role of playmate to white male employers:

I've had to ask some [white male employers] to keep their hands off me and I've had to just give up some jobs if they got too hot behind me. . . . I have lost some money that way, but that's all right. When you lose control of your body, you have just about lost all you have in this world (Gwaltney, 146-47).

Nancy White makes it clear that some white female employers approved of black women standing in their places to provide sexual favors for their husbands. White says:

One day that woman [her white female employer] told me that she wouldn't be mad if I let her husband treat me the same way he treated her. I told her I would be mad . . . if he tried to treat me like I was as married to him as she was (Gwaltney, 151).

Nancy White goes on to describe her method of declining this surrogate role her female and male employers wanted to assign her. Says White: "I had to threaten that devil [the white male employer] with a pot of hot grease to get him to keep his hands to hisself" (Gwaltney, 150).

While black women and men did realize a small measure of success in determining the surrogate roles black women would not fill after emancipation, certain social and economic realities limited black women's power to choose full exemption from all surrogacy roles. Poverty and the nature of the work available, especially to southern black families, demanded black women's participation in some of the most strenuous areas of the work force. There was also the attempt among newly freed black families to adopt some of the values of the people they took to be "quality white folk" during slavery.[3] This meant that efforts were made to influence black women to choose to continue in two of the surrogate roles they had filled during slavery: substituting female power and energy for male power and energy, and acting in mammy capacities.

After emancipation black women chose to substitute their energy and power for male energy and power in the area of farm labor. Greene and Woodson tell of urban Negro male laborers in 1901 who saved money and invested in farms. "It was not uncommon . . . to see Negro mechanics owning well-kept farms, which were cared for chiefly by wives and families" (Woodson and Greene, 61). The United States Census of 1910 reported that 967,837 black women were farm laborers and 79,309 were farmers (Foner and Lewis, 55). Also in 1910 Addie W. Hunton reported that

More than half of the 2,000,000 wage earning women of the [black] race are engaged in agriculture from its roughest and rudest form to its highest and most attractive form. . . . The 15,792,579 acres owned and cultivated by Negroes, which with buildings and equipment and rented farm lands reach a valuation approaching a billion dollars, represent not only the hardihood and perseverance of the Negro man but the power for physical and mental endurance of the woman working by his side. Many of the farms owned by colored men are managed entirely by the women of the family while these men give themselves to other employment (Foner and Lewis, 55).

It was, however, the surrogate role of mammy that some black males and white people consciously tried to perpetuate into the future beyond slavery and reconstruction. In Athens, Georgia, in the early twentieth century, Samuel Harris, the black principal of Athens Colored High School, dreamed up the idea of starting the Black Mammy Memorial Institute in that city. With the help of prominent white citizens this institute was chartered on September 19, 1910, and was authorized to operate for twenty years. According to a brochure published by the Black Mammy Memorial Association, the institute was to be

a memorial where men and women learn . . . how to work and to love their work; where the mantle of the "Old Black Mammy" may fall on those who go forth to serve; where the story of these women will be told to the generations that come and go; where better mothers for homes will be trained; a building from which those who go forth in life may speak louder in their works than their words. . . . The MONUMENTAL INDUSTRIAL INSTITUTE to the OLD BLACK MAMMY of the South will be devoted to the industrial and moral training of young Negro men and women. The work that is to receive special emphasis is the training of young women in Domestic Art (Patten, 153).

Obviously the prominent white citizens wanted to perpetuate the mammy roles so that the comfort of the white family could be assured by a type of black female servant who (after slavery) was properly trained in the skills of nurturing, supporting, and caring about the well-being of white children. Not so obvious, but probable, is the suggestion that to the black man Mr. Harris, black women trained in the mammy skills could learn to organize and manage the black households in the same way that the slave owners' households were organized and managed. This meant that the black family had to become more patriarchal in its structure and values in order to resemble the slave owners' households.

Mammy had a variety of skills that could accommodate this process. She was skillful at exerting authority in the household while being careful not to offend or usurp the power of the patriarchal authority figures: the slave master and his wife. Mammy was skilled in about every form of what was thought of as women's work: sewing, spinning, cooking, cleaning, tending to children, and so on. Hence she could train female children in this work. According to Deborah Gray White, mammy was often the advisor of the slave master in business matters. With regard to the quality of relationships in the master's family, she knew how to be a diplomat and a peacemaker who often healed relations that had gone awry. The mammy skills could promote and support black males as they became the patriarchal heads of the black household after slavery. And the black family could therefore resemble the patriarchal model of family sanctioned in mainline American society.

One could also suggest that the institution of Mothers of the Church, which developed in some black churches after emancipation, has kinship with the mammy tradition. Like the antebellum mammy, a mother of the church exerts considerable authority in the church family. But more often than not she uses her power in such a way that it does not challenge the power and authority of the patriarchal head of the church, usually a male preacher. She is sometimes called upon to be a healer of relationships within the congregation. She is well-versed in and knows how to pass along the church's highest values for living the Christian life. Her power and influence often extend beyond the church into her community because she has been empowered by one of the central authority agents of the community (the black church) to provide care and nurture for the children of God.

Black women's history of filling surrogacy roles has fed into negative stereotypes of black women that exist until this day. From the mammy tradition has emerged the image of black women as perpetual mother figures, religious, fat, asexual, loving children better than themselves, self-sacrificing, giving up self-concern for group advancement. The antebellum tradition of masculinizing black women through their work has given rise to the image of black women as unfeminine, physically strong, and having the capacity to bear considerably more pain than white women. These kinds of ideas helped create the notion of black women as superwomen. The sexual liaisons between white men and slave women created the image of the black woman as Jezebel, as one "governed almost entirely by her libido ... the counterimage of the mid-nineteenth-century ideal of the Victorian lady" (White, 29). Hence the surrogacy roles black women have filled during slavery and beyond are exploitative. They rob African-American women of self-consciousness, self-care, and self-esteem, and put them in the service of other people's desires, tasks, and goals. This has serious implications for Christian theologians attempting to use black women's history as a source for constructive theology.

FROM BLACK WOMAN SURROGATE TO SURROGATE-JESUS

One of the results of focusing upon African-American women's historic experience with surrogacy is that it raises significant questions about the way many Christians, including black women, have been taught to image redemption. More often than not the theology in mainline Christian churches, including black ones, teaches believers that sinful humankind has been redeemed because Jesus died on the cross in the place of humans, thereby taking human sin upon himself. In this sense Jesus represents the ultimate surrogate figure standing in the place of someone else: sinful humankind. Surrogacy, attached to this divine personage, thus takes on an aura of the sacred. It is therefore altogether fitting and proper for black women to ask whether the image of a surrogate-God has salvific power for black women, or whether this image of redemption supports and reinforces the exploitation that has accompanied their experience with surrogacy. If black women accept this image of redemption, can they not also passively accept the exploitation surrogacy brings?

This essay recognizes that reflection upon these questions causes many complex theological issues to surface. For instance, there is the issue of the part God the Father played in determining the redemptive, surrogate role filled by Jesus, the Son. For black women there is also the question of whether Jesus on the cross represents coerced surrogacy (willed by the father) or voluntary surrogacy (chosen by the son) or both. At any rate, a major theological problem here is the place of the cross in any theology significantly informed by African-American women's experience with surrogacy. Even if one buys into Moltmann's notion of the cross as the meeting place of the will of God to give up the Son (coerced surrogacy?) and the will of the Son to give up himself (voluntary surrogacy?) so that "the spirit of abandonment and self-giving love" proceed from the cross "to raise up abandoned men" (Moltmann, 31-35), African-American women are still left with this question: Can there be salvific power in Christian images of oppression (for example, Jesus on the cross) meant to teach something about redemption?

Theologians since the time of Origen have been trying to make the Christian principle of atonement believable by shaping theories about it in the language and thought that people of a particular time understood and were grounded in. Thus most theories of atonement, classical and contemporary, are time-bound (as well as ideologically bound with patriarchy) and do not respond meaningfully to the questions of people living beyond the particular time period. For instance, Origen (183-253 c.e.), capitalizing on people's belief in devils and spirits, provided what Alan Richardson speaks of as a ransom theory, claiming that the death of Jesus on the cross was a ransom paid by God to the devil for the sins of humankind (Richardson, 96-113). This view of atonement declined when another age dawned. Thus Anselm emerged in the eleventh century and spoke of atonement using the chivalric language and sociopolitical thought of his time. He shaped a theory describing sin as the human way of dishonoring God. People owed honor to God just as peasants and squires owed honor and loyalty to the feudal overlord. However, men had no power to render satisfaction to God for their massive disloyalty to God through sin. According to the codes of chivalry in Anselm's time, one atoned for a crime either by receiving punishment or by providing satisfaction to the injured person. Since God did not want to punish humans forever (which the sin deserved) and since humans had no means to render satisfaction to God's injured honor, the deity, Godself, made restitution for humanity. God satisfied God's own violated honor by sending the Son to earth in human form ultimately to die on the cross.

There were also the theories of atonement associated with Abelard (1079-1142). Since the church in Abelard's time put great stress upon the penitential life of believers, it was reasonable for Abelard to see Calvary as "the school of penitence of the human race, for there men of all ages and races have learned the depth and power of the love of God" (Richardson, 21). Often referred to as the moral theories of atonement (Richardson, 21), these emphasized God's love in the work of atonement and claimed that, when humans look upon the death of Jesus, they see the love of God manifested. The cross brings repentance to humankind and shows simultaneously God the Father's love and the suffering inflicted upon that love by human sin. The moral theories of atonement taught that the cross was "the most powerful moral influence in history, bringing to men that repentance which renders them able to be forgiven" (Richardson, 21).

As the Renaissance approached and the medieval worldview collapsed, the Anselmian and Abelardian ways of understanding the atonement began to fade. The Renaissance was a time of great interest in the revival of ancient law. So it was reasonable to expect the reformers to work out their theories of atonement in legal terms grounded in the new political and legal thought of the sixteenth century. Thus Calvin and others spoke of the justice of God the judge, of the divine law of punishment that could not be ignored, and of the infinite character of human sin that deserved infinite harsh punishment. But, according to the Reformers, God is both just and merciful. Therefore, in infinite mercy God provided a substitute who would bear the punishment for human sin. Jesus Christ came to offer himself as a substitute for humans. He took their punishment upon himself. Thus the Reformers provided a substitution theory of atonement.

While these ransom, satisfaction, substitution, and moral theories of atonement may not be serviceable for providing an acceptable response to African-American women's questions about redemption and surrogacy, they do illustrate a serviceable practice for female theologians attempting today to respond to this question. That practice (as shown by the theologians above) was to use the language and sociopolitical thought of the time to render Christian principles understandable. This fits well the task of the black female theologian. For that task is to use the language and sociopolitical thought of black women's world to show them that their salvation does not depend upon any form of surrogacy made sacred by human understandings of God. This means using the language and thought of liberation to liberate redemption from the cross and to liberate the cross from the "sacred aura" put around it by existing patriarchal responses to the question of what Jesus' death represents. To find resources to accomplish this task, the black female theologian is led to the scriptures.

The synoptic gospels (more than Paul's letters) provide resources for constructing a Christian understanding of redemption that speaks meaningfully to black women, given their historic experience with surrogacy. Jesus' own words in Luke 4 and his ministry of healing the human body, mind, and spirit (described in Matthew, Mark, and Luke) suggest that Jesus did not come to redeem humans by showing them God's love "manifested" in the death of God's innocent child on a cross erected by cruel, imperialistic, patriarchal power. Rather, the spirit of God in Jesus came to show humans *life*—to show redemption through a perfect *ministerial* vision of righting relationships. A female-male inclusive vision, Jesus' ministry of righting relationships involved raising the dead (for example, those appearing to be lost from life), casting out demons (for example, ridding the mind of destructive forces prohibiting the flourishing of positive, peaceful life), and proclaiming the word of life that demanded the transformation of tradition so that life could be lived more abundantly. Jesus was quick to remind his disciples that humans were not made for the Sabbath; rather, the Sabbath was made for humans. God's gift to humans, through Jesus, was to invite them to participate in this ministerial vision ("whosoever will, let them come") of righting relations. The response to this invitation by human principalities and powers was the horrible deed that the cross represents—the evil of humankind trying to kill the ministerial vision of life in relation that Jesus brought to humanity. The resurrection does not depend upon the cross for life, for the cross only represents historical evil trying to defeat good. The resurrection of Jesus and the flourishing of God's spirit in the world as the result of resurrection, represents the life of the ministerial vision gaining victory over the evil attempt to kill it. Thus, to respond meaningfully to black women's historic experience of surrogacy-oppression, the theologian must show that redemption of humans can have nothing to do with any kind of surrogate role Jesus was reputed to have played in a bloody act that supposedly gained victory over sin and/or evil. Black women are intelligent people living in a technological world where nuclear bombs, defilement of the earth, racism, sexism, and economic injustices attest to the presence and power of evil in the world. Perhaps not many people today can believe that evil and sin were overcome by Jesus' death on the cross, that is, that Jesus took human sin upon himself and therefore saved humankind. Rather, it seems more intelligent to understand that redemption had to do with God, through Jesus, giving humankind new vision to see resources for positive, abundant relational life—a vision humankind did not have before. Hence, the kingdom of God theme in the ministerial vision of Jesus does not point to death; that is, it is not something one has to die to get to. Rather, the kingdom of God is a metaphor of hope God gives those attempting to right the relations between self and self, between self and others, between self and God as prescribed in the sermon on the mount and the golden rule.

Though space limitations here prohibit more extensive reconstruction of this Christian understanding of redemption (given black women's surrogacy experience), there are a few things that can be said about sin in this kind of reconstruction. The image of Jesus on the cross is the image of human sin in its most desecrated form. This execution destroyed the body but not before it mocked and defiled Jesus by publicly exposing his nakedness and private parts, by mocking the ministerial vision as they labeled him king of the Jews, by placing a crown of thorns upon his head mocking his dignity and the integrity of his divine mission. The cross thus becomes an image of defilement, a gross manifestation of collective human sin. Jesus, then, does not conquer sin through death on the cross. Rather, Jesus conquers the sin of temptation in the wilderness (Mt 4:1-11) by resistance — by resisting the temptation to value the material over the spiritual ("Man shall not live by bread alone"); by resisting death (not attempting suicide; "if you are the son of God, throw yourself down"); by resisting the greedy urge of monopolistic ownership ("He showed him all the kingdoms of the world and the glory of them; and he said to him, 'All these I will give you, if you will fall down and worship me' "). Jesus therefore conquered sin in life, not in death. In the wilderness he refused to allow evil forces to defile the balanced relation between the material and the spiritual, between life and death, between power and the exertion of it.

What this allows the black female theologian to show black women is that God did not intend the surrogacy roles they have been forced to perform. God did not intend the defilement of their bodies as white patriarchal power put them in the place of white women to provide sexual pleasure for white men during the slavocracy. This was rape. Rape is defilement, and defilement means wanton desecration. Worse, deeper and more wounding than alienation, the sin of defilement is the one of which today's technological world is most guilty. Nature — the land, the seas, the animals in the sea — are every day defiled by humans. Cultures such as Native American and African have been defiled by the onslaught of Western, patriarchal imperialism. The oceans are defiled by oil spills and human waste, destroying marine life. The rain forest is being defiled. The cross is a reminder of how humans have tried throughout history to destroy visions of righting relationships that involve transformation of tradition and transformation of social relations and arrangements sanctioned by the status quo. The resurrection of Jesus and the kingdom of God theme in Jesus' ministerial vision provide black women with the knowledge that God has, through Jesus, shown humankind how to live peacefully, productively, and abundantly in relationship. Humankind is therefore redeemed through Jesus' life and not through Jesus' death. There is nothing of God in the blood of the cross. God does not intend black women's surrogacy experience. Neither can Christian faith affirm such an idea. Jesus did not come to be a surrogate. Jesus came for life, to show humans a perfect vision of ministerial relation that humans had forgotten long ago. However, as Christians, black women cannot forget the cross. But neither can they glorify it. To do so is to make their exploitation sacred. To do so is to glorify sin.

NOTES

1. This is not to suggest that such empowerment led to autonomy for slave women. Quite to the contrary. Slave women, like slave men, were always subject to the control of the slave owners. And as historian Deborah Gray White's description of mammy reveals, the empowerment of mammy was also directly related to the attempt of pro-slavery advocates to provide an image of black women which proved that the institution of slavery was vital for molding some black women in accord with the maternal ideals of the Victorian understanding of true womanhood.

2. Some scholars estimate that about eighty percent of slave women worked in the fields. Twenty percent worked as house servants. See Fogel and Engerman 1974, 38-58.

3. Historian Joel Williamson discusses this in relation to a process of acculturation he says existed among slaves and continued into and beyond the reconstruction. Williamson refers to the slaves as trying to "become more white." See Williamson's article.

WORKS CITED

Brent, Linda. *Incidents in the Life of a Slave Girl.* Boston: By the Author, Stereotype Foundry, 1861.

Brown, William Wells. "Narrative of William Wells Brown." *Puttin' on Ole Massa.* Ed. Gilbert Osofsky. New York: Harper and Row, 1969.

Fogel, Robert and Stanley Engerman. *Time on the Cross.* Boston: Little, Brown and Company, 1974.

Foner, Philip S. and Ronald L. Lewis, eds. *The Black Worker,* vol. 5. Philadelphia: Temple University Press, 1980.

Giddings, Paula. *When and Where I Enter.* New York: William Morrow and Company, 1984.

Gwaltney, John Langston. *Drylongso.* New York: Random House, 1980.

Hooks, Bell. *Ain't I a Woman?* Boston: South End Press, 1981.

Moltmann, Jürgen. "The 'Crucified God': God and the Trinity Today." *New Questions on God.* Ed. Johannes B. Metz. New York: Herder and Herder, 1972.

Patten, June O. "Document: Moonlight and Magnolias in Southern Education: The Black Mammy Memorial Institute." *The Journal of Negro History* LXV 2 (Spring 1980): 153.

Picquet, Louisa. *Louisa Picquet, the Octoroon: A Tale of Southern Slave Life.* Ed. Reverend H. Mattison. New York: 1861. Rpt. in *Collected Black Women's Narratives,* the Schomburg Library of Nineteenth-Century Black Women Writers. Series ed. Henry Louis Gates, Jr. New York: Oxford University Press, 1988.

Prince, Mary. *The History of Mary Prince, A West Indian Slave.* Ed. F. Westley and A. H. Davis. London: 1831. Rpt. in *Collected Black Women's Narratives,* the Schomburg Library of Nineteenth-Century Black Women Writers. Series ed.

Henry Louis Gates, Jr. New York: Oxford University Press, 1988.

Richardson, Alan. *Creeds in the Making.* London: Student Christian Movement Press, 1951.

Veney, Bethany. *The Narrative of Bethany Veney a Slave Woman.* Ed. Henry Louis Gates, Jr. Boston: The Press of George H. Ellis, 1889. Rpt. in *Six Women's Narratives,* the Schomburg Library of Nineteenth-Century Black Women Writers. Series ed. Henry Louis Gates, Jr. New York: Oxford University Press, 1988.

White, Deborah Gray. *Ar'n't I A Woman?* New York: W. W. North's Company, 1985.

Williamson, Joel. "Black Self-Assertion Before and After Emancipation." In *Key Issues in the Afro-American Experience.* Ed. Nathan I. Huggins, Martin Kilson and Daniel M. Fox. New York: Harcourt Brace Jovanovich, 1971.

Woodson, Carter G., and Lorenzo J. Greene. *The Negro Wage Earner.* Washington, D. C.: The Association for the Study of Negro Life and History, Inc., 1930.

2

Kali, the Savior

LINA GUPTA

Atop the golden peak of a mighty mountain, the goddess (Devi) Durga appeared mounted on her lion. Seeing the smiling Durga, the demons Canda and Munda approached with their army to seize her. Realizing she was about to be attacked, Durga became enraged, her face became as black as ink, and suddenly the goddess Kali appeared from her forehead with protruding fangs, a gaping mouth, and a lolling tongue. With a fierce roar she tore the demons into pieces with her hands, crushing and devouring them and their horses. In this magnificent myth depicted in the *Devi Mahatmya* (otherwise known as *Durga Saptasati*) Durga is an unconquerable, invincible warrior-maid, incarnated out of the collective wrath of all the gods joined in a council to save the world from the demons (*Devi Mahatmya* 7.3-22).[1] In Durga we have a manifestation of the dark goddess known to Hinduism as Kali. Who is this goddess? Is she merely another projection of the hostility and masculine fear of the feminine that characterizes patriarchal traditions within Hinduism and many of the other world faiths? Or does the goddess embody traits that can be a source of social and spiritual liberation for all women and men? Is she the mythic Great Mother whose symbolism depends on male fascination with female biology, or is she the goddess who represents the ultimate principle of Hinduism that transcends any form of duality? I argue that we can understand her in either of these ways, and that we can and must emphasize the latter understanding if we are to move into a healthier, more just world after patriarchy.

The evidence that the systematic subjugation of women has often been sanctioned by mythological stories, symbols, and images in world religions is too overwhelming to overlook. However, we have reached a point in history when it is simply not enough merely to recognize and analyze the patriarchal mindset and its effects on our religious and social lives. It is essential for us to seek new forms of religious experience and expression, either through the reinterpretation and reconstruction of our traditions or through alternative models of Ultimate Reality that will emphasize as well as include female experience. In search of an alternative, feminists have realized the overwhelming need for women to identify personally with positive images and role models, models that can reassert the importance of the "feminine" in all religious experience. With this realization has come the recognition of the general lack of such images and stories in most traditions.

I believe that Hinduism does indeed contain a model and image that could be used to fit the needs of today's women, and that this model lies at the very heart of Hinduism itself. This image centers on the goddess Kali and her many manifestations. I also believe this image must be extricated from patriarchal interpretations and understandings that have clouded its essential meaning even while tapping into—and using—the many layers of meaning that surround it. In part, such extrication must occur using a method similar to that of Rosemary Ruether, in which feminists select as resources those aspects of tradition that support the well-being of women (and men). In part, such extrication involves reappropriating the essential messages of the scriptures as those messages are made clear in the Tantric writings.

Even though portrayals of female characters in the Hindu epics and the Hindu scriptures called the Puranas[2] appear to depict traditional roles of mothers and wives, deeper egalitarian connotations and religious interpretations of these images and stories have been accepted by many traditional Hindus. That is, Hinduism is not inherently patriarchal; the equal importance of the gods and goddesses in the pantheon would seem to support this. But despite the equality and importance of the goddesses found in various scriptures, traditional Hindu life by and large has remained patriarchal. The significance of the goddesses in Hinduism is undeniable; even so, the lives of women as subservient daughters and wives is also very real. It seems to me that patriarchal understanding has appropriated the goddesses and the feminine aspects of the Ultimate Reality at the heart of Hinduism in ways that sanction the unequal treatment of women. Still, in the absence of a clearly or totally patriarchal tradition, the question of a post-patriarchal version of Hinduism must be dealt with carefully.

What new religious paradigm for understanding and appropriating the feminine in Hindu traditions is available to post-patriarchal Hindu women? Hinduism itself offers clues for such a paradigm in the image of Kali, not in Kali as she has been understood through patriarchy—although this understanding does indeed involve some truth—but Kali in her deepest and most essential meaning. The goddess, the archetype of Devi, is considered to be one of the most enduring and endearing of all archetypes in Hinduism. In getting to the deepest meaning of the goddess, we approach more completely the central meanings of scriptural Hinduism itself.

After a thousand years of denial and devaluation, the archetype of the goddess is reentering the West; Western feminists have relearned the power of the goddess. It is not so much recent interest in the goddess, however, as my own experience as a woman growing up in the Hindu tradition that leads me to this particular essay on Kali. Looking back, I realize how important Kali was to me. As far as I can remember, both daily worship of Kali at home and weekly visits to the Daksineshwar temple with my parents were part of my life. As a child I saw Kali as something to fear, but also something inspiring and empowering. At the temple I watched as people — male and female, old and young, sick and healthy — joined together in worship, waiting patiently to see their beloved goddess at least once. It was incredible to see the joy and reverence expressed at the slightest hint that the temple door would open.

Soon my daily experiences made me aware of discrepancies between a religious view of the goddess and the everyday lives of women. The scriptures and religious tradition proclaim that the beloved Devi resides in women. But these same women are not simply revered and protected; they are also dominated and excluded from the decision-making process that gives male members of Hindu society significant power and authority. This discrepancy was difficult for me to comprehend; although I personally can recall no direct experience of oppression, a subtle pressure to conform to an ideal form of womanhood was constant, and as a female, I felt at once hindered and exalted by ambiguities implicit in that pressure.

This essay will attempt to review the myth of the Great Goddess, whose power, beauty, independence, and religious importance presents an alternative vision to the limitations of patriarchal consciousness. I shall focus on the goddess as a dramatic embodiment of conflicts found in the struggle of women to assert their social rights through spiritual freedom from within the limiting structure of a patriarchal society. I will show how male domination violates the basic principle of equality integral to Hinduism, and how patriarchal ideology found in certain areas of Hinduism is based on a mistaken assumption about the nature of "femaleness." By taking a critical and reflective approach to the stories of the Puranas and their interpretations in Tantric literature, I will emphasize what I take to be the egalitarian core of Hinduism. According to Tantric interpretations, Kali represents, not only to women but to all people, a way of facing and transcending any limitation, whether the limitation is self-created or imposed by others, thus offering a way of liberating tradition itself from its patriarchal bias.

WOMEN AND THE LAWS OF MANU

In order to understand Kali from a post-patriarchal point of view as a resource for liberation and empowerment, one must see the goddess's femininity and femininity in general both in light of patriarchal interpretations found in the Hindu lawbooks collectively known as the *Dharmasastras (The*

Rules of Right Conduct) and in the religious and more liberating interpretations found in various Tantric and Vedanta texts.

Hindu law was first codified by Manu in the seventh century B.C.E. Under this reform women lost much of their freedom. Restrictions were put upon their autonomy, their movements, and their associations with men. Child marriage became the norm, and women were required to be virgins and chaste. Women were placed under the supervision of their fathers first, later their husbands, and then their sons. In short, the role of women was relegated to wife and mother. Anything other was considered unacceptable. It seems to me that the sources on which the later patriarchal Hindu tradition is based have been interpreted only by Hindu men who had vested interests in, and who were responsible for, defining the sociological and religious status of Hindu women.

The following passages from *Manu Samhita (Laws of Manu)* clarify the basic rules of conduct for women. Here we find examples of restrictions put upon the nature and potentiality of women. Once stated as laws, these passages and countless more established the monolithic structure of the *Dharmasastras* that promoted and perpetuated the patriarchal mentality:

Let the [husband] employ his [wife] in the collection and expenditure of his wealth, in keeping [everything] clean, in [the fulfillment of] religious duties, in the preparation of his food, and in looking after the household utensils (Manu, 329).

Drinking [liquor], associating with wicked people, separation from the husband, rambling abroad, sleeping [at unreasonable hours], and dwelling in other men's houses are the six causes of the ruin of women (Manu, 329).

She who drinks spirituous liquor or is of bad conduct, rebellious, diseased, mischievous, or wasteful, may at any time be superseded by another wife (Manu, 341).

Her father protects [her] in childhood; her husband protects [her] in youth; and her sons protect [her] in old age; a woman is never fit for independence (Manu, 328).

Day and night women must be kept in dependence by the males [of] their families and, if they attach themselves to sensual enjoyments, they must be kept under control (Manu, 328).

[When creating them] Manu allotted to women [a love of their] bed, [of their] seat, and [of] ornament, impure desires, wrath, dishonesty, malice, and bad conduct (Manu, 330).

For women no [sacramental] rite [is performed] with texts; thus the law is settled; women who are destitute of [the knowledge of] Vedic texts are [as impure as] falsehood [itself]; that is a fixed rule (Manu, 330).

It is obvious that societal and psychological constraints inherent in these restrictions leave a woman with very few life options to explore. These restraints create a sense of dependency, a disability that further narrows her chance to fulfill her own creativity in any areas other than allocated household chores. By interfering with their potentiality, Manu seems to be encouraging women to resort to passivity by making them appendages to men. A woman loses not only her freedom to make her own life choices but her self-worth as well.

In order to follow the reasoning behind such restrictions, one needs to consider how the nature of femaleness is defined within the context of these writings. How is the feminine viewed and valued in the *Manu Samhita?* The following passages are revealing:

through their passion for men, through their mutable temper, through their natural heartlessness, they become disloyal toward their husbands, however carefully they may be guarded (Manu, 330).

Where women are honored, there the gods are pleased; but where they are not honored, no sacred rites yield rewards (Manu, 330).

The houses in which female relations are not being duly honored, pronounce a curse, perish completely, as if destroyed by magic (Manu, 85).

Knowing their disposition ... [every] man should most strenuously exert himself to guard them (Manu, 330).

And to this effect many sacred texts are sung also in the Vedas in order to [make] fully known the true disposition of [women] (Manu, 330).

Why is it that "every man should most strenuously exert himself to guard women"? What is the nature or disposition of women that necessitates such precaution on the part of men? Manu speaks of an ambiguous nature of woman. She has a mutable temper and heartlessness, but despite this she is to be revered and honored. Her sacredness is to be preserved and appreciated, otherwise god will be displeased. Most important, there is nothing worse than a dishonored woman whose curse spells danger for the household. Her femininity reflects her paradoxical nature. She is to be guarded because of her profane nature; she is to be revered for her sacredness.

Why is there such an elaborate system of rules to control and protect her unless men are afraid of her inherent power? It is her inherent power that creates man's fear as well as his reverence toward her and finally prompts him either to control her through social restrictions or to honor her through gestures of respect and protectiveness.

KALI

It is in the goddess Kali that I find the inherent power of women made explicit. This is true when we understand Kali in the stories of the Puranas on a superficial level, and it is true even when we examine her in the terms patriarchy has used in dealing with her. It is most powerfully true when we examine more deeply the essential religious, cosmological, and epistemological implications of the goddess.

In order to understand Kali, it is also essential that we clarify the notion of Devi. The word *Devi* in its truest sense refers to Para Brahman, the Ultimate Reality, which is beyond all names and forms. In this sense Devi is neither male nor female; it is a state of being. In the *Yamala,* Siva says:

Devi may, My beloved, be thought of as female or male, or the *Saccidanandarupini* may be thought of as *Niskala Brahman.* But in truth She is neither a female, male, neuter being, nor an inanimate thing. But like the term *Kalpavalli* [a word in feminine gender denoting "tree"] feminine terms are attributed to Her (Avalon 1965, 31).

Since mind cannot grasp the genderless reality of the Devi, she appears in physical forms; she is usually contemplated in her female form. Out of the countless manifestations of Devi, Kali is considered to be one of the most important. Characterization of Kali is not a simple matter because stories and personifications of Kali are extraordinarily diverse. She appears with different names as well as with different forms, manifesting in countless goddesses such as Durga, Dat, Parvati, and so on. Nevertheless, through all these diversities two obvious characterizations of Kali are most pertinent to my topic: Kali the mother and the destroyer, and Kali the independent woman (Kali the Great Mother and Kali the Great Goddess). Each of these characterizations could be understood in a variety of ways. In what follows I will look at Kali's superficial and/or physical iconography; I will then explore the deeper significance of Kali in terms of specific central Hindu notions. In light of these discussions I will examine Kali's behavior and baffling companions and her relationship with Siva, her husband. The discussion of Kali in terms of four Hindu concepts—*Sakti, Prakrti, Avidya,* and *Maya*—should shed light on how patriarchal thinking has understood and used Kali; it should also help us understand Kali in her deeper significance and how she can serve as a liberating force for women—and men. The patriarchal perspective often depicts the goddess as nothing more than a great but biologically dependent mother and wife; such interpretations, I suspect, have been used to legitimate the kind of patriarchal hierarchy espoused by Manu. But I will argue that in terms of scripture and the Tantric interpretations, Kali can be taken to symbolize the Ultimate Principle that transcends any form of duality and that, in doing so, the Great Goddess can be taken as a fruitful post-patriarchal model of the feminine, in whom the beauty, power, and independence of the female can be understood and appreciated.

THE ICONOGRAPHY OF KALI

Kali is almost always pictured in ways that terrify the onlooker: red eyes, disheveled hair, blood trickling at the corners of her mouth, lips saturated with fresh blood, a dangling tongue, long sharp fangs, a gaunt, dark-skinned body, a sunken stomach, and protruding breasts. Her adornment and *lack* of adornment intensify her frightening appearance: she is mostly naked; her necklace contains fifty human heads; her waistband is a girdle made of severed human arms; she is wearing two dead infants for earrings (Avalon 1965, 45). Each of her four arms holds a different object or projects a particular gesture. She holds a blood-smeared cleaver in her upper left hand and a blood-dripping severed head in the lower left. With her upper right hand she says "Fear not," and with her lower right she beckons "Come unto me" (Avalon 1965, 46). A first impression of this terrifying appearance reaffirms the conviction that Kali is a goddess of death and destruction, disorder and chaos.

Seen *simply* in her destructive image, goddess Kali seems neither to portray a specifically patriarchal model of a woman nor to offer any appropriate model for contemporary women. Hindu responses to and understandings of Kali are ambiguous. Even as the numen of the untamed feminine who threatens stability and order, she is approached as the beloved all-protective mother by the Hindus. Gruesome as she may appear, Hindus worship her as the source of power, strength, equality, and justice.

While some Puranic myths as well as Tantric texts paint such a horrifying picture of Kali, other texts and later writings describe Kali in gentler images. The Tantric text *Karpuradi-Stotra* at times depicts her as a young, beautiful woman. According to the text she is *atiyuvatin:* always the same, fresh, unchanging, and unwasting (Avalon 1965, 71). Her fierce laughter often gives way to a bewitching smile. *Karpuradi-Stotra* describes her as *smeravadanam,* as having a gently smiling face (Avalon 1965, 92). Being Bliss herself, she is ever blissful.

Which of these images of Kali can be taken as reflecting the fundamental principle of Hinduism? Is Kali the terrible destroyer who laughs at her enemies and devours them with pleasure? Or is she the beautiful mother who nourishes and preserves her created beings? There is truth in both these images.

Patriarchal understandings of these images have been used to limit the power of women. Kali in her nakedness and unusually gross adornments seems to be affirming the patriarchal description of women as lustful and out of control found in the *Laws of Manu*. In speaking of the relationships of women with men, Manu says: "Women do not care for beauty, nor is their attention fixed on age, [thinking it is enough that] he is a man; they give themselves to the handsome and to the ugly" (Manu, 330). Patriarchal claims regarding the unrefined and emotional nature of women are evident in this passage; this and similar claims would seem to be supported by Kali's image and behavior.

Not only her nakedness and unusual adornments, but also her dark complexion have been the focus of patriarchal mentality, a mentality that typifies black and white as symbols of evil and good. Dislike toward black complexion is quite evident in a story of the *Vamana Purana*. According to the Puranic story, the goddess Parvati at times is called Kali, the Black One, by her husband Siva. Hearing Siva call her by this name, she becomes insulted and enraged. In order to get rid of her dark complexion she undergoes severe austerities, finally receiving a golden complexion as her reward (*Vamana Purana* 25-29).

Kali's dark complexion possibly indicates her ancient origin as a tribal fertility goddess worshipped by the dark-skinned indigenous people who populated India prior to the Aryan invasion. Her dark color apparently suggests her connection to the earth and its fertility and therefore establishes her as the Great Mother. The universal devaluation of women could be explained in terms of the assumption that women are closer to the earth than men; it is natural, in this thinking, for men to dominate and subjugate women just as one tries to dominate the earth. In this view the dark Kali reflects a reality to be dominated (specifically by Siva), as women (and wives) must be dominated by men (their husbands).

Kali's Image in Tantra

Tantric interpretation provides us with a means to understand the deeper significance of Kali's iconography and reveals how her presence can be empowering and liberating in a post-patriarchal context. In seeking to understand the essence of Kali in Hinduism we need to go beyond the mythic layer that presents the Great Goddess merely in terms of a Great Mother who represents the biologically dependent female, and therefore dependent wife. The *Karpuradi-Stotra,* a Tantric text, explains and interprets the image of Kali in the following way:

Kali's "body is imagined to be blue of color because, like the blue sky, she pervades the world."

Kali "is imagined black because she is colorless and above the color gunas."

Kali's "hair is disheveled because though herself changeless she binds infinite numbers of jivas [individual selves] by bonds of Maya [illusion]" and "because she liberates Brahma, Vishnu, and Mahesvara, who are her kesa [hair]" (Avalon 1965, 45).

The Sanskrit word *kesa* in the above quotation refers to "K" as Brahma (god of creation), "A" as Vishnu (god of preservation), and "Isha" as Rudra (god of destruction) (Avalon 1965, 45). That is, Kali's destructive image can be best understood in light of forms she assumes for the purpose of creation and preservation, as well as destruction. She embraces all these processes; indeed, she embraces all. Embracing creation, preservation, and destruction, Kali is a symbol of all that is; she is, at the deepest level, Brahman, or the unmanifested One. As such, she is capable both of placing consciousness and the devotee into bondage—the bondage of illusion and ignorance—and of releasing the devotee into absolute liberation (Avalon 1965, 59).

In the Tantric interpretation parts of Kali's physical appearance represent qualities of consciousness and of all that is: Kali's white teeth represent *sattva guna,* potential consciousness; her lolling tongue refers to *raja guna,* the source of activity; and her wine drinking stands for *tamas gunas,* the source that resists activity (Avalon 1965, 45). By destroying the *tamas gunas,* inertia, and by increasing one's *sattva guna,* potential consciousness, Kali finally grants her devotees liberation.

The human skull in her hand is the seat of the ultimate knowledge that finally leads one from bondage to liberation. With her upper left hand depicted as holding a sword of wisdom, she severs the bonds of illusion and mistaken identity that are holding her devotees in bondage. She is naked because she is beyond the shackles of *Maya* or illusion.

The fifty human heads of her necklace refer to the fifty letters of the Sanskrit language. These fifty letters are used for hymns and mantras; they are Brahman itself in the form of sound energy. Her girdle of human arms with folded palms suggests how to perform action without any attachment in order to avoid further entrenchment in the bondage of the cycle of cause and effect (the law of karma). Her heavy hips and *yoni* (sexual organ) stand for the creative process. Her three eyes represent energy radiated in three directions: as moon, sun, and fire. The well-developed breasts of the goddess Kali are filled with over-flowing milk. With the over-flowing milk of one breast she sustains the created world, and with the other she feeds and shows the path of liberation to her devotees. Like a child sleeping safely and peacefully in the lap of its mother, every human being at the end of worldly life rests in eternal peace in the crematorium ground, the dwelling place of mother Kali and the god Siva (Avalon 1965, 84).

Kali as a Contemporary Role Model

In Western tradition the depiction of goddesses' nakedness (Eve, Diana, Aphrodite, or—on the opposite pole—Medusa, whose head and snaky hair call to mind the exposed female sex organ) leads to the temptation and spiritual destruction of men. Kali's nudity, however, does not seem primarily to reflect this projection of men's inner fear at the power of women's sexuality or the cause of man's downfall. Rather, her choice to be naked reveals a choice to be free from social constraints. Kali neither adorns herself for others nor conceals her natural being. She is what she is.

In my mind, Kali's use of jewelry and adornment, while it would never make the cover of *Vogue* magazine, also offers us interesting insights into the way her myths reveal a subtle critique of the limitations of patriarchal consciousness. Kali's iconography, as we have pointed out, depicts her with necklaces of skulls and severed heads. Here the mythic image takes the *form* of a traditional female subservience to male desires in which the female turns herself into an adorned, bejewelled object for the approval of the men that gaze on her; but Kali totally reverses that form's function. Instead of rubies and diamonds, similar to those of other goddesses, Kali wears frightening skulls and corpses whose violent overtones suggest a hidden hostility or rage at this need to adorn and "objectify" oneself. The transformation of jewels into emblems of death also hints at the power of women, with their close connection to the natural cycle of giving birth and nurturing life. Kali's flaunting of her association with nature's destructive powers, symbolized by the skulls, reinforces the link that binds women with mysteries of both life and death.

In addition, Kali, through her peculiar adornments, seems to communicate to others the predicaments she herself faces. Kali asks us to confront the inevitability of death and the unavoidable loss of our identity in death. The Dark Mother teaches us that it is only in accepting our fear and the dark within us that we recognize our true identity as being within a totality of all that is, a recognition that liberates us from all impositions and restrictions. Darkness absorbs all colors. In this sense Kali represents a totality that transcends all forms of duality and separation.

KALI IN TERMS OF FOUR CENTRAL HINDU NOTIONS[3]

A creative and interactive reading in the light of Tantric scriptural interpretation of the Great Goddess can allow Kali with her terrifying appearance to emerge as a powerful symbol of life and liberation to women in their passage to post-patriarchy. Beyond mother and wife, she encourages us to challenge our assumptions, ambiguities, negativities, uncertainties, and fears about "others." Under her assurance we confront who we are in reality as opposed to what we perceive ourselves to be through the subjugated roles we play.

What then do we mean when we speak of a true identity? In the answer to this question we find where the strongest power of Kali lies. In order to understand Kali's nature, her gender, and her inherent power, we must turn to the Tantric understandings of the goddess, interpretations that will shed light on how frequently the later patriarchal traditions have misunderstood the dual or paradoxical nature of her femininity.

An examination of some central cosmological and epistemological Hindu terms that have been applied to Kali reveals the power of the goddess to be that of a liberating image. It also leads us to an understanding of the intensity and depth of the justification and legitimation of the kind of oppressive attitudes toward women that have been expressed in later Hindu writings and specifically in the *Laws of Manu*.

In this section I will focus on four key concepts by which scriptures frequently address, invoke, or explain Kali. Interestingly, these words are in the feminine gender and often designate women as well. In *Devi Mahatmya* Kali "is both form and without form, and is termed variously. She is called *Prakrti* by the followers of Samkhya; *Avidya* by the Vedantins; the power of words by grammarians; *Sakti* of Siva by Saivites; *Visnumaya* by the Vaisnava; *Mahamaya* by the Saktas; and *Devi* by Pauranikas" (*Devi Mahatmya* 4, 55). These terms are interrelated, but due to the complexity of the topic and the limited scope of this essay, I will limit my discussion to the four words *Sakti, Prakrti, Avidya,* and *Maya.* Although all four of these words often are used interchangeably, it is the uniqueness of each one of them that gives us a broader picture of the femaleness and true nature of Kali. I shall try to explain each of these concepts both from a scriptural point of view and from a patriarchal perspective. My intention is to point out how patriarchal and merely literal interpretations (and misinterpretations) of these words sometimes reflect an inability to move beyond a male-centered approach to understanding Kali.

Sakti

Wishing to multiply, One Brahman, the nameless, formless Reality, becomes dual and the universe comes into being as a result of the association between these dual principles—male and female, Siva (consciousness) and Sakti (energy). At the end of the cosmic cycle, however, the created universe with all its diversities returns to its source and Sakti comes to repose with Siva. The word *Sakti* means "power or energy," the female counterpart of the divine male, existing eternally in Siva as his inseparable attribute. To say, however, that Sakti resides in Siva or in the Brahman is merely a figure of speech—in truth, they are one and the same. Sakti as pure potentiality and as devoid of consciousness initiates and continues the process of creation (only) in the presence of Siva. As such she—with Siva—is the cause of manifestations and is responsible for the differentiation of objects.

If we look at the relationship of Sakti (Kali) with Siva *without any critical reflection,* Sakti could be imagined as having no identity of her own. Literally speaking she not only resides *in* Siva, she begins her creation only at the presence of Siva and ultimately returns to him. Whether in her divinity or in her femininity, she belongs to Siva. When Siva is proclaimed to be spirit or consciousness, he is given authority over Sakti. Her active power of manifestation remains a mere potential unless activated by his presence. Her weakness is rooted in her lack of consciousness and inherent in her potentiality. She is a woman captive by her own power and lacking spirit or consciousness, and is therefore a woman to be delivered. That is, deliverance from her unguided, unstructured power is possible only through her subordination to the structure provided by conscious Siva. As power out of control, merely winning in a battle does not satisfy Kali. Her power, unguided by any rationality, takes the form of savagery. When she is on the warpath, all of creation is in peril; all of creation appeals to Siva to save the world from imminent danger. Such an uncritical and superficial understanding of the relationship of Siva and Sakti (Kali) provides fuel for patriarchy as exemplified in *The Laws of Manu*. But in both Vaisnavism and Saivism, Ultimate Reality united with its Sakti is understood in terms of a female principle. In spite of the description of Kali or Sakti as the consort-wife of Siva, understood in her highest form—that is, understood as the Ultimate One—she is his creator. As Adyasakti she is primordial energy itself; she is the Brahman existing before creation. In the later Sakta phase the Devi, the goddess, is transformed into the eternally existing, all-powerful female principle who in her concrete form is often personified as Kali or Durga. Sakti, Devi, or Kali is thus the Brahman manifested in its mother aspect as the Creator and Sustainer of the world. As Sakti, Kali grants prosperity and prowess to her devotees. The sound *s* in *Sakti* stands for welfare and prosperity and *kti* refers to prowess. As Sakti she is the embodiment as well as giver of this blessing. In her ultimate unity with Brahman, Kali is creator and sustainer, as well as destroyer of the world. Kali, the personification of Sakti, the female principle of creation, is present in all. All of creation therefore embodies some aspect of her femaleness.

Prakrti

The word *prakrti* usually is translated as "nature." In Hindu understanding, Prakrti has been taken as the feminine, the object, nature, matter, and the unconscious; this has been distinguished from Purusa, which has been understood as the masculine, the subject, structure, mind, consciousness.

In understanding the word *prakrti*, we may fruitfully look at its constituent parts, and do so from various perspectives. In one understanding *pra* means before; *kriti* refers to creation. Thus, the word can refer to that which existed before creation. *Pra* also means primary or principal; the word can therefore be translated as the principal factor in creation. In the *Brahma Vaivarta Purana*, Devi is addressed as Prakrti, existing before creation as Mula Prakrti or the unmanifested Brahman. At the presence of Purusa or spirit, the male principle, she is manifested in the created universe of name and form.

In yet another translation, *pra* can refer to *sattvic guna,* "quality that reveals"; *kri* means *rajasic guna,* "activity"; *ti* means *tamasic guna,* "quality that suppresses." The unrevealed, unmanifested Prakrti or Devi is the state of equilibrium of these three gunas or characteristics. The three gunas constitute the very substance of Prakrti; when their state of equilibrium is disturbed the manifested universe appears. This being so, all nature is composed of these same gunas in different states of relationship to one another. Prakrti as unconscious matter veils the true nature of Purusa or consciousness; but as the manifested world, it reveals the nature of Purusa (spirit or consciousness). As we have noted, the goddess Kali has both the power to bind and the power to liberate.

The literal meaning of the word *prakrti* is "nature." Nature as it is ordinarily understood is spontaneous, unstructured, and the embodiment of various resources. This aspect of the word might then be emphasized by a patriarchal mindset that also believes in the domination of nature and therefore women. One's life depends on the gift of nature, yet nature's (and Kali's) precariousness and unpredictability make her unreliable. Being unconscious, Prakrti is in need of the presence of Purusa, the spirit. Again, these notions have provided substance for hierarchy and for the subjugation of women. When the dependence of Prakrti on Purusa is emphasized, Manu's hierarchy seems justified. But this reading again does not take into account the absolute unity of Prakrti with Brahman (and indeed, Prakrti with Purusa). To do this without understanding the deep significance of Prakrti (and Kali) is to ignore the truly liberating message and power in the oneness of nature (and women and self) with divinity.

As nature, Devi is the source of both joy and sorrow. She nourishes as well as destroys. Kali, the divine mother, the emblem of femininity, personifying Prakrti, exemplifies the dual nature of Prakrti in its entirety. She is its wildness, its spontaneity, but she is also the power of the unmanifested Brahman.

Avidya

The word *avidya* originated from the word *vidya,* which stands for knowledge. *A* (not) *vidya* therefore refers to the absence of knowledge, ignorance, and sometimes to wrong knowledge as well. Still, from another standpoint, *avidya* can be seen in a positive light; it is our ignorance that—in some ways—creates the world as we perceive it.

Avidya has an apparent existence. It imposes forms on the formless. It apparently limits the limitless. Just as a wave is essentially one with the ocean and yet appears to be differentiated from it because of the limitations of a mere form, so Avidya creates a semblance of separation between the Supreme Brahman, the ocean, and the individual soul, Atman, the wave (Satprakashananda, 140).

Samkara, an eighth-century south Indian philosopher, describes the process of *avidya* in terms of *Adhysa* or superimposition. In the case of a rope being mistaken for a snake, one erroneously attributes remembered qualities of a snake to a present perception of a rope. Similarly, as Elliot Deutsch puts it, it "is the superimposition on the Self (Atman, Brahman) of what does not belong to the Self (finitude and change) and the superimposition on the non-self of what does properly belong to the Self (infinitude and eternality) that constitutes avidya" (Deutsch, 34). Advaita Vedanta distinguishes *Tulavidya* that explains the individual's temporary illusions, from *Mulavidya,* the universal ignorance that accounts for experience of the empirical world. In other words, through *avidya,* reality is assumed of the phenomenal world; the phenomenal world *is. Avidya* is not ignorance in a debilitating sense; it is ignorance in a cosmically creative sense; it is a power of Brahman. Escape from ignorance is precisely this recognition: *Avidya,* and hence the phenomenal world itself, does not have existence on its own but is, rather, the divine One in and of itself.

The identification of Kali or the Devi with Avidya, taken literally, provides patriarchy with an ample opportunity to view woman as the absolute embodiment of ignorance. Patriarchy, rather than focusing on Avidya as the creative power reflecting potential accessible to both men and women, implies a debilitating and consequently destructive power inherent in all women.

Kali, however, can both bind (as Avidya) and liberate. Arthur Avalon in the introduction of *Karpuradi-Stotra* explains: "Devi is *avidya* because she binds; she is called *vidya* because, destroying the wrong knowledge, she liberates her devotees" (Avalon 1965, xxvii). That is, Avidya as the creative power of the goddess binds all beings to her creation, but the goddess is also *embodiment* of all knowledge and therefore delivers all beings from the bondage of *samsara.*

Maya

Like *avidya, maya* is a deceptive and apparently negative power. And like *avidya, maya* creates in its deception. It is creative power, and though we must escape the delusion associated with *maya* through a full realization that *maya* is a power (like *avidya*) of Brahman, such a full realization is a source of real power for us as we live in relation to each other.

The word *maya,* according to the ancient Vedic usage, refers to the mysterious deceptive power of deities. Advaita Vedantists explain this power from two different standpoints. From the metaphysical standpoint, Deutsch explains, "*maya* is that mysterious power of Brahma that deludes us into taking the empirical world as reality. Epistemologically, *maya* is ignorance *(avidya)"* (Deutsch, 30). Maya not only has the power to conceal *(avarana sakti)* reality so that one fails to see it in its true essence, it also has the power to project a distorted view of reality, so one sees reality differently from what it truly is.

Literally translated, the word *maya* could be taken to mean "trickery, deceit, or illusion." In the context of *Manu Samhita*, which stressed the dangerous power of women and their need to be controlled, the equation of Kali and goddess with Maya could be dangerously powerful in supporting a view of women as having the power to distort, confuse, or deceive. But the anthropomorphizing tendencies of these literalisms have to be seen as reflecting a larger, more pervasive male fear of women's power; that power is a creative power—a power to act creatively in the world, to critique and create societal structures, to literally create the world. That power is also one that can be destructive to the limitations of patriarchy. Maya is a power of Brahman, essentially one with the Ultimate.

Readings and Misreadings

From the scriptural point of view the female principle understood in terms of Sakti, Prakrti, Avidya, and Maya reveals Reality (Brahman, Devi, Kali) in all its facets: the creator, the creativity, and the created world. The patriarchal, more literal interpretation of these words, on the other hand, presents a lethal combination of raw unrestricted power or energy (*sakti*), unpredictable nature (*prakrti*), ignorance or wrong knowledge (*avidya*), and deceitful nature capable of concealment and false projection (*maya*). A female, under this definition, while devoid of knowledge, radiates a natural power or potency. Uncontrolled and unrestricted, her power leads to danger and destruction for all concerned.

It is difficult to criticize Manu's way of thinking without appearing to question the entire fabric of Hinduism. However, the whole fabric of Hinduism is not to be understood in terms of Manu's presuppositions about the dangerous emotional disposition of women. Manu's idea is not a solution; rather, we find in Manu a clear statement of a problem, which has an irreplaceable value in making our task so explicit. I find it a clear statement of how a denigrating view and evaluation of femaleness is ingrained in the social structure. Language, which is the prime reflection of attitudes held, reveals how a society defines the nature of male and female and assigns power accordingly. The more the concept of Purusa or Siva is defined in terms of spirit or consciousness without acknowledging its deeper connotation and the oneness of Purusa or Siva with Prakrti or Sakti, the more the concept of Sakti or Prakrti assumes the role of an unconscious raw power to be restricted and subjugated. The rationality of Purusa automatically assigns irrationality to Prakrti, to Kali, and to the female. It is this kind of understanding that a post-patriarchal reading must de-emphasize, and that a post-patriarchal appropriation of Kali through scriptural analysis will help us overcome.

KALI'S BEHAVIOR AND ASSOCIATIONS

Not only do the images and iconography of Kali reveal her essence, her behavior also offers a clue to her true nature. Most of the Puranic stories present her as a deity who delights in death and destruction. Her madness is evident in her diabolical howl and in the way she deals with her enemies in war. She appears to be out of control both on and off the battlefield. She is often found "intoxicated on blood," eating raw and rotten flesh with a smile on her face. She sits on corpses drinking their blood from a human skull. She doesn't appear to be in need of any "proper" friend other than her constant companions: snakes, jackals, and ghosts. Her human associates come from what traditional Hinduism has seen as the lowest caste, the sudras. Moreover, she is the "patron deity" of thugs and thieves. She is found in two preferred localities—battlefields and cremation grounds—and appears fully at ease in both places.

Kali's Behavior

There are many legends that illustrate the bloodthirsty and malevolent aspects of this goddess in her fury. According to the story of the *Devi Mahatmya,* the baffled Durga, in her battle with the demon Raktabija, who has incredible power to recreate himself from every drop of his own blood, summons Kali for assistance. Kali as Camunda, who sprang from Durga's body in her previous battle with the demons Canda and Munda, appears suddenly in her usual fury. She sucks the last drop of blood out of Raktabija's body and makes him unable to regenerate himself any further. She then murders his countless progeny by swallowing them whole, and finally rescues Durga from the imminent danger she faces on the field of war.

In the *Malati-Madhaba* of Bhabhuti we find that near Padmavati there was a temple of the goddess Camunda, who was worshipped with human sacrifice. Aghoroghanta, a devotee of Kali, was reported to have kidnapped a heroine in order to sacrifice her at the goddess's altar (see Kate). This reveals that Kali's worshippers reflect the same tendencies to violence as their deity, who appears to be satisfied with nothing less than the spilling of blood as a reflection of her power. In the *Bhagavata-Purana* Kali is approached by a leader of a band of thieves who plans to sacrifice the young Brahmin boy whom he kidnapped in order to obtain a blessing. As they approach the altar, the purity of the Brahmin burns the goddess and in her anger she decapitates the band of thieves and consumes their blood completely (*Bhagavata-Purana* 5.9 12-20).

In light of these stories Kali's behavior seems baffling and unpredictable. Although her benevolent side cannot be ignored, as when she saves the young boy's life and constantly aids other gods and goddesses in their distress, her malevolence is undeniable. The paradoxical mixture of compassion and violence evident in these stories is only the beginning of mysteries and ambiguities that surround her character. Although she is known as the Mother Goddess, she herself is barren. Although she is the wife of Siva, she is rarely found with her mate. She is not a hermit, but she lacks a proper household; in fact, she lives mostly outdoors and haunts the crematoriums. She is a woman, yet she excels in the normally male domains. Why is it so difficult to comprehend Kali's nature? Is it because we are trying to understand her divine nature in terms of the "femininity" she portrays and because she reflects a form of femininity that does not conform to the established role of women in Hinduism or in *any* other tradition informed by patriarchy?

The concept of liberation within a Hindu context is understood in terms of realizing one's true nature as Brahman. Liberation within the social context could then be understood as realizing one's potential as an individual, as well as a woman. Kali, in her actions, shows that the world of action is not compartmentalized into masculine and feminine spheres. These sexual roles are, rather, only modes of operation one assumes as he or she attempts to fulfill an inner potentiality with regard to what is being presented in a particular time and place. Neither her physical constitution nor her social status constrains or determines Kali's behavior. Her body is not in her way and definitely does not stop her from anything she plans on doing. Whether in her role at the battlefields or at the cremation ground, she neither highlights the sexual difference nor obliterates it but overcomes both possibilities in a meaningful way.

The myth of Kali offers a story of a woman in a plight. She is the personified wrath of all women in all cultures. As we read Kali's stories, we repeatedly encounter her wrathful image appearing from various goddesses who are portrayed to be either docile daughters or devoted wives. In the *Devi Mahatmya* Kali appears as the personified anger of Durga as she faces the demons. In the *Adbhuta Ramayana,* a late work highly favored by the Kashmiri Saktas, Sita, having killed Ravana, assumes the form of Kali (*Adbhuta Ramayana* xxv. 29-31). Kali plays a similar role in Parvati, who is otherwise known to be a benevolent goddess. Kausiki appears from the muscles of Parvati, turns black, and becomes known as Kalika, dwelling in the Himalayas (Bhattacharya, 149). In another such story Sati becomes angry when her husband Siva refuses to allow her to attend her father's sacrificial ceremony (Avalon 1960, 208-13). In her anger she assumes the form of Kali and appears in ten directions in her terrifying forms.

Kali's anger is an expression of a deep, long-buried emotion, a character trait that symbolizes deep emotional response to her situations and surroundings. She is not simply malevolent. Her "terrifying howls" are also a demand for equality where femininity is equated with meekness and subservience, since such anger is the only language that can be heard.

Power, especially the power of the warrior, has always been thought of in exclusively masculine terms. When a female deity is described as excelling in any male function—as Kali does on the battlefield—she is described either as a masculinized female or as out of control and destructive, as if strength and valor are constructive character traits only as long as they are part of a male deity. When these "destructive" traits are part of a female deity in a patriarchal system, the goddess no longer portrays a positive role model. But despite her violence and bloodthirstiness, Kali does indeed portray a model of strength and of self-liberation from constraint for post-patriarchal women.

Kali's Associations

Kali's association with animals that are not domesticated—such as jackals and so on—suggests her relationship goes beyond any type of hierarchical structure. Moreover, her relationship with animals such as snakes verifies her interconnectedness with every life form, regardless of how lowly it may be. From the psychological standpoint animals may very well suggest various parts of the human psyche, and familiarizing oneself with one's own thoughts and feelings regardless of their nature, confronting and associating with one's own inner being, however difficult that may be, is the first step to freedom.

Furthermore, she associates with the sudras. Sudras, according to the social stratification of the Hindu caste system, fall at the bottom of the social structure and lack any possibility of ever transcending that role and status in one lifetime. Consequently they are looked down upon by the rest of the community. Social stratification becomes counterproductive because it segregates and separates people and ultimately leads to oppression and bondage. Kali's companionship with the sudras throws an interesting insight on her rebellion against any structure that is oppressive in any form, and on her determination to reverse that destructive order. For example, the conception of the nation in the form of Divine Mother proved to be a strong basis for India's movement for freedom from the British. Narendra N. Bhattacharya articulates this view very clearly:

a constant characteristic of the Sakta religion, which we must not overlook or underestimate, is that throughout the ages the Female Principle stood for oppressed peoples, symbolizing all the liberating potentialities in the class-divided, patriarchal, and authoritarian social set up of India, the rigidity of which was mainly responsible for the survival and development of the opposite principles represented mainly by Saktism (Bhattacharya, 165).

Kali's Habitations

This interpretation gains further support in Kali's choice of dwelling place, namely cremation grounds. In the Hindu community cremation grounds usually are located at the fringe of human localities, almost at the borderline of the world and beyond. Most important, until recently women were not allowed to go to the cremation ground. One of the reasons for such a restriction is that a woman was assumed to be too emotional to witness the finality of death. Kali, by contrast, breaks away from the existing structure in search of an alternative. To her, the cremation ground is no more natural or unnatural than any other place in the world. Just as the cremation ground does not exist separately from society, death does not exist separately from life. To Kali, the dichotomy does not exist.

Breaking away from existent structures, stereotypes, and limitations necessitates facing an unknown and uncertain future. Similarly, the freedom and absolute liberation, which Kali in the cremation ground signifies, goes beyond the restrictions imposed on our understanding, on our perception and energy; it implies freedom from one's ego and from one's attachment to particularity and separateness.

KALI AND SIVA

Lastly, and most importantly, we must examine Kali from the point of view of her relationship with her husband Siva. As a wife, she can be taken — as she has been understood in patriarchy — solely as a loving mother and spouse. In some versions of her myth, indeed, this appears to be a valid reading. But when we look toward Kali's other, most striking characteristics, and when we look toward her most essential meaning, we are able to see her as moving beyond the patriarchal view of womanhood and marriage.

The Virtuous Wife in the Laws of Manu

For Manu there are some clear expectations for an ideal wife:

Though destitute of virtue, or seeking pleasure [elsewhere], or devoid of good qualities, a husband must be constantly worshipped as a god by a faithful wife (Manu, 196).

She who, controlling her thoughts, words, and deeds, never slights her lord, resides [after death] with her husband [in heaven] and is called a virtuous wife (Manu, 197).

Whatever be the qualities of the man with whom woman is united, according to the law, such qualities even she assumes, like a river [united] with the ocean (Manu, 331).

An ideal wife for Manu is a virtuous wife. Although a woman is devoid of natural virtues, as a wife she must earn them through her fidelity to her husband. She is to strive to control all facets of her thoughts and behavior with regard to her husband. Most important of all, a wife should worship her husband as her god. A woman, married according to religious and social law, must relinquish her identity and individuality and assume her husband's character traits, regardless of their nature. An ideal wife, therefore, is one who neither questions the validity of the rules nor disobeys them, but rather follows them with her whole being. Although a husband also has to follow certain restrictions, and the text contains a few injunctions with regard to his husbandly conduct, it is the wife who must account for the success or failure of a marriage and be the responsible partner for the happiness or unhappiness therein. Moreover, it is also her virtue as a wife that guarantees her own individual fulfillment as a woman here and hereafter in heaven. Manu seems to be defining the institution of marriage in terms of the total submission of a wife to her husband. In his definition of a virtuous wife he is emphasizing adherence to a person—the husband—more than adherence to any moral principle. That is, a wife's virtue solely depends on her total surrender and submission to her husband's will and power—and nothing else.

Kali as Wife

When Kali is seen with a god, she is always with Siva as his consort, Sakti. True to her nature, in her relationship she is paradoxical. There are times when she is not only the domineering one in the relationship, but even the active, initiating partner in the destructive, cosmic dance. In one south Indian story we find Kali celebrating her victory over Sumbha and Nishumbha with a destructive dance (Sivaramamurti, 378-79, 381; also summarized in Kinsley 1986, 119). A devotee of Siva appeals to Siva to remove Kali from the forest. But Kali refuses to move from the area or to stop her destruction. Instead, at the end of the story we find Siva in the forest with Kali, engaged in the same destructive dance. Kali has a disruptive influence on Siva; at the same time, it is in his presence that her own destructive behavior continues.

On the other hand, Siva sometimes brings out the hidden, gentler instinct in her. According to one Puranic story, after defeating her enemies on the battlefield and getting drunk with the blood of her slain enemies, Kali becomes absorbed in her destructive dance. Fearing imminent destruction of the world, Siva appears in the middle of the battlefield in the guise of an infant crying out in thirst. As Kali sees the crying infant, she stops her dancing and puts the infant in her arms. Here, as in other stories, she is presented as a loving mother moved by the sight of the slightest distress in her child. In another story Siva places himself on the battlefield like a corpse in order to stop Kali from her destructive dance and to protect the stability of the world itself. Though intoxicated and mad in her dance, she stops as she recognizes her husband lying under her feet. Like a proper Hindu woman she bites her tongue in shame (Kinsley 1975, 108; Nivedita).

In other stories she behaves like a devoted wife who is unconcerned about her own safety and concerned for the well-being of her husband. Kali is the helpmate who repeatedly risks her life as she is called by her husband to assist him on the battlefield. Still other stories present her as a gentle mother and wife.

But in most of her myths Kali appears to be independent and unattached, without any consort or male deity at her side. Even when she appears as the spouse of Siva, Kali projects a form of womanhood through her relationship with Siva that is beyond any normative behavior prescribed by Manu. Kali is a wife, yet she is far too domineering and destructive to be a wife as Manu envisioned. She appears to be an affectionate and devoted mate, but her changeable and unpredictable behavior does not let her continue in the role as a "proper wife." In short, she does not fulfill any of her wifely duties and obligations. Most important, her defiant nature reminds one of her unrestricted raw energy, which if uncontrolled, according to Manu, leads to chaos and calamity, but which, taken from another perspective, can serve as an imagistic resource for moving beyond patriarchy.

PATRIARCHAL vs. SCRIPTURAL READINGS

The biological differences between men and women are undeniable, but the hierarchical order established by Manu on the basis of such differences can neither be verified nor established in Vedic or Upanishadic terms. The Veda says that all things are Brahman. All distinctions — including the one that allows men of the priestly class but not women to say Vedic mantras — are "wholly opposed to the Spirit of the Great Word (*MahaVakya*)." One Brahman becomes dual, appears as Siva and Sakti, man and woman, two complementary principles involved in the process of creation. They are one and the same. The duality of Siva and Sakti is grounded in the unity and oneness of the Brahman. As Avalon notes, "In the Tantrasastra also Siva has said that there is no difference between them who are inseparably connected. He who is Siva is also Sakti, and she who is Sakti is also Siva" (Avalon 1965, 31).

That is, *scripturally*, both the husband and the wife are considered to be reflections of the divine nature. Therefore any hierarchical order such as that present in Manu's vision of marriage negates the very premise on which it appears to be based. Manu used the symbols of duality found in the principles of Siva and Sakti (or Purusan and Prakrti) to support a hierarchical and patriarchal system in which women's understanding and experience of their own power have been severely restrained. In doing so he violated the very spirit of those symbols.

The more the patriarchal mind recognized the force of the creative power present in the divine female, the more it created an environment for the feminine to be restricted and restrained. The more one understood

Prakrti as mere potentiality, who needs the presence of Purusa for her evolution, the more the sovereignty and absolute authority of the husband became established. In the relationship of man and woman Manu legitimated a sexually imbalanced society where man is to be regarded as a god. In this relationship it is the female who has been imagined to be acting out the unintegrated negative aspect (Prakrti, Avidya, Maya) of this union. Prakrti or woman as *object,* in this reading, requires a subject or the Purusa for fulfillment and existence itself. Marriage, according to Manu, is a form of union between a man and a woman where the feminine is required to be the subservient, dependent companion to the masculine. Rather than speaking of a union in terms of the transcendence of sexual differences and individual ego in a meaningful unity, Manu advocates gender difference that allows for a negative vision of the female.

But the patriarchal reading neglects the source of both subject and object, the One, unmanifested Brahman who is neither a subject nor an object, male nor female. Both subject and object in reality are the same. Union transcends sexual differences and the individual ego. Kali illustrates this. Not conscious of the kind of union Manu advocates, Kali symbolizes a form of marriage that necessitates equality and individuality. Her femininity belongs to her and not to her husband. Kali as a woman, as a wife, knows what her status should be. As she dances the dance of destruction she communicates her responses to the way things are and the way they should be. That is, in her destructive dance she creates her own reality. Only by moving beyond Manu to a less gender-centered reinterpretation of Kali's supposed destructiveness can we appreciate her as the fountain of creative energy she is.

CONCLUSION: THE PRESENCE OF KALI

Behind the diverse characters of Sati, Sita, Durga, and Parvati, lies the single, unchanging face of the true hero, the wrathful goddess Kali, the savior. As these goddesses face oppressing realities of life, Kali the true hero appears in all of them and saves them in their battle of life. How can contemporary women identify themselves with a mythical character? I think there is an interaction between a contemporary woman's psyche and the mythic behavior patterns of the goddess, patterns that inform and are played out in a woman's life. For example, when a woman is outraged by her husband's lack of understanding or refusal to follow through on a request, her acting out is comparable at some level to the story of outraged Sati, who appears as Kali to confront and terrify an uncooperative Siva. When a woman feels a tremendous need to subordinate her welfare to the welfare of the other, she is encountering self-sacrificing Sita. By identifying ourselves with the ways Kali acts on the mythic level, with the actual and potential embodiments of Kali, we begin to find a transpersonal source of liberation within her character and nature. As we listen to the various stories of the goddess Kali we see them take shape into a definite pattern of experience. In emphasizing or de-emphasizing certain elements—in particular, those dealing with the potential of women—we can see how some of the stories were told from a male point of view. By reviewing these stories over and over again, understanding them in their most liberating sense, as do the Tantric interpretations, and reappropriating from them those elements which are most powerful as resources for the liberation of both men and women—taking as authentic and genuinely spiritual those aspects that promote our over-all welfare—we can eliminate the inessential details and the patriarchal distortions and finally identify the sources and patterns of our oppressed past and present. It is this pattern that finally reveals the way we are now and what we could possibly become. It shows the ways in which the images and the stories of Kali can be liberating and empowering to all through exposing an essence that goes beyond male and female, beauty and ugliness, life and death, and all forms of alienation and separation.

In seeking to go beyond the patriarchal view of the goddess, and woman, as untamed and unsubjugated and therefore in need of control and restriction, we must understand Kali at various levels, at more essential levels than superficial, patriarchal readings reveal. On one level she is Brahman, the all-inclusive Reality that is beyond any form of alienation or separation. On another level Kali is the divine principle that provides us with a tradition of female language and images with which we can speak of the divine: Sakti, Prakrti, Maya, and Avidya. She is also called the Devi, the goddess, literally "the self-manifested one" (Avalon 1965, 66). The term *devi* comes from the root *div* meaning "the shining one." That is, Devi is someone who shines through all that has been imposed upon her. She is also referred to as *Asita* (Avalon 1965, 95), which means that she is free from bondage (*sita* is "bound"; *asita*, "unbounded" or "ultimately liberated"). She is called *Kalika,* "a long-standing cloud threatening to rain." She is *Tara,* "the savior." She saves the world from all forms of oppression (Avalon 1965, 101).

She is called *Matah,* "mother of creation." The Sanskrit term for mother is in the feminine when it refers to mother; it also refers to the knower or measurer, and appears when it does so in the masculine gender. Here, in Kali as Matah or Mother, we have the two aspects—Siva, the masculine knower, and the feminine Sakti, the mother, the creator. Neither masculine nor feminine image and language, then, contains the final truth; neither can be absolutized. They are both aspects of the same, single reality.

On still another level she reflects the behavioral reality of a subjugated woman in search of her identity. The dark goddess is perpetually present in the inner and outer struggles faced by women at all times. Her darkness represents those rejected and suppressed parts of female creativity, energy, and power that have not been given a chance to be actualized. As Sister Nivedita writes, "Our daily life creates our symbol of God" (Nivedita, 461).

In and through the dark images we learn to accept the equality of all names, forms, and genders, taken up as they are within the principles of Siva and Sakti and, finally, in the One. Indeed, Kali is the emblem of two opposites that constitute a composite whole, a power and a wonder that goes beyond all distinctions.

NOTES

1. Many of the Puranas are available in English translation. For a selected bibliography relating to Indian goddesses, see Hawley and Wulff, 383-403.
2. The Puranas are Hindu scriptures that were written down after the (earlier) Vedic scriptures.
3. David R. Kinsley provides a readily accessible analysis of the issues and stories pertaining to Kali in Kinsley 1982, which provides an analysis as well of Kali in terms of *Maya, Prakrti,* and *Sakti.* Kinsley suggests that Kali is seen as a mother by her devotees because she "gives birth to a wider vision of reality than one embodied in the order of *dharma"* (Kinsley 1982, 152). I would add "in the order of *patriarchy."* See also Kinsley 1986.

WORKS CITED

Avalon, Arthur, ed. *Principles of Tantra: The Tantratattva of Sriyukta Siva Candra Vidyarnava Bhattacarya Mahodaya.* Madras: Ganesh and Company, 1960.

————, ed. and trans. *Hymn to Kali (Karpuradi-Stotra).* Madras: Ganesh and Company, 1965.

————, trans. *Tantra of the Great Liberation (Mahanirvana Tantra).* New York: Dover Publications, 1972.

Bhattacharya, Narendra Nath. *History of Sakta Religion.* New Delhi: Munishiram Manohaslar Pub. Pvt. Ltd., 1974.

Deutsch, Elliot. *Advaita Vedanta: A Philosophical Reconstruction.* Honolulu: The University Press of Hawaii, 1973.

Hawley, John Stratton, and Donna Marie Wulff, eds. *The Divine Consort: Radha and the Goddesses of India.* Boston: Beacon Press, 1982.

Kate, M. R., ed. and trans. *Bhavabhuti's Malaimadhava, with the Commentary of Jagadhara.* Delhi: Motilal Banarasidass, 1967.

Kinsley, David. *The Sword and the Flute: Kali and Krsna, Dark Visions of the Terrible and the Sublime in Hindu Mythology.* Berkeley and Los Angeles: University of California Press, 1975.

————. "Blood and Death Out of Place: Reflections on the Goddess Kali." In *The Divine Consort.* See Hawley and Wulff, 1982.

————. *Hindu Goddesses.* Los Angeles: University of California Press, 1986.

Manu. *The Laws of Manu.* Sacred Books of the East, 25. Trans. G. Buhler. Delhi: Motilal Banarasidass, 1964.

Nivedita. *Kali the Mother.* I. Calenlta: Ramkrishna Sarada Mission, 1967.

Ruether, Rosemary. *Sexism and God-Talk.* Boston: Beacon Press, 1983.

Satprakashananda. *Methods of Knowledge.* Calcutta: Advaita Ashram, 1976.

Sivaramamurti, C. *Natarajain Art, Thought and Literature.* New Delhi: National Museum, 1976.

3

Muslim Women and Post-Patriarchal Islam

RIFFAT HASSAN

THE ISLAMIC TRADITION: SOURCES AND INTERPRETATION

Before engaging in any meaningful discussion of a post-patriarchal Islam, I consider it necessary to clarify what I mean by the Islamic tradition, since much confusion surrounds the use of this term. The Islamic tradition — like other major religious traditions — does not consist of, or derive from, a single source. Most Muslims if questioned about its sources are likely to refer to more than one of the following: The Qur'an (the Book of Revelation believed by Muslims to be the Word of God); Sunnah (the practical traditions of the Prophet Muhammad); Hadith (the sayings attributed to the Prophet Muhammad); Fiqh (Jurisprudence) or Madahib (Schools of Law); and the Shariah (the code of life that regulates all aspects of Muslim life). While all these "sources" have contributed to what is cumulatively referred to as the Islamic tradition, it is important to note that they do not form a coherent or consistent body of teachings or precepts from which a universally agreed upon set of Islamic norms can be derived. Many examples can be cited of inconsistency between various sources of the Islamic tradition, and also of inner inconsistency within some, for example, the Hadith literature. In view of this fact it is inappropriate, particularly in a scholarly work, to speak of the Islamic tradition as if it were unitary or monolithic. Its various components need to be identified and examined separately before one can attempt to make any sort of generalization on behalf of the Islamic tradition in general.

Of the various sources of the Islamic tradition — at least insofar as it is understood theoretically or normatively — the two most important are the Qur'an and the Hadith. Of these two, undoubtedly, the Qur'an is the more important. In fact, the Qur'an is regarded by virtually all Muslims as the primary source of Islam, having absolute authority since it is believed to be God's unadulterated message conveyed through the agency of Archangel Gabriel to the Prophet Muhammad, who then transmitted it to others without change or error. However, since the early days of Islam, the Hadith literature has been the lens through which the words of the Qur'an have been seen and interpreted.

Before mentioning the importance of the Hadith literature to the Islamic tradition, it is necessary to point out that every aspect of this literature is surrounded by controversy. In particular, the question of the authenticity of individual *ahadith* (plural of *hadith*), as well as of the Hadith literature as a whole, has occupied the attention of many scholars of Islam since the time of Ash-Shafi'i (died in 809). As stated by Fazlur Rahman in his book, *Islam*, "a very large proportion of the Hadiths were judged to be spurious and forged by classical Muslim scholars themselves" (Rahman, 70). This fact has generated much skepticism regarding the Hadith literature in general among "moderate" Muslims. Though few of them are willing to go as far as Ghulam Ahmad Parwez, leader of the *Tulu' e Islam* or the Dawn of Islam movement in Pakistan, who rejects the Hadith literature virtually *in toto*, many of them are likely to be in agreement with the following observations of Moulvi Cheragh Ali, an important Indian Muslim scholar, who wrote in the nineteenth century:

> The vast flood of tradition soon formed a chaotic sea. Truth, error, fact, and fable mingled together in an undistinguishable confusion. Every religious, social, and political system was defended when necessary, to please a Khalif or an Ameer to serve his purpose, to support all manner of lies and absurdities or to satisfy the passion, caprice, or arbitrary will of the despots, leaving out of consideration the creation of any standards of test. ... I am seldom inclined to quote traditions having little or no belief in their genuineness, as generally they are inauthentic, unsupported and one-sided (quoted in Guillaume, 97).

Though valid grounds exist for regarding the Hadith literature with caution, if not skepticism, Fazlur Rahman is right in saying that "if the Hadith literature *as a whole* is cast away, the basis for the historicity of the Qur'an is removed with one stroke" (Rahman, 73). Furthermore, as pointed out by Alfred Guillaume in his book, *The Traditions of Islam:*

> The Hadith literature as we now have it provides us with apostolic precept and example covering the whole duty of man: it is *the basis* of that developed system of law, theology, and custom which is Islam (Guillaume, 15).

However skeptical we are with regard to the ultimate historical value of the traditions, it is hard to overrate their importance in the formation of the life of the Islamic races throughout the centuries. If we cannot accept them at their face value, they are of inestimable value as a mirror of the events which preceded the consolidation of Islam into a system (Guillaume, 12-13).

Not only does the Hadith literature have its own autonomous character in point of law and even of doctrine (Hodgson, 232), it also has an emotive aspect whose importance is hard to overstate since it relates to the conscious as well as to the subconscious patterns of thought and feeling of Muslims, individually and collectively, as H. A. R. Gibb has observed perceptively:

It would be difficult to exaggerate the strength and the effects of the Muslim attitude toward Muhammad. Veneration for the Prophet was a natural and inevitable feeling, both in his own day and later, but this is more than veneration. The personal relationships of admiration and love which he inspired in his associates have echoed down the centuries, thanks to the instruments which the community created in order to evoke them afresh in each generation. The earliest of these instruments was the narration of hadith. So much has been written about the legal and theological functions of the hadith that its more personal and religious aspects have been almost overlooked. It is true, to be sure, that the necessity of finding an authoritative source which would supplement the legal and ethical prescriptions contained in the Koran led to a search for examples set by Muhammad in his daily life and practice. One could be certain that if he had said this or that, done this or that, approved this or that action, one had an absolutely reliable guide to the right course to adopt in any similar situation. And it is equally true that this search went far beyond the limits of credibility or simple rectitude, and that it was in due course theologically rationalized by the doctrine of implicit inspiration (Gibb, 194).

PATRIARCHAL ISLAM: IMPACT UPON MUSLIM WOMEN

Having underscored the importance of the Qur'an and the Hadith as primary sources of the Islamic tradition, it is necessary to point out that through the centuries of Muslim history, these sources have been interpreted only by Muslim men, who have arrogated to themselves the task of defining the ontological, theological, sociological, and eschatological status of Muslim women. While it is encouraging to know that women such as Khadijah and A'ishah (wives of the Prophet Muhammad) and Rabi'a al-Basri (the outstanding woman Sufi) figure significantly in early Islam, the fact remains that the Islamic tradition has, by and large, remained rigidly patriarchal until the present time, prohibiting the growth of scholarship among women particularly in the realm of religious thought. In view of this it is hardly surprising that until now the overwhelming majority of Muslim women have remained totally or largely unaware of the extent to which their "Islamic" (in an ideal sense) rights have been violated by their male-centered and male-dominated societies, which have continued to assert, glibly and tirelessly, that Islam has given women more rights than any other religious tradition. Kept for centuries in physical, mental, and emotional confinement and deprived of the opportunity to actualize their human potential, most Muslim women find beyond their capability even the exercise of analyzing their personal life-experiences as Muslim women. Here it is pertinent to mention that while the rate of literacy is low in many Muslim countries, the rate of literacy of Muslim women, especially those who live in rural areas where most of the population lives, is among the lowest in the world.

In recent times, largely due to the pressure of anti-women laws which are being promulgated under the cover of "islamisation" in some parts of the Muslim world, women with some degree of education and awareness are beginning to realize that religion is being used as an instrument of oppression rather than as a means of liberation. To understand the strong impetus to "islamise" Muslim societies, especially with regard to women-related norms and values, it is necessary to know that of all the challenges confronting the Muslim world perhaps the greatest is that of modernity. The caretakers of Muslim traditionalism are aware of the fact that viability in the modern technological age requires the adoption of the scientific or rational outlook, which inevitably brings about major changes in modes of thinking and behavior. Women, both educated and uneducated, who are participating in the national work force and contributing toward national development think and behave differently from women who have no sense of their individual identity or autonomy as active agents in a history-making process and regard themselves merely as instruments designed to minister to and reinforce a patriarchal system, which they believe to be divinely instituted. Not too long ago many women in Pakistan were jolted out of their dogmatic slumber by the enactment of laws, such as those pertaining to women's testimony in cases of their own rape or in financial and other matters, and by "threatened" legislation, such as proposals pertaining to "blood-money" for women's murder, that aimed at reducing their value and status systematically, virtually mathematically, to less than that of men. It was not long before they realized that forces of religious conservatism were determined to cut women down to one-half or less of men, and that this attitude stemmed from a deep-rooted desire to keep women *in their places*, which means secondary, subordinate, and inferior to men.

In the face both of military dictatorship and religious autocracy, valiant efforts have been made by women's groups in Pakistan to protest against the instituting of manifestly anti-women laws and to highlight cases of gross injustice and brutality toward women. However, it is still not clearly and fully understood, even by many women activists in Pakistan and other Muslim countries, that the negative ideas and attitudes pertaining to women that prevail in Muslim societies in general, are rooted in theology and that unless, or until, the theological foundations of the misogynistic and androcentric tendencies in the Islamic tradition are demolished, Muslim women will continue to be brutalized and discriminated against despite improvement in statistics relating to women's education, employment, social and political rights, and so on. No matter how many sociopolitical rights are granted to women, as long as these women are conditioned to accept the myths used by theologians or religious hierarchs to shackle their bodies, hearts, minds, and souls, they will never become fully developed or whole human beings, free of fear and guilt, able to stand equal to men in the sight of God.

In my judgment the importance of developing what the West calls feminist theology in the context of the Islamic tradition is paramount today with a view of liberating not only Muslim women but also Muslim men from unjust structures and laws that make a peer relationship between men and women impossible. It is good to know that in the last hundred years there have been at least two significant Muslim men scholars and activists—Qasim Amin from Egypt and Mumtaz Ali from India—who have been staunch advocates of women's rights, though knowing this hardly lessens the pain of also knowing that even in this age characterized by knowledge, all but a handful of Muslim women lack any knowledge of Islamic theology. It is profoundly discouraging to contemplate how few Muslim women there are in the world today who possess the competence, even if they have the courage and commitment, to engage in a scholarly study of Islam's primary sources in order to participate in the theological discussions on women-related issues that are taking place in much of the contemporary Muslim world. Such participation is imperative if a post-patriarchal perspective is to emerge in Muslim societies or communities.

PATRIARCHAL ISLAM: THREE FUNDAMENTAL THEOLOGICAL ISSUES

How one envisions post-patriarchal Islam depends in large measure upon how one understands patriarchal Islam and its fundamental assumptions and attitudes regarding women and women-related issues. Much of what has happened to Muslim women through the ages becomes comprehensible if one keeps one fact in mind: Muslims, in general, consider it a self-evident fact that women are not equal to men, who are "above" women or have a "degree of advantage" over them. There is hardly anything in a Muslim woman's life that is not affected by this belief; hence it is vitally important, not only for theological reasons but also for pragmatic ones, to subject it to rigorous scholarly scrutiny and attempt to identify its roots.

The roots of the belief that men are superior to women lie—in my judgment—in three theological assumptions: (a) that God's primary creation is man, not woman, since woman is believed to have been created from man's rib and therefore derivative and secondary ontologically; (b) that woman, not man, was the primary agent of what is customarily described as *Man's Fall* or expulsion from the Garden of Eden, and hence "all daughters of Eve" are to be regarded with hatred, suspicion, and contempt; and (c) that woman was created not only *from* man but also *for* man, which makes her existence merely instrumental and not of fundamental importance. The three theological questions to which the above assumptions may appropriately be regarded as answers are: (1) How was woman created? (2) Was woman responsible for the Fall of man? and (3) Why was woman created? While all three questions have had profound significance in the history of ideas and attitudes pertaining to women in the Islamic as well as the Jewish and Christian traditions, I consider the first one, which relates to the issues of woman's creation, more basic and important, philosophically and theologically, than any other in the context of man-woman equality. This is so because if man and woman have been created equal by Allah, who is the ultimate arbiter of value, then they cannot become unequal, essentially, at a subsequent time. On the other hand, if man and woman have been created unequal by Allah, then they cannot become equal, essentially, at a subsequent time.

It is not possible, within the scope of this essay, to deal exhaustively with any of the above-mentioned questions.[1] However, in the brief discussion of each question that follows, an attempt is made to highlight the way in which sources of normative Islam have been interpreted to show that women are inferior to men.

How Was Woman Created?

The ordinary Muslim believes, as seriously as the ordinary Jew or Christian, that Adam was God's primary creation and that Eve was made from Adam's rib. While this myth has obvious rootage in the Yahwist's account of creation in Genesis 2:18-24, it has no basis whatever in the Qur'an, which in the context of human creation speaks always in completely egalitarian terms. In none of the thirty or so passages that describe the creation of humanity (designated by generic terms such as *an-nas, al-insan,* and *bashar*) by God in a variety of ways is there any statement that could be interpreted as asserting or suggesting that man was created prior to woman or that woman was created from man. In fact, there are some passages[2] that could—from a purely grammatical/linguistic point of view—be interpreted as stating that the first creation (*nafs in wahidatin*) was feminine not masculine.[3] The Qur'an notwithstanding, Muslims believe that *Hawwa'* (the Hebrew/Arabic counterpart of *Eve*), who incidentally is never mentioned in the Qur'an, was created from the "crooked" rib of Adam, who is believed to be the first human being created by God. Here it needs to be mentioned that the term *Adam* is not an Arabic term but a Hebrew one meaning *of the soil* (from *adamah*, "the soil"). The Hebrew term *Adam* functions generally as a collective noun referring to *the human* (species) rather than to a male human being.[4] In the Qur'an also the term *Adam* refers, in twenty-one cases out of twenty-five,[5] to humanity. Here it is of interest to note that though the term *Adam* mostly does not refer to a particular human being, it does refer to human beings in a particular way. As pointed out by Muhammad Iqbal:

> Indeed, in the verses which deal with the origin of man as a living being, the Qur'an uses the words *Bashar* or *Insan*, not *Adam*, which it reserves for man in his capacity of God's viceregent on earth. The purpose of the Qur'an is further secured by the omission of proper names mentioned in the Biblical narration—Adam and Eve. The term *Adam* is retained and used more as a concept than as a name of a concrete human individual. The word is not without authority in the Qur'an itself (Iqbal, 83).

An analysis of the Qur'anic descriptions of human creation shows how the Qur'an evenhandedly uses both feminine and masculine terms and imagery to describe the creation of humanity from a single source. That God's original creation was undifferentiated humanity and not either man or woman (who appeared simultaneously at a subsequent time) is implicit in a number of Qur'anic passages.[6] If the Qur'an makes no distinction between the creation of man and woman—as it clearly does not—why do Muslims believe that Hawwa' was created from the rib of Adam? Although the Genesis 2 account of woman's creation is accepted by virtually all Muslims, it is difficult to believe that it entered the Islamic tradition directly, for very few Muslims ever read the Bible. It is much more likely that it became a part of Muslim heritage through its assimilation in the Hadith literature. That the Genesis 2 idea of woman being created from Adam's rib did, in fact, become incorporated in the Hadith literature is evident from a number of *ahadith*. Of these, six are particularly important since they appear to have had a formative impact on how Muslims have perceived woman's being and sexuality (as differentiated from man's). The *matn* ("content")[7] of these six *ahadith*—three from *Sahih Al-Bukhari* and three from *Sahih Muslim* and all ascribed to the Companion known as Abu Hurairah[8]—is given below:

> 1. Treat women nicely, for a woman is created from a rib, and the most curved portion of the rib is its upper portion, so if you would try to straighten it, it will break, but if you leave it as it is, it will remain crooked. So treat women nicely (M. M. Khan, 346).

2. The woman is like a rib, if you try to straighten her, she will break. So if you want to get benefit from her, do so while she still has some crookedness (M. M. Khan, 80).

3. Whoever believes in Allah and the Last Day should not hurt (trouble) his neighbor. And I advise you to take care of the women, for they are created from a rib and the most crooked part of the rib is its upper part; if you try to straighten it, it will break, and if you leave it, it will remain crooked, so I urge you to take care of woman (M. M. Khan, 81).

4. Woman is like a rib. When you attempt to straighten it, you would break it. And if you leave her alone you would benefit by her, and crookedness will remain in her (Siddiqui, 752).

5. Woman has been created from a rib and will in no way be straightened for you; so . . . benefit by her while crookedness remains in her. And if you attempt to straighten her, you will break her, and breaking her is divorcing her (Siddiqui, 752).

6. He who believes in Allah and the Hereafter, if he witnesses any matter he should talk in good terms about it or keep quiet. Act kindly towards women, for woman is created from a rib, and the most crooked part of the rib is its top. If you attempt to straighten it, you will break it, and if you leave it, the crookedness will remain there so act kindly towards women (Siddiqui, 752-53).

I have examined these *ahadith* elsewhere and have shown them to be flawed both with regard to their formal (*isnad*) as well as their material (*matn*) aspects. The theology of woman implicit in these *ahadith* is based upon generalizations about her ontology, biology, and psychology contrary to the letter and spirit of the Qur'an. These *ahadith* ought, therefore, to have been rejected—since Muslim scholars agree on the principle that any Hadith that is inconsistent with the Qur'an cannot be accepted. However, despite the fact that the *ahadith* in question contradict the teachings of the Qur'an, they have continued to be an important part of the ongoing Islamic tradition. Undoubtedly one of the major reasons for this is that these *ahadith* come from the two most highly venerated Hadith collections by Muhammad ibn Isma'il al-Bukhari (810-70) and Muslim bin al-Hallaj (817-75). These two collections known collectively as *Sahihan* (from *sahih*, meaning "sound" or "authentic") "form an almost unassailable authority, subject indeed to criticism in details, yet deriving an indestructible influence from the *ijma* or general consent of the community in custom and belief, which it is their function to authenticate" (Guillaume, 32). While being included in the *Sahihan* gives the *ahadith* in question much weight among Muslims who know about the science of Hadith, their continuing popularity among Muslims in general indicates that they articulate something deeply embedded in Muslim culture—namely that women are derivative[9] creatures who can never be considered equal to men.

Theologically, the history of women's subjection in the Islamic (as well as the Jewish and Christian) tradition began with the story of Hawwa"s creation. In my view, unless Muslim women return to the point of origin and challenge the authenticity of the *ahadith* that make all representatives of their sex ontologically inferior and irremediably crooked, male-centered and male-controlled Muslim societies are not at all likely to acknowledge the egalitarianism evident in the Qur'anic statements about human creation.

Was Woman Responsible for the Fall of Man?

Many Muslims, like many Jews and Christians, would answer this question in the affirmative, though nothing in the Qur'anic descriptions would warrant such an answer. Here it may be noted that in Genesis 3:6 the dialogue preceding the eating of the forbidden fruit by the human pair in the Garden of Eden is between the serpent and Eve (though Adam's presence is also indicated, as contended by feminist theologians) and this has provided the basis for the popular casting of Eve into the role of tempter, deceiver, and seducer of Adam; but in the Qur'an, the Shaitan (Satan) has no exclusive dialogue with Adam's "zauj." In two of the three passages that refer to this episode, namely, Surah 2:*Al-Baqarah*:35-39 and Surah 7:*Al-A'raf*:19-25, the Shaitan is stated to have led both Adam and "zauj" astray though in the former (verse 36) no actual conversation is reported. In the remaining passage, namely, Surah 20:*Ta-Ha*:115-124, it is Adam who is charged with forgetting his covenant with God (verse 115), who is tempted by the Shaitan (verse 120) and who disobeys God and allows himself to be seduced (verse 121). However, if one looks at all three passages as well as the way in which the term *Adam* functions generally in the Qur'an, it becomes clear that the Qur'an regards the act of disobedience by the human pair in *al-jannah* (the Garden) as a collective rather than an individual act for which exclusive, or even primary, responsibility is not assigned to either man or woman. Even in the last passage, in which Adam appears to be held responsible for forgetting the covenant and for allowing himself to be beguiled by the Shaitan, the act of disobedience, that is, the eating from the Tree, is committed jointly by Adam and "zauj" and not by Adam alone or in the first place.

Having said that, it is extremely important to stress the point that the Qur'an provides no basis whatever for asserting, suggesting, or implying that Hawwa', having been tempted and deceived by the Shaitan, in turn tempted and deceived Adam and led to his expulsion from *al-jannah*. This fact notwithstanding, many Muslim commentators have ascribed the primary responsibility for man's Fall to woman, as may be seen from the following extract:

> In al-Tabari's *Tarikh* (1:108) the very words Satan used to tempt Eve are then used by her to tempt Adam: "Look at this tree, how sweet is its smell, how delicious is its fruit, how beautiful is its color!" This passage is concluded by God's specifically accusing Eve of deceiving Adam. Later in the narrative (1:111-112) al-Tabari mentions a report that is also cited by other commentators, the gist of which is to say that Adam while in his full reasoning faculties did not eat of the tree, but only succumbed to the temptation after Eve had given him wine to drink. Al-Tha'labi in citing the same report also stresses the loss of Adam's rationality through the imbibing of wine, and al-Razi (*Tafsir* 3:13) says that such a story, which he has seen in several "tafsirs," is not at all far-fetched. Implicit in this specific act, of course, is both Eve's culpability and Adam's inherent rationality. Lest any should miss the point that Eve is actively and not just innocently involved in Adam's temptation, Ibn Kathir asserts that as God surely knows best, it was Eve who ate of the tree before Adam and urged him to eat. He then quotes a saying attributed to the Prophet, "But for Banu Isra'il meat would not have spoiled (because they used to keep it for the next day), and but for Hawwa' no female would be a traitor to her husband!" (*Bidaya* 1:84) (Smith and Haddad, 139).

There is hardly any doubt that Muslim women have been as victimized as Jewish and Christian women by the way in which the Jewish, Christian, and Islamic traditions have generally interpreted the Fall episode. However, it needs to be pointed out that the Qur'anic account of the episode differs significantly from the biblical account, and that the Fall does not mean in the Islamic tradition what it means in the Jewish, and particularly in the Christian, traditions.

To begin with, whereas in Genesis 3 no explanation is given as to why the serpent tempts either Eve alone or both Adam and Eve, in the Qur'an the reason why the Shaitan (or "Iblis") sets out to beguile the human pair in *al-jannah* is stated clearly in a number of passages (see Surah 15: *Al-Hijr*:26-43; Surah 17: *Bani Isra'il*:61-64; Surah 18: *Al-Kahf*:50; and Surah 38:*Sad*:71-85). The refusal of the Shaitan to obey God's command to bow in submission to Adam follows from his belief that being a creature of fire he is elementally superior to Adam, who is a creature of clay. When condemned for his arrogance by God and ordered to depart in a state of abject disgrace, the Shaitan throws a challenge to the Almighty: He will prove to God that Adam and Adam's progeny are unworthy of the honor and favor bestowed on them by God, being—in general—ungrateful, weak, and easily lured away from the straight path by worldly temptations. Not attempting to hide his intentions to come upon human beings from all sides, the Shaitan asks for—and is granted—a reprieve until "the Day of the Appointed Time." Not only is the reprieve granted, but God also tells the Shaitan to use all his wiles and forces to assault human beings and see if they would follow him. A cosmic drama now begins, involving the eternal opposition between the principles of right and wrong or good and evil, which is lived out as human beings, exercising their moral autonomy, choose between "the straight path" and "the crooked path."

In terms of the Qur'anic narrative what happens to the human pair in *al-jannah* is a sequel to the interchange between God and the Shaitan. In the sequel we learn that Adam and "zauj" have been commanded not to go near the Tree lest they become "zalimin." Seduced by the Shaitan, they disobey God. However, in Surah 7: *Al-A'raf*:23 they acknowledge before God that they have done "*zulm*" to themselves and earnestly seek God's forgiveness and mercy. They are told by God to "go forth" or "descend" from *al-jannah*, but in addressing them the Qur'an uses the dual form of address (referring exclusively to Adam and "zauj") only once (in Surah 18:*Ta-Ha*:123); for the rest the plural form is used, which necessarily refers to more than two persons and is generally understood as referring to humanity as a whole.

In the framework of Qur'anic theology, the order to go forth from *al-jannah* given to Adam or Children of Adam cannot be considered a punishment because Adam was always meant to be God's viceregent on earth as stated clearly in Surah 2: *Al-Baqarah*:30. The earth is not a place of banishment but is declared by the Qur'an to be humanity's dwelling place and a source of profit to it (Iqbal, 84).

There is, strictly speaking, no Fall in the Qur'an. What the Qur'anic narration focuses upon is the moral choice that humanity is required to make when confronted by the alternatives presented by God and the Shaitan. This becomes clear if one reflects on the text of Surah 2: *Al-Baqarah*:35 and Surah 7: *Al-A'raf*:19, in which it is stated: "You (dual) go not near this Tree, lest you (dual) become of the 'zalimin.'" In other words, the human pair is being told that *if* they will go near the Tree, *then* they will be counted among those who perpetrate *zulm*. Commenting on the root *zim*, Toshihiko Izutsu says,

> The primary meaning of ZIM is, in the opinion of many authoritative lexicologists, that of "putting in a wrong place." In the moral sphere it seems to mean primarily "to act in such a way as to transgress the proper limit and encroach upon the right of some other person." Briefly and generally speaking "zulm" is to do injustice in the sense of going beyond one's bounds and doing what one has no right to (Izutsu, 152-53).

By transgressing the limits set by God, the human pair become guilty of *zulm* toward themselves. This *zulm* consists in their taking on the responsibility for choosing between good and evil. Here it is important to note that the

Qur'anic legend of the Fall has nothing to do with the first appearance of man on this planet. Its purpose is rather to indicate man's rise from a primitive state of instinctive appetite to the conscious possession of a free self, capable of doubt and disobedience. The Fall does not mean any moral depravity; it is man's transition from simple consciousness to the first flash of self-consciousness, a kind of waking from the dream of nature with a throb of personal causality in one's own being. Nor does the Qur'an regard the earth as a torture-hall where an elementally wicked humanity is imprisoned for an original act of sin. Man's first act of disobedience was also his first act of free choice; and that is why, according to the Qur'anic narration, Adam's first transgression was forgiven. ... A being whose movements are wholly determined like a machine cannot produce goodness. Freedom is thus a condition of goodness. But to permit the emergence of a finite ego who has the power to choose, after considering the relative values of several courses of action open to him, is really to take a great risk; for the freedom to choose good involves also the freedom to choose what is the opposite of good. That God has taken this risk shows His immense faith in man; it is now for man to justify this faith (Iqbal, 85).

There is no Fall in the Qur'an, hence there is no original sin. Human beings are not born sinful into this world, hence do not need to be redeemed or saved. This is generally accepted in the Islamic tradition. However, the association of the Fall with sexuality, which has played such a massive role in perpetuating the myth of feminine evil in the Christian tradition, also exists in the minds of many Muslims and causes untold damage to Muslim women.

It is remarkable to see that though there is no reference to sexual activity on the part of man or woman even in their postlapsarian state of partial or complete nakedness in either Genesis 3 or the Qur'an, many Muslims and scholars have jumped to the conclusion that exposure of their *sau'at* ("the external portion of the organs of generation of a man, and of a woman, and the anus," Lane, 1458), generally translated as "shameful parts," necessarily led the human pair to sexual activity that was "shameful" not only by virtue of being linked with their "shameful parts," but also because it was instigated by the Shaitan. The following explanation by A. A. Maududi — one of contemporary Islam's most influential scholars — represents the thinking of many, if not most, Muslims on this point:

The sex instinct is the greatest weakness of the human race. That is why Satan selected this weak spot for his attack on the adversary and devised the scheme to strike at their modesty. Therefore the first step he took in this direction was to expose their nakedness to them so as to open the door of indecency before them and beguile them into sexuality. Even to this day, Satan and his disciples are adopting the same scheme of depriving the woman of the feelings of modesty and shyness, and they cannot think of any scheme of "progress" unless they expose and exhibit the woman to all and sundry (Maududi 1976, 16, n. 13).

The initial statement leaves no doubt about Maududi's negative view of the sex instinct, which he describes as "the greatest weakness of the human race." Associating sexuality with the Shaitan's "attack on the adversary," Maududi assumes that on discovering their state of physical exposure, the human pair resorted irresistibly to an act of "indecency," that is, sexual intercourse. In fact, according to the text, the human pair's first act on discovering their exposed state was one of "decency," namely, that of covering themselves with leaves.

That Maududi—like many other Muslims, Jews, and Christians—sees women as the primary agents of sexuality, which is regarded as the Shaitan's chief instrument for defeating God's plan for humanity, is clear from the way in which he shifts attention from the human pair to the woman in the above passage. In turning his eyes away from the "nakedness" of the sons of Adam to focus on the nakedness of the daughters of Hawwa', he is typical of Muslim culture.

Though the branding of women as "the devil's gateway"[10] is not at all the intent of the Qur'anic narration of the Fall story—as the foregoing account has shown—Muslims, no less than Jews and Christians, have used the story to vent their misogynistic feelings. This is clear from the continuing popularity of *ahadith* such as the following:

The Prophet said, "After me I have not left any affliction more harmful to men than women" (Kahn, 22).

Ibn Abbas reported that Allah's Messenger said: "I had a chance to look into Paradise and I found that the majority of the people were poor and I looked into the Fire and there I found the majority constituted by women."

Abu Sa'id Khudri reported that Allah's Messenger said: "The world is sweet and green (alluring) and verily Allah is going to install you as viceregent in it in order to see how you act. So avoid the allurement of women: verily, the first trial for the people of Isra'il was caused by women" (Siddiqui, 1431).

Why Was Woman Created?

The Qur'an, which does not discriminate against women in the context of creation or the Fall episode, does not support the view—held by many

Muslims, Christians, and Jews—that woman was created not only *from* man but also *for* man. That God's creation as a whole is "for just ends" (Surah 15: *Al-Hijr*:85) and not "for idle sport" (Surah 21: *Al-Anbiya'*:16) is one of the major themes of the Qur'an. Humanity, fashioned "in the best of moulds" (Surah 95: *At-Tin*:4) has been created in order to serve God (Surah 51: *Adh-Dhariyat*:56). According to Qur'anic teaching, service to God cannot be separated from service to humankind, or—in Islamic terms—believers in God must honor both *"Haquq Allah"* (rights of God) and *"Haquq al'ibad"* (rights of creatures). Fulfillment of one's duties to God and humankind constitutes the essence of righteousness. [11] That men and women are equally called upon by God to be righteous and will be equally rewarded for their righteousness is stated unambiguously in a number of Qur'anic passages such as the following:

> And their Lord . . . answered them
> "Never will I suffer to be lost
> The work of any of you,
> Be he male or female:
> Ye are members, one of another."
> (Surah 3: *Al-Imran*:195;
> *The Holy Qur'an*, 174-75)

> If any do deeds
> of righteousness, —
> be they male or female —
> And have faith,
> They will enter Heaven,
> And not the least injustice
> Will be done to them.
> (Surah 4: *An-Nisa'*:124;
> *The Holy Qur'an*, 219)

> The Believers, men
> And women, are protectors,
> One of another: they enjoin
> What is just, and forbid
> What is evil: they observe
> Regular prayers, practice
> Regular charity, and obey
> God and His Apostle.
> On them will God pour
> His mercy: for God
> Is Exalted in power, Wise.
> God hath promised to Believers,
> Men and women, Gardens

Under which rivers flow,
To swell therein,
And beautiful mansions
In Gardens of everlasting bliss.
But the greatest bliss
Is the Good Pleasure of God:
That is the supreme felicity.
> (Surah 9: *At-Taubah*:71-72;
> *The Holy Qur'an*, 461)

Whoever works righteousness,
Man or woman, and has Faith,
Verily, to him will We give
A new Life, a life
That is good and pure, and We
Will bestow on such their reward
According to the best
Of their actions.
> (Surah 16: *An-Nahl*:97;
> *The Holy Qur'an*, 683)

For Muslim men and women, —
For believing men and women,
For devout men and women,
For true men and women,
For men and women who are
Patient and constant, for men
And women who humble themselves,
For men and women who give
In Charity, for men and women
Who fast (and deny themselves),
For men and women who
Engage much in God's praise, —
For them has God prepared
Forgiveness and great reward.
> (Surah 23: *Al-Ahzab*:35;
> *The Holy Qur'an*, 1116-17)

Not only does the Qur'an make it clear that man and woman stand absolutely equal in the sight of God, but also that they are "members" and "protectors" of each other. In other words, the Qur'an does not create a hierarchy in which men are placed above women (as they are by many formulators of the Christian tradition), nor does it pit men against women in an adversary relationship. They are created as equal creatures of a universal, just, and merciful God whose pleasure it is that they live—in harmony and in righteousness—together.

In spite of the Qur'anic affirmation of man-woman equality, Muslim societies in general have never regarded men and women as equal, particularly in the context of marriage. Fatima Mernissi's observations on the position of a Muslim woman in relation to her family in modern Morocco apply, more or less, to Muslim culture generally:

> One of the distinctive characteristics of Muslim sexuality is its territoriality, which reflects a specific division of labor and a specific conception of society and of power. The territoriality of Muslim sexuality sets ranks, tasks, and authority patterns. Spatially confined the woman was taken care of materially by the man who possessed her, in return for her total obedience and her sexual and reproductive services. The whole system was organized so that the Muslim "ummah" was actually a society of male citizens who possessed among other things the female half of the population. . . . Muslim men have always had more rights and privileges than Muslim women, including even the right to kill their women. . . . The man imposed on the woman an artificially narrow existence, both physically and spiritually (Mernissi, 103).

Underlying the rejection in Muslim societies of the idea of man-woman equality is the deeply-rooted belief that women—who are inferior in creation (having been made from a crooked rib) and in righteousness (having helped the Shaitan in defeating God's plan for Adam)—have been created mainly to be of use to men who are superior to them.

The alleged superiority of men to women that permeates the Islamic (as also the Jewish and Christian) tradition is grounded not only in Hadith literature but also in popular interpretations of some Qur'anic passages. Two Qur'anic passages—Surah 4: *An-Nisa'*:34 and Surah 2: *Al-Baqarah*:288—in particular, are generally cited to support the contention that men have a "degree of advantage" over women. Of these, the first reads as follows in A. A. Maududi's translation of the Arabic text:

> Men are the managers of the affairs of women because Allah has made the one superior to the other and because men spend of their wealth on women. Virtuous women are, therefore, obedient; they guard their rights carefully in their absence under the care and watch of Allah. As for those women whose defiance you have cause to fear, admonish them and keep them apart from your beds and beat them. Then, if they submit to you, do not look for excuses to punish them: note it well that there is Allah above you, who is Supreme and Great (Maududi 1971, 321).

It is difficult to overstate the impact of the general Muslim understanding of Surah 4: *An-Nisa'*:34 that is embodied in Maududi's translation. As soon

as the issue of woman's equality with man is raised by liberals, the immediate response by traditionalists is, "But don't you know that God says in
the Qur'an that men are *'qawwamun'* in relation to women and have the
right to rule over them and even to beat them?" In fact, the mere statement
"ar-rijal-o qawwamun-a 'ala an-nisa" (literally, the men are *qawwamun* —
"managers" in Maududi's translation — in relation to the women) signifies
the end of any attempt to discuss the issue of woman's equality with man
in the Islamic *ummah*.

It is assumed by almost all who read Surah 4, verse 34, that it is addressed
to husbands. The first point to be noted is that it is addressed to *"ar-rijal"*
(the men) and to *"an-nisa'"* (the women). In other words, it is addressed
to all men and women of the Islamic community. This is further indicated
by the fact that in relation to all the actions that are required to be taken,
the plural and not the dual form (used when reference is made to two
persons) is found. Such usage makes clear that the orders contained in this
verse were not addressed to a husband or wife but to the Islamic ummah
in general.

The key word in the first sentence of this verse is *qawwamun*. This word
has been translated variously as "protectors and maintainers [of women],"
"in charge [of women]," "having preeminence [above women]," and "sov-
ereigns or masters [over women]." Linguistically, the word *qawwamun*
means "breadwinners" or "those who provide a means of support or livelihood." A point of logic that must be made here is that the first sentence
is not a descriptive one stating that all men as a matter of fact are providing
for women, since obviously there are at least some men who do not provide
for women. What the sentence is stating, rather, is that men ought to have
the capability to provide (since ought implies can). In other words, this
statement, which almost all Muslim societies have taken to be an actual
description of all men, is in fact a normative statement pertaining to the
Islamic concept of division of labor in an ideal family or community structure. The fact that men are *qawwamun* does not mean that women cannot
or should not provide for themselves, but simply that in view of the heavy
burden that most women shoulder with regard to childbearing and rearing,
they should not have the additional obligation of providing the means of
living at the same time.

Continuing with the analysis of the passage, we come next to the idea
that God has given the one more strength than the other. Most translations
make it appear that the one who has more strength, excellence, or superiority is the man. However, the Qur'anic expression does not accord superiority to men. The expression literally means "some in relation to some,"
so that the statement could mean either that some men are superior to
some others (men and/or women) and that some women are superior to
some others (men and/or women). The interpretation that seems to me to
be the most appropriate contextually is that some men are more blessed
with the means to be better providers than are other men.

The next part of the passage begins with "therefore," which indicates that this part is conditional upon the first; in other words, if men fulfill their assigned function of being providers, women must fulfill their corresponding duties. Most translations describe this duty in terms of the wife being "obedient" to the husband. The word *salihat*, which is translated as "righteously obedient," is related to the word *salahiat*, which means "capability" or "potentiality," not obedience. Women's special capability is to bear children. The word *qanitat*, which succeeds the word *salihat* and is also translated as "obedient," is related to a water bag in which water is carried from one place to another without spilling. The woman's special function, then—according to this passage—is that, like the bag in which water is transported without loss to its destination, she carries and protects the fetus in her womb until it can be safely delivered.

What is outlined in the first part of this passage is a functional division of labor necessary for maintaining balance in any society. Men who do not have to fulfill the responsibility of childbearing are assigned the function of being breadwinners. Women are exempted from the responsibility of being breadwinners in order that they may fulfill their function as child-bearers. The two functions are separate but complementary and neither is higher or lower than the other.

The three injunctions in the second part of the verse were given to the Islamic *ummah* in order to meet a rather extraordinary possibility: a mass rebellion on the part of women against their role as childbearers, the function assigned to them by God. If all or most of the women in a Muslim society refused to bear children without just cause as a sign of organized defiance or revolt, this would mean the end of the Muslim *ummah*. This situation must, therefore, be dealt with decisively. The first step taken is to counsel the rebels. If this step is unsuccessful, the second step to be taken is isolation of the rebellious women from significant others. (It is to be noted here that the prescription is "to leave the women alone in their beds." By translating this line as "keep them apart from your beds," Maududi is suggesting, if not stating, that the judging party is the husband and not the Islamic community—an assumption not warranted by the text.) If the second step is also not successful, then the step of confining the women for a longer period of time may be taken by the Islamic *ummah* or its representatives. Here, it is important to point out that the Arabic word generally translated "being" has numerous meanings. When used in a legal context, as it is here, it means "holding in confinement" according to the authoritative lexicon *Taj al-'Arus* (Shehab, 117). (In Surah 4: *An-Nisa'*:15, unchaste women are also prescribed the punishment of being confined to their homes.)

While Muslims through the centuries have interpreted Surah *An-Nisa'*:34 as giving them unequivocal mastery over women, a linguistically and philosophically/theologically accurate interpretation of this passage would lead to radically different conclusions. In simple words what this passage is saying is that since only women can bear children (which is not to say either that all women should bear children or that women's sole function is to bear children)—a function whose importance in the survival of any community cannot be questioned—they should not have the additional obligation of being breadwinners while they perform this function. Thus during the period of a woman's childbearing, the function of breadwinning must be performed by men (not just husbands) in the Muslim *ummah*. Reflection on this Qur'anic passage shows that the division of functions mandated here is designed to ensure justice in the community as a whole. While there are millions of women all over the world—and I am one of them—who are designated inaccurately as single parents (when, in fact, they are *double parents*), who bear and raise children single-handedly, generally without much support from the community, this surely does not constitute a just situation. If children are the wealth and future of the *ummah*, the importance of protecting the function of childbearing and childraising becomes self-evident. Statistics from all over the world show that women and children left without the care and custodianship of men suffer from economic, social, psychological, and other ills.

What Surah *An-Nisa'*:34 is ensuring is that this does not happen. It enjoins men in general to assume responsibility for women in general when they are performing the vitally important function of childbearing (other passages in the Qur'an extend this also to childrearing). Thus, the intent of this passage that has traditionally been used to subordinate women to men in fact is to guarantee women the material (as well as moral) security needed by them during the period of pregnancy when breadwinning can become difficult or even impossible for them.

The second passage that mentions the "degree of advantage" men have over women is Surah 2: *Al-Baqarah*:228, which reads

> Divorced women
> Shall wait concerning [remarriage after divorce]
> For three monthly periods.
> Nor is it lawful for them
> To hide what God
> Hath created in their wombs,
> If they have faith
> In God and the Last Day.
> And their husbands
> Have the better right
> To take them back
> In that period, if
> They wish for reconciliation.
> And *women shall have rights*
> *Similar to the rights*
> *Against them, according*

> To what is equitable;
> But men have a degree
> (Of advantage) over them,
> And God is exalted in Power, Wise.
> (*The Holy Qur'an*, 89-90. Emphasis mine)

As can be seen, the above-cited passage pertains to the subject of divorce. The "advantage" that men have over women in this context is that women must observe a three-month period called *iddat* before remarriage, but men are exempted from this requirement. The main reason why women are subjected to this restriction is because at the time of divorce a woman may be pregnant and this fact may not become known for some time. As men cannot become pregnant, they are allowed to remarry without a waiting period.

In my judgment, the Qur'anic passages—in particular the two discussed above on which the edifice of male superiority over women largely rests—have been misread or misinterpreted, intentionally or unintentionally, by most Muslim societies and men. A correct reading of these passages would not, however, make a radical or substantial difference to the existing pattern of male-female relationships in Muslim societies unless attention was also drawn to those *ahadith* that have been used to make man not only superior to a woman but virtually into her god. The following Hadith is particularly important:

> A man came . . . with his daughter and said, "This my daughter refuses to get married." The Prophet said, "Obey your father." She said, "By the name of Him Who sent you in truth, I will not marry until you inform me what is the right of the husband over his wife." He said, . . . "If it were permitted for one human being to bow down (sajada) to another I would have ordered the woman to bow down to her husband when he enters into her, because of God's grace on her." (The daughter) answered, "By the name of Him Who sent you, with truth, I would never marry!" (Sadiq Hasan Khan, 281).

A faith as rigidly monotheistic as Islam cannot conceivably permit any human being to worship anyone but God, therefore the hypothetical statement "If it were permitted" in the above cited Hadith is, *ipso facto*, an impossibility. But the way this Hadith is related makes it appear that if not God's, at least it was the Prophet's will or wish to make the wife prostrate herself before her husband. Each word, act, or exhortation attributed to the Prophet is held to be sacred by most of the Muslims in the world and so this Hadith (which in my judgment seeks to legitimate *shirk*, associating anyone with God—an unforgivable sin according to the Qur'an) becomes binding on the Muslim woman. Muslims frequently criticize a religion such as Hinduism in which the wife is required to worship the husband (*patipuja*) but in practice what is expected from most Muslim wives is not very different from *patipuja*. In India and Pakistan, for example, a Muslim woman learns almost as an article of faith that her husband is her *majazi Khuda* (god in earthly form). This description, undoubtedly, constitutes a *shirk*.

Man and woman, created equal by God and standing equal in the sight of God, have become very unequal in Muslim societies. The Qur'anic description of man and woman in marriage: "They are your garments/And you are their garments" (Surah 2: *Al-Baqarah*:187) implies closeness, mutuality, and equality. However, Muslim culture has reduced many, if not most, women to the position of puppets on a string, to slave-like creatures whose only purpose in life is to cater to the needs and pleasures of men. Not only this, it has also had the audacity and the arrogance to deny women direct access to God. Islam rejects the idea of redemption, of any intermediary between a believer and the Creator. It is one of Islam's cardinal beliefs that each person—man and woman—is responsible and accountable for his or her individual actions. How, then, can the husband become the wife's gateway to heaven or hell? How, then, can he become the arbiter not only of what happens to her in this world but also of her ultimate destiny? Surely such questions must arise in the minds of thoughtful Muslim women, but so far they have not been asked aloud and my own feeling is that not only Muslim men but also Muslim women are afraid to ask questions the answers to which are bound to threaten the existing balance of power in the domain of family relationships in most Muslim societies.

MUSLIM WOMEN AND POST-PATRIARCHAL ISLAM: IN SUMMATION

The foregoing account provides much evidence for arguing that the patriarchal assumptions and attitudes that are deeply entrenched and universally present in Muslim culture have had serious negative implications—both theoretical and practical—for Muslim women throughout Muslim history up until the present time. At the same time, it has been amply demonstrated that the Qur'an, which to Muslims in general is the most authoritative source of Islam, does not discriminate against women despite the sad and bitter fact of history that the cumulative (Jewish, Christian, Hellenistic, Bedouin, and other) biases that existed in the Arab-Islamic culture of the early centuries of Islam infiltrated the Islamic tradition, largely through the Hadith literature, and undermined the intent of the Qur'an to liberate women from the status of chattel or inferior creatures and make them free and equal to men. Not only does the Qur'an emphasize that righteousness is identical in the case of man or woman, but it affirms, clearly and consistently, women's equality with men and their fundamental right to actualize the human potential that they share equally with men. In fact, when seen through a non-patriarchal lens, the Qur'an goes beyond egalitarianism. It exhibits particular solicitude toward women as also toward other classes of disadvantaged persons. It also provides particular safeguards for protecting women's special sexual/biological functions such as carrying, delivering, suckling, and rearing offspring.

In view of what women in the major religious traditions of the world have suffered in the name or interest of patriarchal values or systems and structures of thought and conduct, it is hardly surprising that many feminist theologians consider the rejection of patriarchy a prerequisite for the liberation of women from various forms of injustice. However, when patriarchy is seen as indissolubly linked with the "core" of a religious tradition—for instance, with God in the context of Judaism, Christianity, and Islam—then the rejection of the one generally involves the rejection of the other. This is why a number of feminist theologians have in the post-patriarchal phase of their thinking gone beyond their religious traditions altogether. Rejecting God, who is identified by them with maleness, they have also, oftentimes, rejected men-women relationships and childbearing, seeing both heterosexual marriage and childbearing as patriarchal institutions used to enslave and exploit women.

However, to me, patriarchy is not integral to the Islam embodied in the Qur'an nor is God thought of as male by Muslims in general. Rejection of patriarchy does not, therefore, have to lead to rejection of God in whom a Muslim's faith is grounded. Here it needs to be pointed out that being a Muslim is dependent essentially only upon one belief: belief in God, universal creator and sustainer who sends revelation for the guidance of humanity. As Wilfred Cantwell Smith has remarked insightfully, "A true Muslim . . . is not a man who believes in Islam—especially Islam in history; but one who believes in God and is committed to the revelation through His Prophet" (Smith, 146).

God, who speaks through the Qur'an, is characterized by justice, and it is stated with the utmost clarity in the Qur'an that God can never be guilty of *zulm* (unfairness, tyranny, oppression, or wrongdoing). Hence, the Qur'an, as God's Word, cannot be made the source of human injustice, and the injustice to which Muslim women have been subjected cannot be regarded as God-derived. Historically, as this essay has shown, some of the passages in the Qur'an have been interpreted in such a way that they appear to support what seems—from a twentieth-century Muslim feminist perspective—to be unjust ways of thinking and behaving. However, given the incredible richness of the Arabic language, in which virtually every word has multiple meanings and nuances, it is possible—and necessary—to reinterpret these passages differently so that their import or implication is not contrary to the justice of God.

To me, in the final analysis, post-patriarchal Islam is nothing other than Qur'anic Islam, which is profoundly concerned with freeing human beings—women as well as men—from the bondage of traditionalism, authoritarianism (religious, political, economic, or any other), tribalism, racism, sexism, slavery, or anything else that prohibits or inhibits human beings from actualizing the Qur'anic vision of human destiny embodied in the classical proclamation, "Towards God is thy limit" (Surah 53: *An-Najm*:42; trans. by Iqbal, 57).

The goal of Qur'anic Islam is to establish peace, which is the very meaning of *islam*. However, from the perspective of the Qur'an, peace is not to be understood to be a passive state of affairs, a mere absence of war. It is a positive state of safety or security in which one is free from anxiety or fear. It is this state that characterizes both *islam*, self-surrender to God, and *iman*, true faith in God, and reference is made to it, directly or indirectly, on every page of the Qur'an through the many derivatives of the roots "s-l-m" and "a-m-n" from which *islam* and *iman* are derived respectively. According to Qur'anic teaching, peace can only exist within a just environment. In other words, justice is a prerequisite for peace. Without the elimination of the inequities, inequalities, and injustices that pervade the personal and collective lives of human beings, it is not possible to talk about peace in Qur'anic terms. Here it is of vital importance to note that there is more Qur'anic legislation pertaining to the establishment of justice in the context of family relationships than on any other subject. This points to the assumption implicit in much Qur'anic legislation, namely, that if human beings can learn to order their homes justly so that the rights of all within its jurisdiction—children, women, and men—are safeguarded, then they can also order their society and the world at large justly. In other words, the Qur'an regards the home as a microcosm of the *ummah* and the world community, and emphasizes the importance of making it "the abode of peace" through just living.

Despite everything that has gone wrong with the lives of countless Muslim women down the ages due to patriarchal Islam, I believe strongly that there is hope for the future. As an increasing number of Muslims—men and women—begin to reflect more and more deeply upon the teachings of the Qur'an, they begin to see more and more clearly that the supreme task entrusted to human beings by God, of being God's deputies on earth, can only be accomplished by going beyond patriarchal views and values. The message contained in Surah 4: *An-Nisa'*:34, which ensures justice between men and women in the context of childbearing, can be extended and universalized to embrace all aspects of human interaction and relatedness. As this happens, the shackles of patriarchal traditions will fall away and the Qur'anic vision of what it means to be a Muslim will begin to be actualized in a world from which the myth of woman's inferiority and "crookedness" has finally been expelled.

NOTES

Bibliographic information on works cited is to be found in the bibliography following the notes.

1. For a more detailed discussion of the issue of woman's creation, see Hassan 1985 and 1987.

2. For instance, Surah 4: *An-Nisa'*:1; Surah 7: *Al-A'raf*:189; and Surah 39: *Az-Zumar*:6.

3. In the aforementioned passages (as also in Surah 6: *Al-An'am*:98 and Surah 31: *Luqman*:28) reference is made to the creation from one source or being (*nafs in wahidatin*) of all human beings. Muslims, with hardly any exceptions, believe that the one original source or being referred to in these passages is a man named Adam. This belief has led many translators of the Qur'an to incorrect translation of simple Qur'anic passages. For instance, Surah 4: *An-Nisa'*:1, if correctly translated, reads as follows: "O 'an-nas' be circumspect in keeping your duty to your Sustainer who created you (plural) from one being ("nafs in wahidatin") and spread from *her* ("min*ha*") her mate ("zauja*ha*") and spread from these two beings many men and women." However, most translators translate the feminine attached pronoun "*ha*" in *minha* and *zaujaha* as "his" instead of as "her." How is such a mistake possible? Could it be the case that given their preconceptions and psychological orientation, these interpreters of the Qur'an, who all happen to be men, are totally unable to imagine that the first creation could have been other than male? Or are they afraid that a correct translation of "*ha*" might suggest the idea—even for an instant—that woman, not man, was the prior creation and therefore superior if priority connotes superiority, and that man was created from woman and not the other way around (which, in a reversal of the Eve-being-created-from-the-rib-of-Adam story, would give Eve the primacy traditionally accorded to Adam)? Certainly no Qur'anic exegete to date has suggested the possibility that *nafs in wahidatin* might refer to woman rather than man.

4. In this context, Leonard Swidler remarks:

> It is a mistake to translate it (*ha adam*) in Genesis 1:22 either as man in the male sense or as a proper name, Adam ... until Genesis 4:25 the definite article "ha" is almost always used with *adam*, precluding the possibility of its being a proper name; in 4:25 it becomes a proper name, "Adam" without the "ha." Moreover, it is clearly a collective noun in Genesis 1:22, as can be seen in the plural "let *them* be masters" (Genesis 1:22) (Swidler, 76).

5. *Adam* is used as a proper name in Surah 3: *Al-'Imran*:35 and 59; Surah 5: *Al-Ma'idah*:30; and Surah 19: *Maryam*:58.

6. For instance, in Surah 75: *Al-Qiyamah*:36-39. This passage reads: "Does *al-insan* think that he will be left aimless? Was he not a drop of semen emitted? Then he became something which clings. Then He (Allah) created and shaped and made of him two mates: the male and the female."

7. Each Hadith consists of two parts: *isnad* (or *sanad*) and *matn*. The *isnad* contains the names of persons who have handed on the substance of the Hadith to one another. The *matn* is the text or actual substance of the Hadith.

8. Since the early centuries of Islam it has been axiomatic for (Sunni) Muslim masses to regard the Companions of the Prophet as being totally above the suspicion of being untrustworthy in any way, least of all as transmitters of the Prophet's *ahadith*. Given such an attitude of absolute devotion, a critical examination of the credentials of the Companions as transmitters could hardly have been undertaken.

As Ignaz Goldziher has observed: "To be a Companion of the Prophet was the highest dignity obtainable. The person and honor of such people were considered untouchable, and to slight them would have been considered a capital crime" (Goldziher, 163). However, in the earliest phase of the development of Islam, a more critical attitude prevailed toward the Hadith literature and its transmitters. Here it is of interest to note that according to the well-known Muslim scholar 'Abdul Wahab Ash-Shairani, Imam Abu Hanifah, considered to be the founder of the largest school of law in Sunni Islam, did not consider Abu Hurairah to be a reliable transmitter of *ahadith* (Ash-Shairani, 59).

9. It is interesting to observe that while in the Genesis 2 story, woman is derived from Adam's rib, there is no mention of Adam in any of the *ahadith* under discussion. This is a further "dehumanization" of woman since she could—in the *ahadith* in question—have been created from a disembodied rib which may not even have been human.

10. The famous expression comes from Tertullian, a church father from North Africa who wrote:

And do you not know that you are (each) an Eve? The sentence of God on this sex of yours lives in this age: the guilt must of necessity live too. You are the devil's gateway: you are the unsealer of that (forbidden) tree: you are the first deserter of the divine law: you are she who persuaded him whom the devil was not valiant enough to attack. You destroyed so easily God's image, man. On account of your desert—that is, death—even the Son of God had to die (*De cultu feminarum* 1:1, cited in Swidler, 346).

11. The Qur'anic understanding of "righteousness" is described in Surah 2: *Al-Baqarah*:177, which states:

> It is not righteousness
> That ye turn your faces
> Towards East or West;
> But it is righteousness—
> To believe in God
> And the Last Day,
> And the Angels,
> And the Book,
> And the Messengers;
> To spend of your substance,
> Out of love of Him,
> For your kin,
> For orphans,
> For the wayfarer,
> For those who ask,
> And for the ransom of slaves;
> To be steadfast in prayer,
> And practice regular charity;
> To fulfill the contracts
> Which ye have made;

And to be firm and patient,
In pain (or suffering)
And adversity,
And throughout
All periods of panic.
Such are the people
Of truth, the God-fearing
(*The Holy Qur'an*, 69-70).

WORKS CITED

Ash-Shairani, 'Abdul Wahab. *Al-Mizan al-Kubra*. Vol. 1. Cairo.

Gibb, Hamilton A. R. *Studies on the Civilization of Islam*. Ed. Stanford J. Shaw and William R. Polk. Boston: Beacon Press, 1962.

Goldziher, Ignaz. *Muslim Studies*. Vol. 2. Trans. C. R. Barber and S. M. Stern. Chicago and New York: Aldine and Atherton, 1971.

Guillaume, Alfred. *The Traditions of Islam*. Beirut: Khayats, 1966.

Hassan, Riffat. "Made from Adam's Rib? An Analysis of the Concept of Woman's Creation in the Qur'an and the Hadith with Comparisons with the Jewish-Christian Tradition." *Al-Mushir* XXVII, 3 (Autumn 1985): 124-55.

———. "Equal Before Allah? Woman-Man Equality in the Islamic Tradition." *Harvard Divinity Bulletin* XVII, 2 (Jan-May 1987): 2-4. Rpt. *Pakistan Progressive*. University of Wisconsin: 9, 1 (Summer 1987):46-59.

Hodgson, Marshall, G. S. *The Classical Age of Islam*. Vol 1 of *The Venture of Islam: Conscience and History in a World Civilization*. Chicago: University of Chicago Press, 1974.

Iqbal, Muhammad. *The Reconstruction of Religious Thought in Islam*. Lahore: Shaikh Muhammad Ashraf, 1962.

Izutsu, Toshihiko. *The Structure of the Ethical Terms in the Koran*. Mita, Siba, Minatoku, Tokyo: Keio Institute of Philosophical Studies, 1959.

Khan, M. M., trans. *Sahih Al-Bukhari*. Lahore: Kazi Publications, 1971.

Khan, Sadiq Hasan. *Husn al-Uswa*. Publication details unavailable.

Lane, E. W. *Arabic-English Lexicon*. London: Williams and Norgate, 1963.

Maududi, A. A. *The Meaning of the Qur'an*. Vol. 2. Lahore: Islamic Publications Ltd., 1971.

———. *The Meaning of the Qur'an*. Vol. 4. Lahore: Islamic Publications Ltd., 1976.

Mernissi, Fatima. *Beyond the Veil*. Cambridge: Schenkman Publishing Company, 1975.

Rahman, Fazlur. *Islam*. Garden City, New York: Doubleday and Co., 1968.

Shehab, Rafi ullah. *Rights of Women in Islamic Shariah*. Lahore: Indus Publishing House, 1986.

Siddiqui, A. H., trans. *Sahih Muslim*. Vol. 2. Lahore: Shaikh Muhammad Ashraf, 1972.

Smith, Jane I., and Yvonne Y. Haddad. "Eve: Islamic Image of Woman." *Women and Islam*. Ed. Azizah al-Hibri. New York: Pergamon Press, 1982.

Smith, Wilfred Cantwell. *Islam in Modern History*. Princeton: Princeton University Press, 1957.

Swidler, Leonard. *Biblical Affirmations of Woman*. Philadelphia: The Westminster Press, 1979.

4

Buddhism after Patriarchy?

RITA M. GROSS

Can a religion founded by a man who abandoned his wife and newborn infant because he was convinced that they were an obstacle to his own salvation possibly serve women's interests and needs? Can a religion founded by a man who also resisted women's similar attempts to abandon their domestic responsibilities to seek salvation possibly serve women's interests and needs?

Such questions suggest the more basic question of whether there can be a post-patriarchal form of Buddhism. All current conventional religions must face the essential feminist question of whether, stripped of sexist privilege to men, patriarchal hierarchies, and androcentric interpretations of key texts and concepts, anything remains of the religion. Buddhism is no exception. Thus the question mark in the title of this chapter. Nevertheless, since an essay follows the title, this chapter concludes that no matter how difficult the transition, there can be Buddhism after patriarchy and that patriarchal and post-patriarchal Buddhism share enough to justify being grouped under the same name. Nevertheless, the chapter title also conveys my conviction that Buddhism as currently constituted is patriarchal and, therefore, seriously inadequate.

The two stories to which I have already alluded convey many of the basic questions that must be asked if one questions whether there is Buddhism after patriarchy. On the one hand, for people who value women's conventional and traditional domestic pursuits, the first story provides little comfort. Buddhism has frequently been interpreted as a world-denying religion, the goal of which is to cut all involvement in ordinary existence by means of radical denial of conventional concerns. Thus the future Buddha abandoned his family because such conventionality is counterproductive to true spiritual concerns. In the Buddhist world this story is lovingly retold and reenacted as indication of the future Buddha's concern for universal rather

65

than private well-being. That his acts could have been radically misogynist is not generally perceived in the Buddhist world. On the other hand, once the young prince had become An Enlightened One (a Buddha), one may well question why he taught the methods of release that had proved effective for him to men, but denied them to women. In contemporary scholarship the authenticity of stories about how the Buddha put off his aunt and foster-mother when she sought to follow his way of rejection of conventional ties is questioned by many scholars. Even if textual criticism prevails and the texts in question are deemed to be later additions, they have had great impact historically in Buddhism (Falk, 162). Furthermore, most forms of Buddhism still discriminate against women who would gladly enter into the unconventional paths recommended by Buddhism (Tsomo; Havenik).

These two popular stories, and many stories, values, and interpretations familiar in the Buddhist tradition, make abundantly clear that Buddhism needs to be significantly reconceptualized and re-imaged to become post-patriarchal. But for such reconceptualization to be genuine and authentic, one must also find a core in Buddhism that is already beyond patriarchy. In this vision both liberal feminist concerns, such as women's equal participation in all aspects of Buddhism, and radical feminist concerns, such as the reconceptualization of key Buddhist concepts, are relevant.

My methodology for carrying out this assignment is varied, but two major strands stand out. On the one hand, I am deeply committed to the comparative perspective in religious studies and that perspective for me includes the impact of the social sciences, especially anthropology. On the other hand, Buddhism is, for me, not merely material for comparative analysis, but also personal perspective. Thus, I work simultaneously as a comparativist and as a Buddhist theologian, both as an insider and as an outsider. I see no conflict in this method; rather, it is a complete and well-rounded approach.

BUDDHISM AS FREEDOM WITHIN THE WORLD

Many textbooks present Buddhism as a world-denying, otherworldly religion. Certainly much within Buddhist tradition fosters this interpretation. Nevertheless, some of the force of this interpretation results from Western misperceptions of Buddhism. One standing authentically within the Buddhist tradition can just as cogently see Buddhism as a path to freedom *within* the world process as a path to freedom *from* the world process. To see Buddhism as providing freedom within the world is more compatible with post-patriarchal vision than the more familiar interpretation of Buddhism as freedom from the world.

Thus the core of the Buddhist quest has something to do with *freedom*. Though it is not a literal translation, what I am calling freedom would roughly correspond to *nirvana* in classical Buddhist and Indian thought.

Pinning down precisely what this term means is notoriously difficult in Buddhology; whole books have been written about the question. Nevertheless, one can with some certainty say that *nirvana* means freedom from *samsara*, that is, "cyclic existence," which by definition is understood to be painful. One can, of course, further interpret and debate what precisely such freedom would entail. If one is free *from* painful cyclic existence, what is one free *for?* The answer to that question is less clearly and definitively spelled out in Buddhist tradition, but always involves some way to help and serve one's fellow sentient beings. We may again take our cue from the Buddha's life story. He was persuaded to attempt to teach his insights when he doubted that anyone would understand and wished only to remain in the bliss of his own freedom.

Whether one understands freedom as "freedom from" or as "freedom within" the world, one must begin with the Four Noble Truths, the conceptual heart of Buddhism and the existential discovery of every Buddha in her or his enlightenment experience. Freedom is proclaimed in the third truth, the truth of cessation. Cessation of what? Cessation of the causes of suffering, proclaimed in the first and second truths. The first truth states that (conventional) existence inevitably produces suffering. That suffering, according to the second truth, results from the desire and ignorance that characterize conventional existence. But, according to the third truth, if one can be free from such desire and ignorance, one can be free from the suffering they produce. The fourth truth declaims the lifestyle that is conducive to such freedom. One should pursue wisdom, moral discipline, and spiritual depth—my rendition of the classic goals of *prajna, sila,* and *samadhi.*

One of the most influential Buddhist conceptualizations of the meaning of freedom from suffering has been that such freedom means freedom from rebirth. Birth into the world inevitably brings the pain of "birth, old age, sickness, and death"[1]—an unenviable lot. Rebirth into those patterns is inevitable for all who are not free from desire and ignorance. This interpretation of Buddhism easily leads to otherworldly and anti-worldly concerns. Birth (rebirth) is undesirable; far better to remain in the timeless "untime" of the unborn than to take form in the realms of "birth, old age, sickness, and death." Life, as known by those of us who inhabit human bodies in this realm, is inadequate and undesirable compared to some other transcendent state of existence. Furthermore, that other state of existence is attainable by those who can properly renounce the usual human mode of existence and emotionality. Those who no longer experience ignorance and desire will never again be reborn into *samsara,* or cyclic existence, and will live out the remainder of this life in tranquility, undisturbed by conflicting emotions.

Clearly this classic interpretation of *samsara* and *nirvana* is otherworldly and anti-worldly, seeing existence as the problem, and release as freedom from existence. This dualistic and anti-worldly interpretation of Buddhism can be further intensified by familiar and popular descriptions of the life-style that will promote freedom from desire and ignorance. As is well known, the preferred Buddhist lifestyle in traditional Buddhist countries has always been the monastic lifestyle. One of the primary motivations for this preference is the observation that family and profession, the lot of ordinary people, tend to enmesh one in desires, negative emotions, and large-scale ignoring. Those who have no families and professional concerns, which tend to promote worry and desire, will be more likely to attain *nirvana* and cessation, both of conventional concerns and of conventional existence. Thus the tradition evaluates very positively the actions of the young man who abandoned his wife and child, praises other men who resisted the pleadings of their wives to return to them and their children, and praises couples who mutually decided to dissolve their marriage at any cost to pursue anti-worldly lives. Only women who independently decide on such a lifestyle are ambiguously evaluated by the tradition, as is evidenced by the fact that their monastic order was allowed to die out in most of the Buddhist world and contemporary efforts to revive it often meet with resistance and hostility.

World-denying, anti-worldly, dualistic spiritualities are often very negatively evaluated in contemporary culture, especially by feminists but also in general. Later, we will weigh this evaluation, but first it is important to establish an alternative, but at least equally valid and authentic interpretation of Buddhism, not as freedom *from* the world, but as freedom *within* the world.

We must return to the discussion of *samsara* and *nirvana*, and to the four noble truths. Freedom remains the essential term, but freedom that merely escapes the world of conventional existence may not be real freedom and in fact may well be impossible. Rather, the only freedom is, in the perceptive words of Suzuki, *roshi*, "to find our ease in impermanence" (Suzuki, 102-4). Dissatisfaction with impermanence, which is to say dissatisfaction with the inevitable finitude of our existence, *rather than* impermanence and finitude themselves, is the fundamental unfreedom. As the four noble truths state, we suffer because of our desires; the most basic desire is for things to be different than they are. Conventionally, our deepest desires are for permanence (immortality), ease or bliss, and security, but these desires are unfulfillable, despite the fact that whole religions are based on promising these impossible goals. Thus, the real problem addressed by Buddhism is not an unsatisfactory world that we somehow transcend or escape *from*, but improper and unsatisfactory desires regarding that world.

Freedom, the cessation proclaimed by the third noble truth, remains the heart and core of Buddhism. And, as Buddhism always proclaims, that freedom is achieved when the desires and ignorance that cause suffering are given up. But is cessation of desire really a matter of "renouncing the world" rather than "living in the world"? To transcend desire and ignorance, one needs to change one's attitudes, which is not guaranteed by a change of lifestyle. The world we live in and the existence we experience are not the problem, are not the source of suffering and the barrier to freedom. Rather, the problem is unrealistic hopes and demands regarding that world—essentially hopes and demands for permanence, ease, and security. We need to go beyond these attitudes to be truly free. When this occurs, we are not, in fact, free *from* the world process, since we are still inevitably subject to "birth, old age, sickness, and death," as well as impermanence, lack of security, and insufficient ease or pleasure. In short, finitude is, was, and will be our lot. However, to "find our ease in impermanence" is to live and die untroubled by finitude, untroubled by our world and by the conditions of our existence. We are free *within* the world and therefore, are unlikely to be otherworldy or anti-worldly in our basic values and orientations. We live, in the classic words of Buddhist vision, "neither wandering in *samsara* nor dwelling in *nirvana.*"[2]

Both interpretations of Buddhism, as freedom from the world, and as freedom within the world, are authentic and traditional. Though they intertwine throughout Buddhist history, an accurate generalization would see the anti-worldly and dualistic interpretation of Buddhism as dominant in early Indian Buddhism, while the non-dualistic interpretation of Buddhism as freedom within the world becomes more important some centuries after the historical Buddha but never entirely displaces the earlier emphasis. Thus Buddhism follows the general lines of religious evolution from a more other-worldly to a more this-worldly orientation pointed out by Robert Bellah in his classic essay on that topic (Bellah). Buddhism also participated fully in, and in fact may have helped initiate, the kind of dualistic, anti-worldly, and otherworldly spirituality that was so critical to religious development in the West in the formative late pre- and early Christian centuries.

That style of spirituality has been thoroughly delineated and critiqued in the last decade by many feminist scholars. Usually they evaluate that type of spirituality very negatively because in the West such spirituality tends to be both misogynist and patriarchal. Furthermore, feminist scholars often find links between otherworldly, dualistic spiritualities and the most serious problems that currently afflict us—widespread glorification of aggression and war as methods of solving conflicts and the exploitation of global ecology without regard for the earth as a finite matrix of existence. Misogyny and patriarchy are often seen as the critical links between anti-worldly outlooks and aggression or exploitation.

If this feminist analysis is correct, one might easily conclude that viewing Buddhism as freedom within the world rather than as freedom from the world is more conducive to post-patriarchal Buddhism. Though I share that conclusion, I do not arrive at it by the same analysis. First of all, though in its historical manifestations Buddhism is as patriarchal as Western religions, it is not as misogynist as Western religions were at the height of their misogynist phases. Furthermore, I do not see a logical necessity for anti-worldly and otherworldly spiritualities to develop misogyny as well. Dualistic, otherworldly spiritualities should not be rejected because historically, in the West, they were linked with misogyny, but because they are inadequate spiritually. If we were convinced that freedom from the world really is our proper spiritual goal, then our task would be to engage in the social re-construction that would permit a non-patriarchal and non-misogynist but otherworldly spirituality. But very few are today convinced that anti-worldliness really is our true spiritual goal. Whatever once made otherworldliness spiritually attractive, those forces now seem exhausted, at least in the non-popular level of religious practice where the leading edge of religious and spiritual thinking is found. Today we seek non-dualistic, world- and life-affirming spiritualities. We also seek post-patriarchal spirituality. These two goals are compatible, but do not logically entail each other. Recognizing this complexity helps us avoid the rather simplistic conclusions that otherworldly spiritualities developed only because men were the religious elite in them, or that women could create and favor only this-worldly spirituality. However, Buddhism understood as freedom within the world and informed by the concerns of feminist and post-patriarchal women (and men) will undoubtedly address concerns and issues unthinkable to patriarchal and male-created Buddhism understood as freedom from the world.

BUDDHISM AFTER PATRIARCHY

Two rather different sets of issues need to be considered when describing Buddhism after patriarchy. First, one needs to discuss changes necessary to Buddhism as currently constituted and conceptualized. The second, much more difficult task is contemplating what needs to be reconstituted and reconceptualized in Buddhism after patriarchy. In the Buddhist world to date there have been some discussions of the first set of issues, but almost no discussion of the latter set. Because I have dealt with the first set of issues in several other contexts, I will only summarize those conclusions here, devoting most of the remaining space to the more radical question of a post-patriarchal reconceptualization of Buddhism.

In my previous feminist analyses of Buddhism I have advocated the conclusion that the basic Buddhist teachings are not misogynist or patriarchal; I have also demonstrated that the basic teachings of Buddhism *as currently constituted* do not in any way condone gender hierarchy and, in fact, militate against such practices. However, I could not conclude that therefore Buddhism is immune to a feminist critique. The institutions of Buddhist life are male-dominated and disadvantageous to women in general; as a result Buddhist historical records include few (though some) women important to the history of the tradition (see Dowman; Allione; Gross 1989; Paul). This obviously involves an irresolvable contradiction. Why women have fared so badly in Buddhism despite its teachings can, I believe, be explained, but not justified, by two facts: 1) Buddhism emerged in a religious context already riddled with patriarchal gender roles, and 2) to the present Buddhism has not been noted for its willingness to advocate social change.

This situation can readily be analyzed in classic liberal feminist terms. Using arguments familiar from the first layer of recent feminist analysis, the problem is discrimination against women, to be solved by "equal rights," in this case the same access to Buddhist training and leadership positions that men have always had. Women were excluded from Buddhist institutions; if they are now equally included in these institutions, justice and fair play will be rendered. The Buddhist situation can also be discussed in terms that are quite similar to reformist Christian feminist theology. The core teachings and concepts of the tradition are essentially egalitarian and liberating for all; the patriarchal overlay is unfortunate, but just that—an overlay that does not affect the heart of the teachings. That patriarchal overlay can and should be cut immediately by righting past wrongs and belatedly granting women their rightful full participation in Buddhist institutions. I have summarized my own advocacy of this position in a statement that has become a slogan for me. "Since the problem in Buddhism is not with theoretical vision but with practical application, the need is to *mandate and institutionalize gender equality,* to build it into the fabric of Buddhist life and institutions completely, in a thoroughgoing fashion" (Gross, forthcoming).

Clearly, I am in complete sympathy with the liberal and reformist feminist position vis-à-vis Buddhism. However, I no longer feel that it is likely to be the end of the story of Buddhism after patriarchy. This is because the liberal and reformist agenda would produce the one thing Buddhism has always lacked—large numbers of thoroughly trained, well-practiced and *articulate* female Buddhist teachers who are not male-identified. That is to say that for the first time the Buddhist world would experience significant numbers of female gurus. In the non-theistic tradition of Buddhism, I feel that this new situation will have the same transformative potential as the introduction of female god-language into the patriarchal monotheisms. Minimally, in line with the liberal reformist agenda, at least Buddhist women will have the same kind of role models that Buddhist men have always had. But, to quote again from the conclusion of my article on Buddhist attitudes toward gender, "The question remains. Has everything that needs to be said about liberation already been said by male Buddhists? Or when women finally participate in Buddhist speech, will they add to the *sum total* of Buddhist wisdom about liberation? The example of Western religions, especially Christianity, in which feminist analysis is far more developed than in Buddhism, suggests that the androgynous voice does not merely amplify what has always been said, but also adds to that message significantly" (Gross, forthcoming).

To add to what has already been said rather than merely to amplify it is to suggest the post-liberal, radical agenda of an androgynous reconceptualization of Buddhism. To date very little, if any such reconceptualization has been attempted. Therefore, beginnings will necessarily be modest, tentative, and somewhat idiosyncratic.

However, Buddhist texts often state that the liberated state is beyond gender, not obtainable in either a male body or a female body. If that is true, and I believe that it is, then what could women possibly say or understand that is not already part of the teachings? The *dharma*, the truth, is not only beyond gender; *it is also beyond words*. On this point Buddhists agree. The words of *dharma* texts are, however, men's words. In a society that constitutes itself by means of strong gender roles and in which only men articulate the religious experience and its vision of liberation, religious speech will grow out of male experience. The more rigid are gender roles, the more impossible it is for a member of either sex to speak adequately for the whole human experience. Clearly these conditions have prevailed in Buddhism. The men who wrote Buddhist *dharma* texts lived in patriarchal, not androgynous societies, and had little access to women's experiences. Therefore, it is quite likely that their words are incomplete, however accurate they may be.

In this early attempt at Buddhist androgynous reconceptualization, I will focus on three areas of concern, all of which are interrelated in that they focus on issues of the connection between "spirituality" and "ordinary" communal or domestic life. In classic formulations of Buddhism, especially those that interpret Buddhism as freedom from the world, little discussion of these topics is found; communal and especially domestic existence are often seen as irrelevant, or even antithetical to spirituality. Therefore, not surprisingly, the interpretation of Buddhism as freedom within the world is central to this reconceptualization.

The most important point in this reconceptualization urges deeper appreciation of the absolute centrality of the *sangha*, the Buddhist community, and the third of the Three Refuges in Buddhist life. This reconceptualization draws its inspiration from experience and from widespread feminist theses. Recent feminist thought often emphasizes that, for women, relationship is far more central than separation and individuation (Gilligan; Schauf), and it also emphasizes that the centrality of community and relationship to human well-being have not been sufficiently recognized in patriarchal and androcentric thought. Deriving from this central insight into the absolute centrality of the *sangha* are two subsidiary questions. Ordinary, everyday domestic life, which has never received much attention in formal Buddhist thought, needs to be addressed much more directly as a *Buddhist*, rather than merely a secular or a lay problem. Finally, one can ask, but probably not answer adequately, the very basic question of what is spirituality, and where is it found, in the light of feminist-androgynous reconceptualization of Buddhism.

"I GO FOR REFUGE TO THE *SANGHA*": COMMUNITY AND SPIRITUALITY

To appreciate what is at stake in this evaluation of the *Sangha*, it is necessary to have some understanding of traditional definitions and perceptions of the *Sangha*. The most basic and foundational categories in Buddhism are the Three Jewels, also known as the Three Refuges—the Buddha, the *Dharma*, and the *Sangha*. They are so basic that the transition from being a non-Buddhist to becoming a Buddhist is made by "going for refuge to the Three Jewels." The act of going for refuge to the Three Jewels is also so basic that it is found universally in all forms of Buddhism—one of the few features found in all forms of this far-flung and geographically separated religion. The concept of going for refuge is especially poignant given Buddhism's non-theism. Many religions promise help and comfort from unseen but powerful forces; Buddhism usually proclaims that there is no external savior and no remote possibility of vicarious enlightenment. But Buddhists do have the Three Refuges as models, inspirations, and guides. The meaning of these Three Refuges is commonly explained by saying that the Buddha is the example of human potential, the *Dharma* is trustworthy teaching, and the *Sangha* is the companionship and feedback of fellow travelers on the path to freedom.

Thus, it would seem that Buddhism, at least in its vision, recognizes the centrality of community to the task of achieving well-being and liberation. Nevertheless, Buddhism as currently constituted and usually interpreted does not manifest that vision. Both outsiders and insiders (both Buddhologists and Buddhists) often present the *Sangha* as a poor third and devote significantly more energy to presentations of the Buddha and the *Dharma*. Lavish Buddhist art in all Buddhist countries attests to the centrality of various Buddhas; an immense literature explores innumerable philosophical nuances of the *Dharma*; millions of hours are spent in meditation practices; popular devotional practices bring these concerns to the general population. But, though everyone takes refuge in the *Sangha* as well, very little attention is devoted to exploring the meaning of this refuge. Textbooks on Buddhism describe the various philosophical schools of Buddhism in some detail. Buddhist ethics are often barely mentioned and few descriptions of Buddhist communal life are found. These emphases may not result entirely from the common overemphasis of academic religious studies on matters of belief and creed; Buddhists themselves often seem both to take *Sangha* for granted and to emphasize self-reliance and aloneness as the essence of the Buddhist path. Rarely does one find explicit statements interpreting the *Sangha* as the matrix necessary for the accomplishment of Buddhist concerns such as freedom.

The situation is familiar to feminist theologians. The categories of the tradition are full and provocative, but important meanings of those categories have been overlooked, underplayed, or ignored by androcentric interpreters. Why is the *Sangha* one of the Three Refuges? Surely not to be taken for granted in the pursuit to understand *Dharma* and to emulate Buddha, and surely not to be ignored in favor of individualistic self-reliance, but because *Sangha* is the essential matrix for the Buddha and the *Dharma*. If the *Sangha* is unhealthy and unsupportive, very few people will successfully emulate the Buddha or understand the *Dharma*. Therefore, one would expect to find keen appreciation of the *Sangha,* not "poor third" status for it. One would also expect detailed instructions and explicit emphasis on how to be a companion of the way — a *Sangha* member — and one should be able to expect such companionship from one's fellow travelers. These have not, however, been emphasized in the Buddhist world; philosophical training, meditation practice, popular devotional practices, and patronizing Buddhist art and institutions all receive far more emphasis and attention. A feminist can easily explain this curious omission and fill in the missing elements.

Buddhists unsympathetic to my claims might at this point object in two opposite, yet curiously similar ways. Some might say that the *Sangha,* meaning the (male) monastic community, already does receive significant attention. It is greatly honored as the central institution in the Buddhist world and much attention is devoted to detailed rules regulating its members. Others might say that the real *Sangha* consists of its monastic members and that lay Buddhists are secondary members whose main function is to revere and economically support the monastic community. Both positions share the view that the purpose of the *Sangha* is to facilitate freedom from the world rather than to provide a community of comfort and support and, furthermore, both regard the proper attitude toward the *Sangha* as reverence for world renouncers rather than concern for communal well-being. Many would also claim that this is the normative Buddhist attitude toward the *Sangha* — an attitude which is fully sufficient. Many also fear that emphasizing the *Sangha* as psychological matrix for enlightenment would somehow be dangerous and misleading. In fact, many who have been sympathetic to my liberal feminist discussions of Buddhism are quite uncomfortable with this suggested reconceptualization.

My own route to this concern was lengthy. I first needed to absorb myself as thoroughly as possible in Buddhism as it was being taught to me, or as I perceived it being taught. I heard a great deal about Buddhism as a "lonely journey," which was the emphasis of the explanatory comments given at the ceremony at which I took refuge. In fact, it was explained that taking refuge in the *Sangha* "is the final statement of being alone." That suited me fine at the time; having been utterly alone much of my life, I had coped by romanticizing aloneness, a common though unconscious strategy in our hyper-masculine and highly alienated culture. I also attentively listened to great teachers as living exemplars of the Buddha, studied a great deal, and meditated in exemplary fashion, which seemed to be the recommended Buddhist way of dealing with the enigma of existence. Sometimes I complained of feeling lonely, but all my Buddhist friends told me that that was the Buddhist way of non-theism. Years later, with the wisdom of hindsight, I feel that another message was also being beamed to us by our Buddhist teachers, but we were missing it, still are missing it, because it doesn't accord with the values of a highly alienated and individualistic culture. We were also being told, "We take refuge in the *Sangha* as companionship. . . . The *Sangha* acts as the source of the learning situation as much as the teacher does. . . . Without that *Sangha*, we have no reference point. . . . We are lost" (Trungpa, 25).

For some time I didn't notice that clear message. Instead, I began to experience intensely that there can be too much aloneness—that while aloneness is integral to human experience and spiritual development, it can be overdone. I also began to notice more clearly the extreme contrast between the personal ineffectiveness accompanying too much aloneness and the sane joy of proper communal and relational existence, of genuine friendship and closeness, of true *Sangha* experience. With these in place, it was so much more possible to be a decent person and to study or meditate effectively! I was discovering what I had not been taught. The Three Jewels are completely interdependent; without the *Sangha*, there is no Buddha and no *Dharma*. The *Sangha* as community, as source of psychological comfort, is the indispensable matrix of spiritual existence. It is not something to be taken for granted, not a poor third, not to be ignored to focus on self-reliance and non-theism.

At the same time I was slowly beginning to agree with two basic theses of more recent feminist thought. I am ever more willing to concede that there are real and profound differences between men's and women's cultures. I do not regard these differences as inevitable or biologically based; if they are in fact based in biology, I see little cause for optimism regarding the human future. A friend of mine once put the difference between women's and men's cultures succinctly, perhaps in an oversimplified and certainly very harsh fashion: "Men achieve identity through separation and women through relationship, which creates a lot of hell." The hell is compounded by the fact that we live in a hyper-masculine society, a society in which alienation, loneliness, and lack of community have reached dangerous levels but are still tolerated and even encouraged—a society in which violence and separation receive more support and approval than nurturance and relationship.

In patriarchal thought those same differences between women and men are also posited, though they are interpreted in different fashion negative to women, and are used to keep women in their very limited, private roles. Evaluated by less patriarchal standards, it becomes clear that these stereotypical women's values and concerns are, *and always have been*, essential to the well-being and survival of the species. Because they are so healthy and normative for humanity, one of the greatest needs of our time is for these values to enter the realms of public discourse rather than to be privatized and minimized. Stereotypical "feminine values" need to become the basis of public life and community; otherwise the rate of acceleration toward oblivion will only increase. So much that is wrong with the society, both on the macro- and the micro-levels, is clearly the result of too much separation, not enough relationship. In this situation the values of female culture need to become much more normative and universal. They are so profoundly human, humane, healing, and enlightening; in many ways and contexts, they are more worthy and more helpful than the masculine values of isolation and aloneness.

My suggested reconceptualization is simply to fill the profound and provocative category *Sangha* with the feminist values of community, nurturance, communication, relationship, and friendship, which have not been in the forefront of traditional descriptions of the *Sangha*. To emphasize these values is to recognize how critical they are, *and always have been,* as matrix and container for emulation of the Buddha and for meditative or philosophical pursuits of the *Dharma*.

Looking backward, we can now easily explain the common perception that the *Sangha* is less essential than the Buddha and the *Dharma*. At the same time we can also appreciate that the *Sangha* as matrix of psychological support has always been important, though its importance has largely gone unrecognized. Men, speaking out of masculinist culture, have written most Buddhist texts and been far more numerous as teachers. So they said less about *Sangha* than about philosophy, meditation practice, or devotion, and when they did speak of *Sangha,* they tended to emphasize its loneliness more than its relationality. American Buddhists, also brought up in a masculinist culture, imbibe that bias until it is possible to develop deeper insights about the proper relationship between relationship and isolation. What pushes those insights is the experience of too much separation and not enough relationship in a context in which one can discover the positive, feminist evaluation of stereotypical feminine values and women's culture.

But why would men reared in a masculinist culture emphasize the joys of being alone, the values of self-reliance and separation to the exclusion of recognizing the values of relationship and community? Feminist theory again suggests an answer, though there is no consensus on the answer. Insofar as this answer is correct, and I believe it has a great deal of cogency, it strongly recommends important restructuring of parenting activity consonant with, in fact mandated by, understanding post-patriarchy as freedom from gender roles. A great deal has been written in a variety of contexts about the difficulty of the male experience of growing up, about a boy's difficulties in separating from rather than identifying with his mother and his consequent reluctance ever again to trust and be vulnerable to intense feelings of connection. A great deal has also been written in a variety of contexts about the need for such separation to achieve masculinity (Chodorow; Nelson). What all this speculation ignores is the patriarchal assumption that parenting, especially of infants and young children, should be almost solely the responsibility of females. With less patriarchal, more androgynous parenting practices, the exaggerated need to glorify self-reliance and aloneness may well disappear.

In the meantime it is important to emphasize that even though the men who formulated Buddhist tradition to date did not emphasize the *Sangha* as nurturing matrix of psychological health, as container for Buddhist meditation and philosophy, nevertheless, the *Sangha* did function for them as such. Without proper nurturing these men would not have renounced conventional life to enter the positive and valued role of monk and world renouncer; they would have renounced the world of convention to become sociopaths, destructive social deviants. Even more important is the comradeship, support, and encouragement, often unacknowledged and uncelebrated, of like-minded companions. It is doubtful that they really accomplished all that they did solely in lonely self-reliance.

This feminist or androgynous reconceptualization turns on the realization that human beings simply do not do well in the absence of deeply satisfying, supportive, and comforting human relationships. It recognizes that unavoidable human aloneness is no excuse for unfriendliness, alienation, or deliberate isolation. The best statement of this position, the best definition of *Sangha* according to this reconceptualization that I have ever found comes from the writings of Trungpa, a great contemporary teacher of Buddhism, a teacher very familiar with Western thought, including some aspects of feminism. "You are willing to work with your loneliness in a group. The *Sangha* is thousands of people being alone together, working with their own loneliness."

When *Sangha* really functions as people working "alone together," rather than fundamentally alone, then people can study and practice Buddhism far more effectively. Anyone who has ever experienced too much aloneness can easily verify this fact from personal experience. When such community and the quality of communication entailed by it are stable and ongoing, psychological trauma and disorientation readily give way to some level of sanity. One can again take one's seat and practice the *Dharma*, both by study or meditation and by helping others. Without community and communication, a crisis is both prolonged and intensified, and everyday, garden-variety loneliness prevents one from being as effective or insightful as one could be.

These comments should lead to a further recognition. Though "Sanghaship," or being a communicative and supportive *Sangha* member is critical, it is by no means "natural," especially for people trained in a masculinist culture. One must train for it as surely as one trains in Buddhist thought to understand the teachings, and as one trains in Buddhist meditation to develop the mind of awareness and freedom. Therefore, Buddhist discipline needs to be developed that would provide such training, and that training needs to be taken as seriously as training in meditation and philosophy. To take refuge in the *Sangha* should mean to join a community of people sensitive to the importance of communication and companionship, a community of people trained to take communication and companionship as seriously as they take study and practice of the *Dharma* and emulation of the Buddha. And those who aspire to take refuge in the *Sangha* should aspire to be such companions and friends.

Given that Buddhism is non-theistic, this understanding of *Sangha* is even more urgent. The appeal of theism, which is appealing even to Buddhists on some days, is the faith it provides that there is a caring Ultimate Other with whom relationship is always possible, who will always be faithful, even when human companions are faithless. To Buddhists, such a hypothesis, no matter how attractive, seems unrealistic. However, this Buddhist contemplation of the strengths of theism should engender one sobering implication. Since people do need to be in relationship, to be taken care of and to care, and since a non-theist cannot imagine an Ultimate Other with whom that relationship is possible, there's no one left to do it but ourselves, each other, the *Sangha*. After all, according to non-theism, no one is going to save us; we have to do it ourselves. Previously I had thought of that basic teaching in terms of the individual's quest for enlightenment. Now it seems as important to realize that to save ourselves by ourselves it is necessary to create the social, communal, and companionate matrix of a society in which friendship and relationship are taken as categories of utmost spiritual importance.

This most basic reconceptualization of Buddhism may be summarized and concluded by a revision of one of the basic lists found in some schools of Buddhism. To grasp the significance of this revision, it must be remembered that in an educational system and a culture that relies heavily upon oral tradition and memorization, as did most of the pre-modern Buddhist world, such lists encode fundamental values. One such list is called the Three Wheels that promote the *Dharma*, traditionally given as study, practice, and livelihood. The idea of this list is to include all the basics necessary to a balanced lifestyle in which one can practice Buddhism in a well-rounded rather than a one-sided fashion. Thus livelihood is included as a wheel of *Dharma* because of the necessity of a proper economic basis for the Buddhist way of life. One cannot study the *Dharma* or practice meditation lacking an economic base. This recognition is laudatory and realistic. However, it seems self-evident to me that the Three Wheels are, in fact, relationship, livelihood, and study *cum* practice. Study and practice are really one pursuit, not two. And the psychological basis for them is at least as crucial as the traditionally recognized economic basis. It is natural, appropriate, healthy, and mandatory to invest the same energy and intensity in friendships as in work or spiritual discipline.

THE ORDINARY AS SACRED: EVERYDAY LIFE AND PRACTICE

The relationship between spirituality and ordinary existence is complex and variegated throughout religious traditions and within Buddhism. As we have seen, in Buddhism, for the most part, spirituality and ordinary existence are seen as antithetical to each other and Buddhism has little interest in "ordinary" life. However, Buddhism as freedom within the world could not avoid rethinking that traditional evaluation of ordinary life and taking it, as well as the people who live "ordinary" lives, more seriously.

Throughout its history Buddhism's greatest institutional weakness has been its focus on the monastic *Sangha* as the true carrier of the religion and consequent lack of attention to lay members. Though the classic pattern has important alternatives in Tibet and Japan, the usual expectation has been that lay Buddhists would provide economic support to the monastic *Sangha* in exchange for minimal ritual and expository services. Of the multifaceted Buddhist path, only the moral disciplines of right speech, right action, and right livelihood were routinely taught to lay Buddhists. The correct outlook, right views and right intentions, and the meditative disciplines leading to it, were considered too difficult to practice while living the conventional householder's lifestyle. In contemporary Buddhism, not only in North America but also in Asia, this model is being challenged by movements of serious lay practice and study. Many variations are found, but the usual pattern involves short but disciplined regular periods of study and practice interspersed with periods of "retreat" for full-time study and practice, during which normal patterns of household life are set aside.

This development involves a potentially vast transformation of Buddhism, in which monastic practitioners are no longer regarded as the best or the only serious practitioners of Buddhism. Such situations already exist in some versions of Tibetan and Japanese Buddhism, but Western Buddhism, in which the vast majority of Buddhists are both serious practitioners and lay people heavily involved in family and career concerns, may well be the most fertile ground for this development. Interestingly, Western Buddhism is also the only form of Buddhism subject to significant feminist influence and the most likely vanguard of Buddhism after patriarchy. Most teachers of Western Buddhists, who are still Asians in this first generation, are not encouraging the majority of their students to take monastic vows and are encouraging their lay students to be serious full-fledged, full-time Buddhist practitioners who are well-educated in Buddhist thought and significantly involved in meditation practices. Monastic situations are often regarded as temporary retreats in which very complex studies and practices occur; these periods of monastic living are seen as training for everyday life as well.

Clear analysis of what this development entails is important. The traditional Buddhist skepticism of the spiritual value of domestic concerns, both familial and economic, could remain. The development of serious lay Buddhist practice does not necessarily mean a transvaluation of values in which activities that were formerly held in low esteem are accorded value. It means only that lay people now attempt to make time for practices usually engaged in only by monastics and that their efforts are being supported and encouraged. However, if enough lay Buddhists participate long and seriously in such an endeavor, *and especially if significant numbers of them are women,* such a transformation is inevitable. The everyday life of career and family will come to be regarded as Buddhist practice *rather than as the parentheses within which such practice occurs,* a vast transformation of values. This vast transformation and enlargement of Buddhist concerns is far more radical than simply encouraging lay people to engage in extensive study and practice. The traditional hierarchy between the spiritual and the ordinary is erased and the lines between them become blurred. Housework, meditation, business, study, childcare, retreat, marriage, celibacy—all the dichotomies and hierarchies that seemed so clear—vanish. Such a reevaluation enormously enlarges the canon of Buddhist concerns. It also introduces new tensions, which can be difficult to resolve.

This transvaluation of values grows out of conflicts that can occur when people try to combine the monastic and the householder lifestyles. These conflicts have probably been most poignantly articulated by women who have been involved in serious lay Buddhist practice before they become parents with the major responsibility for childcare. On the one hand, there simply is no time for the demanding disciplines of Buddhist practice, and constant interruption when one does make the attempt. On the other hand, more seriously, people often report feelings of deep conflict. They intuitively feel that their childcare activities are spiritually significant, but they find little validation of that point of view in retreat manuals and other traditional Buddhist texts, and often they experience guilt over "not practicing" and "not being serious about Buddhism." These same conflicts can arise regarding a broad range of "ordinary" domestic and work-related concerns of both women and men.

This situation obviously invites feminist reconceptualization, but the task is trickier and more subtle than may at first appear. The standard feminist observation and critique that Buddhism, like all the male-created and male-dominated religions, has little understanding of or advice relevant to women's life cycles, bodies, or reproductive experiences is appropriate. These topics are rarely discussed in classic sources, and if they are, the discussion is remote and of little use, obviously coming from someone who has no direct experience of them. They are never evaluated positively or as of direct spiritual significance. The feminist response is to call for a revalorization of these experiences stressing their dignity as well as their spiritual potential. This revalorization would encompass and include not only parenting but the entire round of domestic and worldly activities usually left behind by "serious Buddhists" and devalued even by lay Buddhists who see study and practice as their "real" Buddhist activity. Thus the feminist reconceptualization calls for seeing "ordinary" activities as sacred—as spiritually significant. This call is an important challenge to the conventional religions, especially to those, including Buddhism, that have a long tradition of seeing spiritual discipline as an otherworldly and anti-worldly pursuit of freedom from the world. The feminist call is for nothing less than finding freedom within the world, within domestic concerns, within emotions, within sexuality, within parenthood, within career. This vision goes far beyond simply encouraging householders to make time in their lives for traditional study and practices. The vision of Buddhism as freedom within the world means that one can be free not only in a monastery, but also in an office or a nursery. If one loses one's freedom in the nursery or office, but not at the meditation center, and becomes petty, trivial, unmindful, or unclear, then one is not truly free.

While this feminist reconceptualization certainly has compelling merit, some care and caution are required in its endorsement. Buddhism has traditionally been suspicious of ordinary, conventional, worldly life for good reason. Often and easily it becomes petty, trivial, distracting, and indulgent. Even people who take care to live contemplative and introspective lives in the midst of worldly activity often feel that they have become distracted and caught up in trivial or indulgent reactions and pursuits; how much more easily would an ordinary life unsuffused with awareness and introspection become petty, unattractive, and undesirable. The point is not that ordinary activities are necessarily sacred, but that they can be sacred when done with the proper mental and spiritual attitude. The corresponding, equally significant point is that one can easily lose that mind of clarity, awareness, and mindfulness. While it sounds attractive to see the sacred in ordinary everyday activities, in dirty diapers and busy schedules, actually being able to do that, rather than simply becoming distracted and petty, is not easy. In fact, such an ability is often claimed to be the acme of spiritual attainment, of true freedom. But it is not attained overnight or without significant spiritual practice, simply by declaring its desirability.

There is inevitable tension connected with this enlargement and revaluing of Buddhist concerns. On the one hand, it is attractive not to dichotomize experience into important spiritual concerns and unimportant worldly concerns, but to see these two arenas of life as interpenetrating and nondistinguishable. On the other hand, it is easy, while attempting to unify one's life, simply to fall into mere unaware, worldly attitudes. Two questions might occur to an outsider. Why is it important to maintain clarity? Return to basic Buddhist principles. Without clarity and insight, one will fall into attachment and ignorance, which inevitably bring suffering in their wake. Is it any easier to maintain awareness and detachment in a monastic than in a household environment? The answer is an unqualified yes, based on my experiences of many periods of retreat into quasi-monastic environments for intensive study and meditation. All-pervasive discipline, a strict schedule, lack of interruptions, and focused attention to meditation practice all conspire to enhance clarity, insight, and awareness. However, the Buddhist and feminist concerned with spirituality as freedom within the world see perpetual retreat into such protected environments as rather limited and artificial, violating the balance sought in the Three Wheels principle discussed earlier. Dichotomizing one's life into "important spiritual" and "unimportant ordinary" activities is similarly unattractive. A whole, balanced lifestyle in which all its parts are valued as important to over-all spiritual well-being, without ever degenerating into mere conventional worldliness, is much more ideal. For this lifestyle we really have no models; to create such models is one of the tasks of post-patriarchal Buddhism seen as freedom within the world.

Thus, I suggest balancing on the razor's edge—a familiar Buddhist metaphor for the life of spiritual discipline. While affirming the sacred potential of ordinary domestic householder concerns, one must also hold firmly to the Buddhist dissatisfaction with conventional attitudes and approaches to them. Genuine freedom within the world involves nothing less.

WHAT IS SPIRITUAL DISCIPLINE AND WHAT'S IT GOOD FOR?
AN UNANSWERED FEMINIST QUESTION

This final section of my essay will discuss many of the same questions and raise many of the same concerns from another point of view. As before, the goal is seeking wholeness and balance in lifestyle and values, which is the same thing as seeking to avoid extremes. In the previous section we discussed how the extreme view of seeing Buddhism's goal as freedom from the world could result in a devaluing of worldly life and activities. We sought alternatives that did not fall into the other extreme of becoming completely caught up in and attached to worldliness. In this section, I will deal with some of the same concerns by discussing another extreme view that can result when Buddhism is interpreted as freedom from the world. This is the extreme of regarding meditation practice as the most, even only, valuable human activity, the only activity conducive to enlightenment and clear seeing into "Things As They Are."

Sometimes I become impatient with some of the models and heroes presented to me by my tradition, not because they are men, but because they seem extreme. Do I really want to emulate them? Does my skepticism have anything to do with a valid feminist critique, or is it simply due to laziness and resistance? Though nothing is more important to me than clear seeing, than seeing Things As They Are, in classic Buddhist terms, I find it difficult to appreciate some of the methods utilized by some who are acclaimed as having achieved this goal. Long periods of isolation are routine in Tibetan Buddhism, and Zen monks do lengthy periods of continuous *zazen.* What can Mila Repa's years-long isolation in his cave, nearly starving himself to death and turning green from his diet of nettles, have to do with enlightenment? I am no more attracted when I read of a contemporary Western woman studying under Tibetan teachers who routinely goes into solitary meditation in her cave, which cannot even be reached for much of the year because it is snowbound. Are such practices necessary? Are they even helpful to anyone? Why are they often praised and admired? Why do so many people seem to think that to realize one's innate enlightened humanity, such anti-human disciplines are helpful? What about seemingly less extreme measures? What about the shorter solitary retreats and the time and expense involved in significant periods of intensive meditation practice?

This line of questioning, especially when combined with feminist skepticism, is deeply troubling. Because the patriarchs have been wrong about so much, and because they hang onto their sexism so desperately even after its demonic nature is pointed out to them, resisting even the uncontroversial agenda of liberal Buddhist feminism, healthy skepticism about anything they say is warranted. One cannot simply trust that the leaders have everything right, that they've picked good and healthy models for us, that we do have to go to such extremes as they recommend to be fully human. Because patriarchal religions will not rid themselves of their patriarchy, a feminist who wishes to remain with that tradition must take nothing on faith and test everything. Ultimately, this includes the beloved heart of Buddhist life — its emphasis on meditative and spiritual disciplines, an emphasis which can seem extreme and one-sided. At some moments one questions whether the demanding meditations actually help one live well and truthfully, or whether they get in the way. Maybe they are simply the creations of patriarchs who use them to control life and distance themselves from others! Maybe that is why Buddhism sometimes seems to glorify aloneness and be deficient in its emphasis on relationship! Clearly, such reflections are frightening to one who has deeply invested in Buddhism.

What is the exact content of these restless questions? I am not questioning whether meditation is or has been very pleasurable — sometimes peaceful, sometimes exhilarating — as well as at least seemingly beneficial. In fact, the various meditations are so conducive to the feeling that one has finally come closer to seeing into the depth of things that one *is* tempted to say, as I have sometimes done after periods of intensive meditation, *"this is the real world!"* Then one can almost believe that those who spend most of their time in meditation, as so many heroes of the tradition have done, are, in fact, the only ones who really see Things As They Are. But if that were true, then all the attempts to create a balanced lifestyle that accommodates both "spiritual" and "ordinary" concerns as being of one flavor would obviously be an impossible waste of time. This conclusion I obviously am not willing to make. Furthermore I reject two common assertions of the tradition. Helpful as meditation may be to some people, I doubt that it is as indispensably necessary as is sometimes claimed. More important, I doubt that one should pursue meditation as single-mindedly to the exclusion of other pursuits, as did many of the heroes of the tradition.

These questions reflect a deeper tension found in all religious traditions and between the religions and feminism. All religions, not only world-denying traditions but also the supposedly world-affirming traditions, have a deep impulse to remake people, to declare that the human condition, unrefined and unreworked by religious disciplines, initiations, or confessions is inadequate. It is filled with original sin, completely consumed by suffering, lacking esoteric knowledge, or even a properly shaped penis. Without the intervention of time-consuming, expensive, painful, and *seemingly unnatural* religious disciplines, we human beings, as we are, are quite hopeless. But religion can cope, can wash away original sin, show the path beyond suffering, fill one with proper knowledge, or remake the body properly. Meditation disciplines designed to achieve these goals abound.

Feminists tend to be quite suspicious of such claims. This suspicion is due to the claim commonly made by religions that women are even worse off than men, that women are the cause of these negative conditions, that women are less capable of being repaired by religious disciplines, and that, therefore, women can be forbidden even to practice the religious disciplines that repair the human situation. Obviously, these strongly anti-female claims are unequivocally rejected by feminism. More important, feminist rejection of anti-female teachings and practices predisposes us to be suspicious of other negative evaluations common to religions. Often feminists say that the tendency of religions to find life deeply unsatisfactory is a patriarchal value and that the more accurate and feminist assessment is to find life joyful and satisfactory, including its dark aspects and its limitations. We do not need to be free of those aspects of life, but to find our ease in them, which will enable us to appreciate them.

In these claims feminism is quite similar to the alternative attitude also espoused by most religions in other moods. Though often lost in the barrage of rhetoric regarding the unsatisfactoriness of life, this alternative assessment is, in fact, the deeper, more normative attitude, especially in Buddhism. All the confusions and defilements that cause so much suffering are not our original true human nature at all, but a veil, a secondary overlay. In this assessment the spiritual need is to be able to accept and settle into our human goodness and our human potential. Life conditions are fundamentally sane and satisfactory, but we have a difficult time seeing that they are. The point of spiritual discipline is to be able to let ourselves be fully human. But how can years of solitary retreat effect that goal? We are back to the original question.

Balancing these two views, both of which intuitively have merit and ring true, without falling into either extreme, will prove as difficult as balancing spiritual and worldly concerns without falling off the razor's edge into mere worldliness or into regarding worldly concerns as insignificant. Feminist first impressions may well be more sympathetic to the view that the human situation is fundamentally good, but eventually the necessity of some kind of difficult, "against the grain" discipline that enables us to return to and rest in the fundamental goodness becomes obvious. The question is not "Whether discipline?" but "What kind of discipline?" Sorting out excesses, many of them due to patriarchal limitations, from genuinely sane, balanced approaches will be difficult. This will be another major task of Buddhism after patriarchy. In general, the same kind of balance or Three Wheels principle sought for in other arenas of post-patriarchal reconceptualization would hold here. Lifelong, regular spiritual discipline is obviously important, but it should not be regarded as the only thing worthwhile, "the one thing needful" in life, and the demands of one's spiritual discipline should not incapacitate one regarding other dimensions of a whole, complete lifestyle. One of the results in this revaluing will be a change in the ideals and heroes of the tradition presented to the wayfarer on the path. No longer will a man who spends most of his life alone in caves attaining esoteric states of mind be regarded as so ideal. Nor for that matter will a woman who raises many children without ever developing herself. In Buddhism after patriarchy, free of gender roles, well-rounded, well-balanced individuals and lifestyles will replace the half-humans who have limited our vision for so long.

Another important post-patriarchal question concerning spiritual discipline asks "For what purpose?" What do we hope will result from the practice of spiritual discipline? What changes will it effect? Freedom from rebirth and communication with unseen beings, often currently the hoped-for results, do not seem to be relevant. One can even question the relevance of exalted, euphoric states of consciousness or esoteric knowledge and understanding. Rather, the point of it all is a basic psychological grounding, deep sanity and peace with ourselves—out of that grows the caring for community, for each other, that is so important for spiritual insight and well-being. Additionally, our sensitivity to, appreciation of, and desire to care for our earth will shine forth. Spiritual discipline will no longer encourage us to seek to leave her behind for a better world or to superimpose another purer visualized world upon her. To become sane, to live in community with each other and our earth is to experience freedom within the world. Who would want freedom from the world instead!

POSTSCRIPT

As I imagine anti-feminist Buddhist critics reading these comments, I try to anticipate their methods of discounting what has been said. The most cogent would be to say that everything I have said is already contained in the traditional resources. To which I would reply, "Yes, and that indicates I've learned my lessons well. Because, though all these themes are found in the tradition, they are muted voices often covered over and obliterated by much louder anti-worldly, anti-domestic voices telling us that if we don't meditate all our lives and drop all worldly concerns, death will be a frightening, terrible experience. But yes, these messages are there as the heart resource of the tradition which we can utilize to inspire us and to build upon. For I am proposing, not a new, unnamed religion after patriarchy, but *Buddhism* after patriarchy."

NOTES

1. The four worldly types of suffering discussed by the Buddha in an early sermon.
2. A recurrent phrase in some Vajrayana Buddhist liturgies.

WORKS CITED

Allione, Tsultrim. *Women of Wisdom.* London: Routledge and Kegan Paul, 1984.
Bellah, Robert. "Religious Evolution." In *Reader in Comparative Religion,* 3d ed. Ed. Less and Vogt. New York: Harper and Row, 1972.
Chodorow, Nancy. *The Reproduction of Mothering: Psychoanalysis and the Sociology of Gender.* Berkeley: University of California Press, 1978.
Dowman, Keith. *Sky Dancer: The Life and Songs of the Lady Yeshe Tsogyel.* London: Routledge and Kegan Paul, 1984.
Falk, Nancy Auer. "The Case of the Vanishing Nuns." In *Unspoken Worlds.* Ed. Falk and Gross. Belmont, California: Wadsworth, 1989.
Gilligan, Carol. *In a Different Voice: Psychological Theory and Women's Development.* Cambridge: Harvard University Press, 1982.
Gross, Rita. "The Feminine Principle in Tibetan Vajrayana Buddhism: Reflections of a Buddhist Feminist." *Journal of Transpersonal Psychology* 16 (1984): 179-92.
———. "Buddhism and Feminism: Toward Their Mutual Transformation." *Eastern Buddhist: New Series.* XIX, 1 and 2 (Spring and Autumn 1986):44-58, 62-74.
———. "Yeshe Tsogyel: Enlightened Consort, Great Teacher, Female Role Model." In *Feminine Ground: Essays on Women and Tibet.* Ithaca, New York: Snow Lion Publications, 1989.
———. " 'The Dharma Is Neither Male nor Female': Buddhism on Gender and Liberation." In *Testimonies of the Spirit: Men's and Women's Liberation.* Ed. Grob, Gordon, and Hassan. Westport, Connecticut: Greenwood Press, forthcoming.
Havenik, Hanna. *Tibetan Buddhist Nuns: History, Cultural Norms, Social Reality.* Oslo: Norwegian University Press, n.d.
Nelson, James B. *The Intimate Connection: Male Sexuality, Male Spirituality.* Philadelphia: The Westminster Press, 1988.
Paul, Diana Y. *Women in Buddhism: Images of the Feminine in Mahayana Tradition.* Berkeley: Asian Humanities Press, 1979.
Schauf, Ann Wilson. *Women's Reality: An Emerging Female System in the White Male Society.* Minneapolis: Winston Press, 1981.
Suzuki, Shun, yu. *Zen Mind: Beginner's Mind: Informal Talks on Zen Meditation and Practice.* New York and Tokyo: Weatherhill, 1974.
Trungpa, Chogyam. "Taking Refuge." *Garuda V.* Boulder, Colorado: Shambala Publications, 1977.
———. *Hinayana-Mahayana Seminary Transcripts: 1980* (privately printed and circulated).
Tsomo, Karma Lekshe. *Sakyadhita: Daughters of the Buddha.* Ithaca, New York: Snow Lion Publications, 1988.

5

Transforming the Nature of Community

Toward a Feminist People of Israel

JUDITH PLASKOW

A post-patriarchal Judaism begins with the insistence that women as well as men comprise Jewish humanity. Confronted with a religious system that projects women as "other," Jewish feminists assert that Jewish women's experience is an integral part of Jewish experience and that women with men make up Jewish community. No account of Judaism is complete unless it considers fully and seriously the experience of women, and no Jewish community is fully Jewish unless women play an equal role in shaping and defining it.

This principle, simple as it seems, necessitates far-reaching changes in Jewish self-understanding. Since the Jewish textual tradition treats men as normative Jews, Jewish history must be rewritten to include the history of women. The boundaries of Jewish memory must be altered and expanded to incorporate women's experience and teachings. Jewish law must be re-argued and reconstructed as the presence of women as lawmakers makes certain new norms imperative and certain old ones unthinkable. New Jewish liturgy must mark important turning points in women's lives and reflect the contours of women's spiritualities. The very concept of God must be rethought, and new symbols for God created.

Since to consider the totality of these changes would require a book rather than a single chapter (see Plaskow 1990), in this article I will limit myself to the implications of the assumption of women's full humanity for the concept of Israel. Defining Israel as the Jewish community and the Jewish people, I will explore the nature of an Israel that takes women's experience seriously. Feminists have argued that women have been marginalized within the community of Israel and excluded from some of the central experiences of Jewish religious life (Koltun; Heschel). What have been the sources and costs of women's marginalization, and what would constitute rectification? What resources for change lie within Jewish self-understanding, and in what ways does Judaism need to be transformed? These questions are at once practical and theological. The issue of Israel is an issue concerning Jewish communal form and practice, the embodied shape and nature of Jewish life. One cannot hope to create a feminist Jewish people, however, without also considering certain theological questions—the significance and spiritual dimensions of community, the conceptualization of difference in Jewish life, and the key concept of chosenness.

THE COMMUNAL NATURE OF PERSONHOOD

Any understanding of Israel must begin with the recognition that Israel is a community, a people, not a collection of individual selves. The conviction that personhood is shaped, nourished, and sustained in community is a central assumption that Judaism and feminism share. To the Jew, the feminist, the Jewish feminist, the individual is not an isolated unit who attains humanity through independence from others or who must contract for social relations. Rather, to be a person is to find oneself from the beginning in community—or, as is often the case in the modern world, in multiple communities (Waskow, 124). To develop as a person is to acquire a sense of self in relation to others and to critically appropriate a series of communal heritages.

For feminists, insistence on the communal character of human selfhood is articulated over against the individualism of the dominant strand in Western culture and represents the intersection of a number of streams of experience and analysis. The consciousness-raising groups of the 1960s that marked the beginning of the second wave of feminism provided important evidence of the communal nature of human life. Examining our experience in the consciousness-raising context, women were able to piece together the processes of socialization and learning that shape the female role. We were able to see that our self-understandings, our life choices, our expectations of ourselves as women were not the products simply of our own growth and development but of powerful social forces that had molded us from birth. Moreover, at the same time we came to see the communal origins of the constraints on our lives, we also experienced community as the source of our liberation. Coming to a clear understanding of gender as socially constructed, we experienced a new opening of self, a sense of freedom to be and become our own persons rather than to live out prescriptive social roles. But this new sense of autonomous selfhood, like the traditional female self, came and could have come only with others. It was only as we sat and spoke together, as many women told of feelings and troubles that each had seen as her own, that "hearing drew forth . . . speech," and we were able to experience and understand the connections between what had been laid out for us and our own choices (Morton, 29; Plaskow 1979, 198-209). We apprehended selfhood not as something brought ready-made to community but as both shaped by community and enlarged by common commitment and struggle.

This direct and powerful experience of the connection between self and community has been supplemented by trenchant analytical critiques of liberal individualism as a basis for feminist theory. In *The Radical Future of Liberal Feminism*, Zillah Eisenstein argues that there is a fundamental contradiction between the liberal view of persons as isolated and self-created and feminist insistence on the social nature of women's oppression. Insofar as mainstream American feminism unconsciously adopts the dominant cultural assumption that individuals can freely and independently form their own lives, it cannot explain the oppression of women as a class or the role of social and political institutions in protecting patriarchal power relations. Only a theory that understands "sex-class oppression" and that "recognizes the importance of the individual within the social collectivity" can generate a politics that will liberate women (Eisenstein, chaps. 1, 8).

Feminist experience of communal personhood and feminist political and philosophical analyses of social selfhood cohere with women's historical experience of embeddedness in and responsibility for relation. As an extensive literature on women and relation attests, women generally have been denied the luxury of believing in the separate individual ego; we have been forced to know ourselves as dependent and depended on by others (Gilligan; Chodorow; Keller; Heyward). While much of the literature of relation is based on white middle-class women's experience, the testimony of minority women only expands and deepens this insistence on connection. For many minority women the sense of group solidarity in oppression has been a basic reality of existence (Hooks 1984). Under the conditions of patriarchy, women's experience of relation has been distorted by sex, race, and class oppression, and women have been kept from self-determination within the web of connection. But this cannot negate the fact that women's relegation to the sphere of relation has kept women alive to a basic dimension of human experience that feminism affirms even as it seeks to transform the material character of human relations.

The knowledge that human beings are located in community is, of course, not limited to women. Shared by many cultures, it is central to both Jewish theology and the Jewish social experience. If to be a woman is to absorb and wrestle with a cultural understanding of femaleness, so to be a Jew is to absorb the history of the Jewish people. Jewish memory is communal memory and centers on community even as it forms and is formed by community. The covenantal history that begins in the Bible with Abraham, Isaac, and Jacob finds its fulfillment only at Sinai, when the whole congregation answers together, "All that the Lord has spoken we will do" (Ex

19:8). Though the Israelites are designated a people even in Egypt (Ex 1:9), it is only when they receive life and teachings as a community at Sinai that their prior history becomes important to remember. If you obey my covenant, God tells them, "you shall be to me a kingdom of priests and a holy nation" (Ex 19:6); at the moment of establishing the covenant, its corporate nature is affirmed (Gendler, 83; Buber, 138). From Sinai on, the Jewish relationship to God is mediated through this community. The Jew stands before God not as an individual but as a member of a people.

The theological significance of community in Judaism finds expression in religious, social, and national life. While the observant Jew is expected to pray three times daily whether alone or with others, there is a definite bias on behalf of public prayer. Maintaining a daily *minyan* (quorum for prayer) is regarded as an important function of the synagogue. Certain key prayers simply cannot be said unless there are ten men (sic) present, and the divine presence is said to rest in a unique way on the congregation. According to Rabbi Johanan, "When God comes to a synagogue and does not find a *minyan* there, [God] is angry, as it is written, 'Why, when I came, was there no one? When I called was there no one to answer?' (Is 50:2)" (*Encyclopedia Judaica*, "Minyan"; Katz, 176-77). It seems that once God establishes a covenant with the people as a whole, God is fully present only with and among the community. The individual who prays privately loses an important dimension of worship, and God hardly recognizes the people unless they are together.

Beyond the requirements of prayer, the sociological exigencies of Jewish existence also made for community. In some areas of the diaspora anti-Semitic legislation compelled Jews to live in certain districts, but even in areas where ghettos were not mandated by law, the Jews' relation to the larger political order was mediated through the Jewish community. Local communities (*kehillot*) operated semi-autonomously both in relation to each other and the wider Gentile culture, offering their members a range of services that today would be provided by a combination of charitable, religious, and state institutions (*Encyclopeda Judaica*, "Community"; Katz). Just as the Jew's relationship to God is mediated through membership in the Jewish people, so the Jew's relationship to society was mediated through the *kehillah*, which, in addition to providing for individual and communal needs, levied the taxes to be paid to the government and generally managed relations with the non-Jewish world.

WOMEN IN THE JEWISH COMMUNITY

The similarities between feminist and Jewish understandings of the relation between self and community are substantial and genuine, and I have addressed the theme of community in Judaism without irony. Yet from a feminist perspective the Jewish emphasis on community is deeply ambiguous and ironic, for it coexists with the subordination of women within

Jewish communal life. Affirming community, Judaism affirms a male community in which the place of women is an open and puzzling question. At times it seems as if women are simply not part of Israel at all; more usually, women's presence in the community is assumed, but assumed as clearly peripheral.

When, for example, God enters into a covenant with Abraham and says to him, "This is my covenant, which you shall keep, between me and you and your descendants after you: Every male among you shall be circumcised" (Gn 17:10), women can hear this only as establishing our marginality. Even if circumcision is not itself the covenant but only the sign of the covenant, what role can women have in the covenant community when the primary symbol of the covenant pertains only to men? This important passage seems to presuppose a religious community composed of males only, an impression reinforced by other texts. The covenant at Sinai is spoken in male pronouns, for example, and its content assumes male hearers (Bird, 49-50). But the very same sources that can be taken to indicate the exclusion of women from Israel are often contradictory or equivocal. The appearance and disappearance of women in many biblical narratives and the legal regulation of women's sexuality and status where unique biology or some anomaly demand it, make clear that, while women are hardly equal in the Israelite community, they are also not simply absent.

The place of women in the community of Israel can be illuminated most fully by Simone de Beauvoir's notion of woman as "other." In her classic work *The Second Sex*, de Beauvoir argues that men have established an absolute human type—the male—against which women are measured as "other." Women cannot simply be excluded from community, for the relationship between men and women is not like other relationships between oppressor and oppressed. Men and women are parts of a totality in which, biologically speaking, both sides are necessary. Without women, it is impossible for any community to continue. Yet as far as normative Jewish texts are concerned, women do not define the values that make the community distinctive or that warrant its perpetuation. Women are not the subjects and molders of their own experiences but the objects of male purposes, designs, and desires (de Beauvoir, xv, xix, xvi). Thus women *are* part of the covenant community, but precisely in a submerged and non-normative way.

It is not simply narrative sources that reveal the place of women in the Jewish community, moreover, but also *halakhah* (Jewish law). *Halakhah* seeks to regulate communal behavior and make communal ideals concrete. In the case of women, legal exemption from public prayer and Torah study and legal subordination within the patriarchal family together carve out a restricted communal role. As Moshe Meiselman suggests (Meiselman, 14), the proper sphere of women is captured by Psalm 45:14, "The entire glory of the daughter of the king lies on the inside." The rabbis saw in this passage confirmation of the supposedly private nature of women's role and enforced this view through *halakhic* rulings. Since in many periods of Jewish history women helped earn the family livelihood, the Jewish division of male and female roles does not correspond exactly to the public/private distinction in our modern sense. What is written into law, however, is male control of public religious values and the male definition of women in terms of female biology.

Jewish feminists have often, and with reason, seen the restricted role of women in the Jewish community as a justice issue. The fact that we have been excluded from the public religious forum and socialized to a limited set of family roles has kept women from fully developing as persons and has deprived the Jewish community of the energy and talents of half its members. *Halakhah* has cordoned off from women just those avenues of religious expression the tradition values most highly. Torah study, Torah reading, leadership of the congregation, daily participation in public prayer are important vehicles of religious experience that women either have not been encouraged to develop or have been altogether denied.

Yet once we see the importance of community in the Jewish experience, we must add to all this another dimension of loss that women suffer. Over and above the value of participation in any particular religious activity is the spiritual aspect of community itself. It is not just that community is the space within which one fulfills a range of religious duties and reaps a range of spiritual rewards, but that community is the primary vehicle and place of religious experience. Thus, God did not enter into the covenant at Sinai because it was easiest to speak to the people when they were gathered together. God's speech established them as a community, and it was as a community that they heard the voice of God. If women are submerged in the Jewish covenant community, then we are excluded from the center of Jewish religious experience. There is no Jewish way to go off into the desert and have an independent relationship to God. Relationship to God is experienced and mediated precisely through the community that maintains women's marginality.

No panegyric on the virtues of private spirituality can disguise the fact that the nature of religious experience in Judaism is fundamentally communal or that the historical importance of public worship has a spiritual grounding. The divine presence rests in community in a uniquely powerful way.

But this means that the exclusion of women from full membership in the Jewish community is *in itself*, apart from exclusion from this or that religious obligation, exclusion of women from a profound and central dimension of Jewish spiritual life. Women's otherness is not just a matter of social and religious marginality but of spiritual deprivation.

TOWARD A REDEFINITION OF ISRAEL

Ending this social and spiritual marginality requires a far-reaching transformation of Jewish life. To recreate Israel from a feminist perspective, we must incorporate women's experience into the understanding and practice of the Jewish people so that women's contributions to Jewish community are not driven underground, thwarted, or distorted, and men's are not given more weight and status than they ought to enjoy. Until that happens, both our concept of Israel and the dynamics of Jewish life will remain thoroughly misshapen by sexism.

As Jewish feminists seek equality in a tradition that takes seriously the importance of community in human life, we must not neglect the centrality of community by repeating in relation to Judaism the liberal feminist mistake of seeing women as individuals who happen to be discriminated against in the Jewish system. Insofar as we fight for equality assuming as given the Judaism in which we are to be equal, we run the risk of gaining access to a community that structures its central ideas and institutions around male norms, but without changing the character of those ideas or institutions. Women in Judaism—like women in any patriarchal culture—are rendered invisible *as a class;* we are seen as "other" *as a class;* we are deprived of agency *as a class.* Until we understand and change the ways in which Judaism as a system supports the subordination of Jewish women as a subcommunity within the Jewish people, genuine equality of women and men is impossible.

The real challenge of feminism to Judaism emerges, not when women as individual Jews demand equal participation in the male tradition, but when women demand equality *as Jewish women,* as the class that has up until now been seen as "other." To phrase the feminist challenge to Judaism in an other than liberal way, we might say that the central issue in the feminist redefinition of Israel is the place of difference in community. Judaism can absorb many women rabbis, teachers, and communal leaders; it can ignore or reinterpret certain laws to allow women to participate fully in a *minyan;* it can make adjustments around the edges; it can live with the ensuing contradictions and tensions without fundamentally altering its self-understanding. But when women, with our own history and spirituality and attitudes and experiences, demand equality in a community that will allow itself to be changed by our differences, when we ask that our memories become part of Jewish memory and our presence change the present, then we make a demand that is radical and transforming. Then we begin the arduous experiment of trying to create a Jewish community in which difference is neither hierarchalized nor tolerated but truly honored. Then we begin to struggle for the only equality that is genuine.

THE ISSUE OF DIFFERENCE IN COMMUNITY

Since the insistence that women be accepted in Judaism as women may seem neither new nor radical, it is important to define where its challenge lies. It is not the recognition of difference that is in itself difficult. Judaism has always recognized—indeed insisted on—the differences between women and men. But it is of the essence of these differences as traditionally understood that they have been stratified and defined from the perspective of the dominant group. What is new about Jewish feminism is that *women* are claiming the right to define and assess our differences, that we are revaluing and renaming what has been used to oppress us. The fact that this undertaking on the part of Jewish feminists is analogous to struggles both of minority feminists and of Jews in the modern West brings into focus the enormous obstacles to creating communities rich in diversity and accountable to different perspectives. Examining some of the connections between the feminist, Jewish, and Jewish feminist situations may help clarify what is at stake in redefining Israel as a community that honors difference.

The feminist context is in some ways the most instructive for understanding the problem of difference in community because contemporary feminism has had a strong ideological commitment to including all women. The consciousness-raising groups of the 1960s tried to free themselves from the structures of domination in the wider society in order to provide spaces where every woman could be heard. Commitment to the bonds of sisterhood in the face of the pervasive nature of sexism was supposedly rooted in affirmation of all women's experience and each woman's struggle. As minority women increasingly have made clear, however, feminist theory and priorities often have ignored the multiple communities that shape women's lives. Assuming that male/female difference is the oldest and only important social difference, white middle-class feminists many times have constructed accounts of women's experience that falsely universalize a particular cultural and class perspective (Moraga and Anzaldua; Hooks 1981 and 1984; Hull, Scott, and Smith; Spelman 1988). The identification of "woman" with white middle-class—often Gentile—women is a continuing problem in feminist writing. It is illustrated by the persistence of anti-Semitic stereotypes in feminist literature, the additive analyses of sexism and racism that ignore the reality of many women's lives, and the exclusionary phrase "women and blacks" that appears and reappears in feminist writing (Spelman 1982, 42-46). The message such work communicates to minority women—Jewish women as well as women of color, although in different ways—is that if we want to be part of the "women's" movement, we should bring ourselves as women in the abstract (i.e. women of the dominant group), leaving aside the particular women we happen to be (Spelman 1988).

Commitment to feminism does not, then, automatically entail willingness to relinquish race, class, and religious privilege—or even to acknowledge they exist. While, in part, the persistence of race and class prejudice within the women's movement can be attributed to a liberal ideology that disguises the real power relations within society, fear of difference is itself a factor that continues to divide women from each other. Once we acknowledge the diversity and multiplicity of women's loyalties, what guarantee is there that we will find a common ground? Moreover, Audre Lorde suggests that when women have been educated in a society that sees all difference in terms of inferiority and superiority, "the recognition of any difference must be fraught with guilt" (Lorde, 118). Concerned that—as has so often happened in the past—recognizing difference will lead to inequality, feminists repeatedly have adopted the strategy of pretending that differences among women do not exist. But, of course, denying differences does not abolish them; it simply allows traditional forms of domination to continue unacknowledged. Moreover, avoiding differences prevents women from mining the knowledge and power that are rooted in our racial, ethnic, and religious particularity and from using "difference as a springboard for creative change" (Lorde, 115).

If feminism claims to respect difference and yet at the same time denies it, the modern West's offer of civil rights to the Jews was never premised on the acceptance of difference, even as a theoretical possibility. Jewish emancipation—the grant of full citizenship and legal equality—was based on the expectation that "in the absence of persecution and enforced segregation, Jews and Judaism would assimilate to the prevailing social and cultural norms of the environment" (Hyman, 165). The dominant groups in various European nations explicitly claimed the right to define the reality to which Jews would accommodate themselves. Jews were granted free access to the wider culture, but only at the cost of the communal autonomy that had characterized Jewish life for centuries and that had provided Jews with community, identity, and a set of common beliefs and values. In the words of a liberal deputy to the French national assembly, "One must refuse everything to the Jews as a nation but one must give them everything as individuals" (Hertzberg, 360). Relinquishing all Jewish particularity, Jews were to become German or Briton or French people of the Jewish religion, a religion that would now stress universal values and give up its peculiar and discriminatory forms. Insofar as Jews insisted on continuing to define their identity in ethnic as well as religious terms, they were regarded as reneging on a clear bargain and as occasioning the discrimination that legal emancipation did not eradicate. As *The Christian Century* asked rhetorically in a 1930's editorial, "Can democracy suffer a hereditary minority to perpetuate itself as a permanent minority, with its own distinctive culture sanctioned by its own distinctive cult form?" (Cited in Eisen, 34.) The writer is unable to imagine a democracy in which citizens share certain common values, yet also maintain allegiance to traditional sub-communities.

In the early period of emancipation Jews embraced the benefits of citizenship, accepting—sometimes willingly, sometimes out of necessity—the implicit or explicit conditions that went along. Two hundred years later, however, the communal and individual costs of emancipation are very clear: assimilation, fragmentation, loss of self-determination, loss of common identity and purpose. In traditional society Jews may have been outsiders, but they had an important defense against indifference or hatred; their own communal self-understanding radically contradicted the world outside. In the modern world Jews have more deeply internalized society's expectations and values, becoming divided from the Jew within the self. Social contempt for Jewish particularity finds its echo in Jewish contempt for Jewish noses, Jewish hair, Jewish assertiveness, Jewish mothers, Jewish history, Jewish religious life. Jews unable to affirm our own Jewishness or even to understand its meaning have little energy or creativity to bring to our Jewish communities.

The long struggle by Jews in the modern era to "prove the religious, intellectual, and social viability of Judaism within an open ... society" (Hyman, 170) — and the struggle of contemporary minority feminists to address differences within the feminist community — makes *The Christian Century's* question anything but rhetorical. Why is it unthinkable for minority communities to perpetuate themselves within a democracy — or within a movement? Is communal identity and cohesion really at odds with participation in a wider society? Given that in the modern world most individuals belong to more than one community, that communal loyalties diverge and overlap, is it not possible to affirm a common commitment to a national or feminist identity without denying other aspects of the self? Is it not possible that the interaction of distinctive sub-communities could enrich a total community? And given the tremendous costs of self-division, is it not in the interests of the state or the women's movement to allow individuals their communal roots? Is not the dream of many Jews in the modern world — acceptance by the broader culture in and through our particularity and not despite it — a worthy starting point for reconceptualizing community?

And what then of Jewish feminists? Jews among feminists, feminists among Jews, Jewish feminists have experienced the burden of difference in all the various communities to which we belong. The distrust of difference that has characterized feminism in relation to minority women and modern nationalist movements in relation to Jews is equally present in the Jewish community. Indeed, non-Orthodox Judaism places women in the same position in the Jewish community that Jews have found ourselves in in relation to the modern state. The bargain is less obvious because the character of Jewish women's bonds and culture is less obvious, being part of the great silence that shrouds women's experience. But insofar as women have distinctive rituals, a history, literature, modes of connection that grow out of centuries of sex-role segregation, these are to be abandoned for the privilege of participating in a dominant male culture that does not recognize anything of value in what will now be lost (Prell, 585). Moreover, since Jewish women, like Jews in modern society, are expected to internalize the values of the dominant group, we are also to forget our own history and forget even that it has been forgotten. Lacking a community of Jewish women to counter the perceptions of a male-defined Jewish culture — or a WASP-defined feminist one — our heritage of power as Jewish women is translated into anxiety lest we be dominating Jewish mothers, lest we be perceived as "taking over," or lest there be a "princess" lurking in our souls. The "other's other," we take in both the images of Jews and specifically Jewish women in the wider society, and also the projections of Jewish men.

Clearly the liberal notion of equality cannot provide an adequate theoretical basis for transforming Israel on feminist terms. Yet the gains of liberalism must not be repudiated in moving beyond it, any more than the costs of emancipation mean it should be revoked. Historically, liberalism made possible the recognition of Jews and women as human beings, an achievement that is the indispensable prerequisite of our true equality. But once we realize that recognizing others as individuals is fully compatible with fostering the power and self-understanding of dominant groups, it becomes necessary to move to an understanding of community that incorporates the accomplishments of liberalism and at the same time responds to its flaws. Jewish feminists want from the Jewish and feminist communities what women of color want from the feminist community, what self-affirming Jews want from the wider culture: equality in our particularity, acknowledgment of the many communities that shape our lives, acknowledgment of our complex history and experience, and attention to that history and experience in the formulation of cultural or religious norms and values.

CHOSENNESS, HIERARCHY, AND DIFFERENCE

It is not sufficient, however, simply to call the Jewish community to an acceptance of difference. To understand more fully those aspects of Judaism that thwart Jewish acceptance of diversity, we must examine further those ideas that have contributed to Judaism's long history of conceptualizing difference in terms of hierarchical separations. Suspicion and ranking of difference have been aspects of Judaism from its beginnings. Thinking of itself as a "kingdom of priests and a holy nation," the Jewish people understood its own holiness partly in contradistinction to the beliefs and behavior of surrounding nations. Serving the Lord meant shunning and destroying foreign gods and morality, thus refusing the "snare" of a different religious system (Ex 23:23-33). Paralleling external differentiation were a host of internal separations that set apart distinct and unequal objects, states, and modes of being. On a religious level, to be a holy people was both to be different from one's neighbors and to distinguish between and differently honor pure and impure; Sabbath and week; kosher and non-kosher; Cohen, Levi, and Israel (grades of priests and ordinary Jews); and male and female. On a social level the "otherness" of women was the first and most persistent among many inequalities that have marked Jewish life. Differences in wealth, learning, and observance; differences in cultural background and customs; differences in religious affiliation and understanding have all provided occasions for certain groups of Jews to define themselves as superior to different and non-normative "others." The distinction between men and women was never a unique hierarchy but emerged as part of a system in which many people and aspects of existence were defined in terms of superiority and inferiority (Setel 1986; Falk).

This hierarchical understanding of difference is perhaps the most significant barrier to the feminist reconceptualization of Jewish community. Jewish feminists cannot transform the place of women's difference within the people of Israel without addressing the larger system of separations in which it is embedded. In the context of the reconceptualization of Israel it is the notion of chosenness that is the chief expression of hierarchical distinction and therefore the most important focus for discussion. As a central category for Jewish self-understanding that is emblematic of other gradations, chosenness provides a warrant and a model for ranked differentiations within the community and between Israel and others. If Jewish feminism is to articulate a model of community in which difference is acknowledged without being expressed in hierarchical distinctions, it will have to engage the traditional Jewish understanding of difference by rejecting the idea of chosenness without at the same time denying the distinctiveness of Israel as a religious community.

Chosenness is a complex and evolving idea in Judaism that is by no means always associated with claims to superiority. While there is a strand in Jewish thinking that attributes chosenness to special qualities in the Jews and that argues for Jewish hereditary spiritual uniqueness and supremacy, by and large Israel's election is viewed not as a matter of merit or attributes but of responsibilities and duties. When the notion of chosenness first appears in the Bible simultaneously with the establishment of Israel as a covenant community, there is no apparent motive for Israel's special status but God's steadfast love and (itself unexplained) earlier promise to the patriarchs (Dt 7:7-8). Israel's standing as God's "own possession among all peoples" (Ex 19:5-6; Dt 7:6) is linked to acceptance and observance of the covenant; this constitutes its specialness in its own eyes and in the eyes of others (Dt 4:5-7). When Deutero-Isaiah shifts emphasis from election of Israel as holy community to election of Israel as servant to the world, he still gives no reason for God's selection. This prophet of exile calls Israel "a light to the nations" and interprets its suffering as a sign of chosenness and future redemption (Is 49:6; 53), but election is marked by suffering, not by exaltation (Eisen, 16-18; *Encyclopedia Judaica,* "Chosen People"; *Encyclopedia of Religion,* "Election"; Atlan, 56-57).

If ascription of supernatural sanctity to Israel is the exception rather than the rule, however, this eliminates only some of the troubling aspects of the notion of chosenness. When election is understood as obligation or taken for granted as the foundation of the *halakhic* life, the privileged nature of Israel's relationship to God remains even while explicit claims to superiority are absent (Atlan, 56). After all, the traditional male Jew who each morning blesses God for not making him a woman is said to be giving thanks for the special burden and responsibility of *halakhic* observance rather than deliberately vaunting his prerogatives. But however humbly he accepts his legal burden, his prayer nonetheless presupposes that women are exempt from *halakhic* responsibility, that the other side of his privilege is their exclusion. This same dichotomy applies to the gift of chosenness, which is similarly acknowledged in the morning blessings. The Jew is grateful to be a Jew because the burden of Jewishness is a boon and privilege others do not share. As the daily liturgy makes amply clear, the lot of the Jews is singular; their special destiny is God's unique choice, not one path among many. Whether this destiny is characterized in terms of the *noblesse oblige* of witness and service or straightforward claims to metaphysical superiority, it still constitutes a hierarchical differentiation.

To express the import of election in relation to the issue of difference, chosenness says that the Jewish difference is different from other people's difference; that Jews are different differently from the way in which other groups are different from one another. Jewish difference is not one among many, the uniqueness of a people as all peoples are unique, having their own history and task. Jewish difference is a matter of God's decision, God's mysterious and singular choice bestowing upon the Jews an unparalleled spiritual destiny. This difference is a hierarchical difference, a statement of privilege—even if burdensome and unmerited privilege—in relation to those who are not chosen.

Feminists troubled by this hierarchical understanding of the relation between Jews and others are hardly alone in our concern. Since emancipation, the concept of chosenness has been as much a source of embarrassment to Jews as of sustenance. Its exclusivity has seemed to many Jews to be in conflict with the desire for civic equality; its assumption of a special destiny to be in tension with the simple humanity of the Jew that was the premise of emancipation. In the last two hundred years the concept of chosenness has been almost endlessly refashioned as Jewish thinkers have tried to find ways to discard and retain it at the same time. Chosenness has been reinterpreted in terms of mission to the nations and universal ethics; the notion of Jewish superiority has been roundly rejected; the boundaries between God's choosing and Jewish God-consciousness have been thoroughly confused (Eisen, 18-22). Yet with the exception of the Reconstructionists' explicit repudiation of election, few of these reinterpretations have eliminated the stubborn implication of privilege the concept of chosenness entails.

In this situation feminist criticism of chosenness may seem simply to add one more small voice to what is already a surfeit of inconclusive discussion. Yet if feminists share many of the concerns of other critics, we also have a distinctive perspective to bring to the conversation. While most reinterpretations of election have focused on the relation of Jews to the wider society—seeking to reconcile chosenness with equality and participation in a pluralistic culture—feminism calls attention to the function of chosenness in relation to Jewish self-conception and the internal dynamics of the community. Feminist objections to the idea of chosenness center not just on its entanglement with external hierarchical differentiations but with internal hierarchies as well.

Chosenness is not just a statement about Jewish relations with other peoples but a focus for Jewish self-understanding. If Jews are set apart from others through a unique call to God's service, this call must first express itself in Jewish communal life. The holiness that leads to external differentiation is lived out through observing the internal separations that mark a holy community. Since chief among these many separations is the differentiation between male and female, chosenness becomes linked to the subordination of women and other groups in the rhythms of Jewish existence. It is not that one can draw a direct line from the idea of chosenness to the creation of "others" within the Jewish community or that the former provides an explicit model for the latter. But both are part of a cluster of important ideas that make graded differentiation a central model for understanding difference, and the two are also linked to each other both historically and psychologically.

It is worthy of note, for example, that in the same period in which Deutero-Isaiah elaborated the notion of chosenness, placing its significance in a world-historic context, there emerged for the first time persistent use of female sexuality as a symbol of evil. In an earlier period, when election was understood primarily in terms of Israel's observance of the commandments, women's sexuality was strictly controlled within the patriarchal family but was not seen as negative in and of itself (Setel 1985, 86, 88-90). This means that as the experience of exile gave rise to a new and more elevated interpretation of chosenness, the status of women diminished. The precise connection between these ideas is difficult to establish, but their historical correlation speaks to the real association between different types of hierarchical thinking. Moreover, the fact that both ideas emerge in relation to the exile suggests that the process of distinguishing between normative and non-normative Jews may be linked to the notion of chosenness through the dynamics of Jewish suffering.

The concept of chosenness has been an important solace to Jews in the face of anti-Jewish oppression, and it was often articulated more strongly where suffering was more severe. Emphasis on the unique destiny of the Jewish people and on the differences between Jew and Gentile would have provided an important counterbalance to the painful messages of the world and helped make Jewish misery intelligible and bearable. The self-concept that emerged as a compensation for suffering and outward rejection, however, was exaggeratedly elevated. As such, it was necessarily in tension both with the constant realities of life in a hostile culture and with the truth of human imperfection. Though nothing in their lives would have made this realization easy, Jews were not really so different from their neighbors, except that the complex of forces that made for their oppression also kept them from acting out their sense of superiority and/or rage. In this situation in which an enlarged self-concept was challenged by daily experience, someone had to bear the weight of "otherness" reflected in the mirror of the Gentile world, and also the pain and anger, lusts and temptations that Jewish flesh is heir to. Although there were many groups within the Jewish community, which in different periods carried part of this burden, the Jewish woman was always a safe recipient of Jewish male projection. Marginalized in the wider society as well as Jewish culture, she represented both the "otherness" the male Jew rejected for himself and the qualities that could not be acknowledged in a chosen people. A member of the elect, she was nonetheless the underside of that election (Breitman 1987, 1988). It is thus no coincidence that a new notion of chosenness and a new image of women entered the world together, for one demanded the other as its psychological complement and completion.

A dynamic in which an over-elevated self-understanding must be balanced by the creation of "others" within the elect community points the way to change, however, through its own reversal. If the notion of the Jews as the chosen people seems to require the subordination of women, the withdrawal of projection from women is the correlate of a measured and clear-eyed understanding of the self. The male Jew's acknowledgment of his own simple humanity is integrally related to the recognition of Jewish women as normative Jewish human beings, just as the acceptance of women as human fosters the recognition of all Jews' simple humanity. The rejection of chosenness and the rejection of women's "otherness" are interconnected pieces of the wider project of finding ways to conceptualize and live with difference that are not based on projection and graded separations.

If feminists reject the concept of election, however, what remains of the distinctiveness of Israel and its relationship to the choosing God? Modern Jewish thinkers have hesitated to give up the idea of chosenness because they have been afraid that, with it, they would surrender the rationale for Jewish existence. But chosenness is necessary to justify Jewish life only on a view that does not take seriously the communal nature of human existence. If human beings are isolated individuals who must be persuaded to link ourselves with others, then Jewish commitment, like any form of communal engagement, requires argument and warrant. If, however, community is constitutive of personhood, then it needs no supernatural vocation to connect the Jew with Jewish living. Jewishness is a rich and distinctive way of being human, of linking oneself with God and with other persons, of finding a pattern within which to live that gives life depth and meaning. That is enough reason to be a Jew.

To argue for the self-justifying nature of Jewish life is not to reduce Judaism to a sense of group belonging or to define Israel without reference to God. The Jewish people came into being as a result of and in response to profound religious experiences, and it has been the purpose of its long history to ever more deeply comprehend and live out the relationship to God that drew it from its first hour. While the notion of a supernatural deity who singles out a particular people is part of the dualistic, hierarchical understanding of reality that the feminist must repudiate, to reject this idea of God is not to reject the God who is met in community and wrestled with in history. Nor is it to deny that loyalty to God has been at the center of Jewish identity and an important part of what makes that identity distinctive.

Indeed, the purpose of a feminist critique of chosenness and redefinition of Israel is not to truncate Jewish spirituality but to liberate it from its connection with hierarchical dualisms. So long as the Jewish people holds onto a self-understanding that perpetuates graded distinctions within the community, Jewish spirituality will be defined by and limited to a small proportion of Jews. Women will be excluded from the relationship with God that comes through full participation in community. The history of their experience and understanding of God will be excluded from Jewish memory. Only a Jewish community that permits and desires its members to be present in their particularity and totality can know in its fullness the relationship to God that it claims as its center.

What must replace chosenness, then, as the model for Jewish self-understanding is the far less dramatic *distinctness*. The Jewish community and the sub-communities within it, like all human communities, are distinct and distinctive. Jewish experience has been variously shaped by gender, by place of dispersion, by language, by history, by interaction with other cultures. Just as the total Jewish experience is always located within a wider world, so the experiences of Jewish subgroups have taken place in some relation to a larger Jewish life and self-understanding. The term *distinctness* suggests, however, that the relation between these various communities — Jewish to non-Jewish, Jewish to Jewish — should be understood not in terms of hierarchical differentiation but in terms of part and whole.

The use of a part/whole model for understanding difference has a number of implications. First of all, it points to the greater unity to which different groups belong, making it possible to acknowledge the uniqueness of each group as part of a wider association of self-differentiated communities (Falk, 122). Jewish women are part of the larger Jewish community as Jews are part of a larger heterogeneous culture. The parts are distinct. They have their own history and experience, and depending on their character, their own institutions, religion, practices, and beliefs. The content of this distinctness creates an internal sense of group identity and community and also allows the group to distinguish itself from others. Without this distinctiveness — were such a "without" even imaginable — we would lack the richness and diversity, the color and the passion, the insights and the wisdom that make up human history and culture. But while distinction is necessary, inevitable, a cause for celebration, the boundaries of distinction need not be rigidly guarded by graded separations. Boundaries can also be places where people can touch. Awareness of the wider communities to which any community belongs fosters an appreciation of distinctness that need not be rooted in hierarchy or in projection onto others of rejected aspects of the self.

Second, if the different groups and subgroups that make up a community or nation are parts of a greater whole, there is no whole without all the pieces. Though Jewish history frequently has been abstracted from its varied surroundings and studied as an independent subject—and though the histories of other peoples often make scant reference to the Jews—Jewish history is part of the history of the peoples and cultures among whom the Jews have lived. Thus, for example, unless European history includes the experience of Jews, it is not truly European history but the poorer and less complex history of dominant Christian cultures. Similarly, unless Jewish history and community include the history and experience of women, it is not truly Jewish history or Jewish community but male Jewish history and community. Such exclusion is destructive not only to the groups ignored but also to the rich tapestry of Jewish life that grows in distinctness and beauty with the distinctness and beauty of its various portions.

Third, what is true of communities is also true of selves. Where the boundaries between communities are marked by hierarchical separations, normative humanity is defined without reference to groups that are less valued. Thus Europeanness is defined without reference to Jews, Jewishness without reference to Jewish women. But the further effect of this separative understanding of community is that individuals within subordinate groups repress those aspects of themselves that are despised in the culture. Jews do not bring the special contributions of Jewishness to bear on wider social issues. Jewish women, as we gain equal access to Jewish communal life, deny our own experience for normative male practice and discourse. Those whose differences might have enriched and challenged the greater communal life learn to forget or keep hidden pieces of themselves.

We are brought back to the spiritual injury that such forgetting entails, and to the potential for liberation in a different model of community. To be wholly present in our lives in all our power is to touch the greater power of being that is the final unity within which all particulars dwell. To deny our complex particularity, as individuals or communities, is to diminish our connection to the God known in and through the experience of community. The community or self that spends its energy repressing parts of its totality truncates its creative power and cuts itself off from its full possibilities (Ackelsberg, March 1983, October 1983). A Jewish community that defines itself by walling itself off from others without and within marshals strength at its boundaries to the detriment of the center. It nourishes selves that must deny parts of themselves and thus cannot bring their uniqueness to the enrichment of a common life. To create Jewish communities that value particularity is to create places where Jews in their complex wholeness can bring their full power to the upbuilding of Jewish community and the other communities in which Jews dwell. It is in the distinctiveness that opens itself to difference that we find the God of Israel and of each and every people.

WORKS CITED

Ackelsberg, Martha. "Personal Identities and Collective Visions: Reflections on Being a Jew and a Feminist." Unpublished lecture, Smith College, March 8, 1983.

―――. "Towards a Feminist Judaism." Unpublished lecture delivered at the Jewish Women's Conference: Challenge and Change, October 1983.

Atlan, Henri. "Chosen People." In *Contemporary Jewish Religious Thought: Original Essays on Critical Concepts, Movements and Beliefs.* Ed. Arthur A. Cohen and Paul Mendes-Flohr. New York: Charles Scribner's Sons, 1987.

Bird, Phyllis. "Images of Women in the Old Testament." In *Religion and Sexism: Images of Women in the Jewish and Christian Traditions.* Ed. Rosemary Ruether. New York: Simon and Schuster, 1974.

Breitman, Barbara. "Psychopathology of Jewish Men." *Letter to Tikkun* 2 (1987).

―――. "Lifting Up the Shadow of Anti-Semitism." In *A Mensch Among Men: Explorations in Jewish Masculinity.* Ed. Harry Brod. Freedom, California: Crossing Press, 1988.

Buber, Martin. *Israel and the World: Essays in a Time of Crisis.* New York: Schocken Books, 1963.

Chodorow, Nancy. *The Reproduction of Mothering: Psychoanalysis and the Sociology of Gender.* Berkeley and Los Angeles: University of California Press, 1978.

De Beauvoir, Simone. *The Second Sex.* Trans. H. M. Parshley. New York: Bantam Books, 1961.

Eisen, Arnold. *The Chosen People in America: A Study in Jewish Religious Ideology.* Bloomington: Indiana University Press, 1983.

Eisenstein, Zillah. *The Radical Future of Liberal Feminism.* New York: Longman, 1981.

Falk, Marcia. Response to "Feminist Reflections on Separation and Unity in Jewish Theology." *Journal of Feminist Studies in Religion* 2 (Spring 1986).

Gendler, Everett E. "Community." In *Contemporary Jewish Religious Thought: Original Essays on Critical Concepts, Movements and Beliefs.* Ed. Arthur A. Cohen and Paul Mendes-Flohr. New York: Charles Scribner's Sons, 1987. See also Atlan, 81-86.

Gilligan, Carol. *In a Different Voice: Psychological Theory and Women's Development.* Cambridge: Harvard University Press, 1982.

Hertzberg, Arthur. *The French Enlightenment and the Jews: The Origins of Modern Anti-Semitism.* New York: Schocken Books, 1968.

Heschel, Susannah, ed. *On Being a Jewish Feminist: A Reader.* New York: Schocken Books, 1983.

Heyward, Carter. *The Redemption of God: A Theology of Mutual Relation.* Washington, D.C.: University Press of America, 1982.

Hooks, Bell. *Ain't I a Woman: Black Women and Feminism.* Boston: South End Press, 1981.

―――. *Feminist Theory: From Margin to Center.* Boston: South End Press, 1984.

Hull, Gloria, Patricia Bell Scott, and Barbara Smith. *All the Women Are White, All* the *Blacks Are Men, But Some of Us Are Brave*. Old Westbury, New York: The Feminist Press, 1982.

Hyman, Paula. "Emancipation." In *Contemporary Jewish Religious Thought: Original Essays on Critical Concepts, Movements and Beliefs*. Ed. Arthur A. Cohen and Paul Mendes-Flohr. New York: Charles Scribner's Sons, 1987. See also Gendler, 165-70.

Katz, Jacob. *Tradition and Crisis: Jewish Society at the End of the Middle Ages*. New York: The Free Press of Glencoe, 1961.

Keller, Catherine. *From a Broken Web: Separation, Sexism and Self*. Boston: Beacon Press, 1986.

Koltun, Elizabeth. *The Jewish Woman: New Perspectives*. New York: Schocken Books, 1976.

Lorde, Audre. *Sister Outsider*. Trumansburg, New York: The Crossing Press, 1984.

Meiselman, Moshe. *Jewish Woman in Jewish Law*. New York: KTAV and Yeshiva University Press, 1978.

Moraga, Cherrie, and Gloria Anzaldua. *This Bridge Called My Back: Writings By Radical Women of Color*. Watertown, Massachusetts: Persephone Press, 1981.

Morton, Nelle. *The Journey Is Home*. Boston: Beacon Press, 1985.

Plaskow, Judith. "The Coming of Lilith: Toward a Feminist Theology." In *Womanspirit Rising: A Feminist Reader in Religion*. Ed. Carol P. Christ and Judith Plaskow. San Francisco: Harper and Row, 1979.

———. *Standing Again at Sinai: Rethinking Judaism from a Feminist Perspective*. San Francisco: Harper and Row, 1990.

Prell, Riv-Ellen. "The Vision of Woman in Classical Reform Judaism." *Journal of the American Academy of Religion* 50 (December 1982):575-89.

Setel, Drorah. "Prophets and Pornography: Female Sexual Imagery in Hosea." In *Feminist Interpretation of the Bible*. Ed. Letty M. Russell. Philadelphia: The Westminster Press, 1985.

———. "Feminist Reflections on Separation and Unity in Jewish Theology." *Journal of Feminist Studies in Religion* 2 (Spring 1986):113-18.

Spelman, Elizabeth V. "Theories of Race and Gender: The Erasure of Black Women." *Quest: A Feminist Quarterly* 5 (1982):36-62.

———. *Inessential Woman: Problems of Exclusion in Feminist Theory*. Boston: Beacon Press, 1988.

Waskow, Arthur. *Rainbow Sign: The Shape of Hope*. Unpublished manuscript, 1987.

6

The Redemption of the Body

Post-Patriarchal Reconstruction of Inherited Christian Doctrine

PAULA M. COOEY

The role of Christian traditions in patriarchy is ambiguous. On the one hand, they have clearly played an active role in sustaining patriarchal culture. Indeed, some feminists have argued that Christianity is essentially and irredeemably patriarchal (see Christ and Plaskow; Daly 1978, 73-112). On the other hand, Christian traditions have provided on occasion alternatives to patriarchy. Some feminists have argued that the earliest communities were radically egalitarian and that patriarchy was later assimilated from the cultures in which the early missionaries evangelized (for example, Fiorenza, 136-47; Ruether). From this latter perspective the patriarchy of Christianity is not essential to it, and one may legitimately seek a vision of a post-patriarchal Christianity. Such vision will include the critical analysis and evaluation of church teaching with a view to its possible value for an egalitarian and environmentally harmonious existence.

Why "egalitarian" and "environmentally harmonious existence"? A post-patriarchal Christianity will simultaneously affirm the full integrity of women as women and the integrity of all who have heretofore suffered under patriarchy. The latter include the human poor and powerless, whatever their sex and gender identification, as well as the earth and other sentient creatures. Through the pioneering work of Rosemary Radford Ruether, Christian feminists have come to realize that the very ways of thinking and feeling in the Christian past that have oppressed women have simultaneously oppressed other humans as well as other living beings. These ways of thinking have been sharply dualistic, ranking spirit and rationality *above* body and sensation. Men have then been associated with spirit and rationality; women, other oppressed peoples, animals, and the earth have been associated with body and sensation. Inasmuch as the body has been denigrated, so also have these others. Thus a post-patriarchal Christianity will be interested in the redemption of all who have been oppressed under patriarchy, and it will focus on redeeming the body.

Those of us attempting to develop post-patriarchal Christian theologies have a mighty theological challenge to address. We need to acknowledge that there is religious and social diversity within the Christian heritage, and that amid this diversity there are constructive resources, destructive resources, and, as is most often the case, ambiguous resources. Aspects of the tradition are retrievable inasmuch as they help us to affirm the integrity of women and others who have suffered under patriarchy. While the entire past must be remembered, including those aspects of the past that have been neglected in patriarchal scholarship and are painful to remember, we can afford to draw upon what to the best of our knowledge does not repeat the injustices of the past. But an appeal to the past is not enough. We must also recognize that our own tradition can grow through the offering of fresh, imaginative understandings of inherited doctrines, understandings which may not have exact parallels in the past. We must supplement the usable aspects of our past with new vision and new voices.

Just what, then, will constitute post-patriarchal Christian teaching or doctrine? We cannot yet be certain. We cannot even know if a post-patriarchal Christianity is possible. Nevertheless, I propose to explore this challenge specifically by suggesting a post-patriarchal understanding of the incarnation and redemption. For it is in these doctrines that images of body—and hence of women, oppressed peoples, other forms of sentient existence, and the earth—are given focus in Christian thinking. In particular I want to show how a post-patriarchal understanding of the incarnation can enable us to affirm the body and all sentient existence on earth.

Let me begin, in the first major section of this essay, by briefly adumbrating my understanding of incarnation, noting its relevance to sacramental life, and illustrating it in the life of a specific woman. In the second part, I will discuss ways this understanding is linked with, and yet also divergent from, inherited understandings of incarnation and redemption. To conclude, I shall return to my constructive proposal concerning incarnation, showing its implications for the themes of salvation and resurrection.

A POST-PATRIARCHAL IMAGE OF THE INCARNATION

In a post-patriarchal context, I suggest, incarnation refers to an immanent, ongoing divine creation, preservation, and regeneration of life. Where there is healing and affirmation of life, there is the redeeming body of God. We participate in this creativity; we cooperate in imagining it into existence and making it real. For Christians, an understanding of incarnation is linked directly with traditional sacraments, for it is in the very materiality of sacraments and sacramental life that abstract doctrines have their richest meaning.

Consider baptism and communion. A post-patriarchal understanding of incarnation connects explicitly the healing waters of baptism and the nurture of the bread and wine at the communion table to the material suffering of sentient existence throughout the planet. This healing and nurture shifts the center of focus in Christian consciousness from death to life. Baptism and holy communion make present to Christians the reality of God's activity in primitive and common elements upon which continued creaturely existence absolutely depends. These two sacraments, central to the ongoing life of faith, call Christians as beneficiaries of healing and nurture to creative action. From the pain of our own bodies, with thanksgiving, hope, and joy, we make up and make real a better world.

As we partake of these sacraments, we realize that we are creatures of God's creativity and preservation, and that we share in a "solidarity of sentience" with the rest of creation. We, like our fellow sentient creatures, are participants in divine creativity and preservation, and our bodies reflect this process. When we participate in the sacraments, we recognize this. As both agents and victims of sin, we share in human accountability for human damage to one another and the rest of planetary life; as creatures of God's repair through the healing and nurture of the sacraments, we are regenerated, re-membered, metaphorically speaking, and called to a new participation in incarnation.

The Body

Our share in the process of making up a better world, and making it real in the flesh, begins with a mighty groan in protest against the violation of the body—its starvation, its malnutrition, its sexual and vocational exploitation, its imprisonment and torture, its murder, and its use as a battleground for establishing the control over many by a few. For the body has served and still serves as a symbolic and actual focus for much that has been oppressive in patriarchy.

An extraordinary wonder in its generation and constitution, the human body provides an essential element in the making of patriarchal cultures by serving as the primary battleground in the creation, accumulation, and sustenance of power. Identified by the earth's dominant civilizations with property, finitude, nature, and human female sexuality, the body provides a major symbolic focus for what a culture permits and what it prohibits; it determines the cultural dividing line between public and private; and extended metaphorically, the body registers social attitudes toward the natural order. As battleground, the human body reflects ongoing struggles for political power through the social institutions of slavery, torture, warfare, and marriage. Those who achieve power further maintain it by regulation of sexual interaction, reproduction, childbearing, medical practices, and work roles, often justified or rationalized on religious grounds. The powerful, as makers of culture, likewise elicit the tacit support of the relatively powerless through the social construction of gender, of class, and of the significance of racial and ethnic differences.

The degree to which one is culturally defined by the body stands in inverse proportion to his or her economic and political power, social status, and sense of personal value.[1] For all its wonder, the leaking, heaving, flatulating, needy, vulnerable, finite human body more often than not culturally symbolizes a horrible bondage to natural, social, and personal corruption and death in the West. The body provides a source of seemingly never-ending conflict and a locus for social and environmental violence. Those whose bodies have been abused, or who have been symbolically associated with the body, are particularly victimized by this conflict. These victims include women, animals, and even the earth. A post-patriarchal understanding of incarnation must be committed to a redemption of the body. In so doing, it must recognize that the transfiguration of pain begins with giving voice or bearing witness to injustice with a view to healing and nurture.

Alicia Partnoy

The life and work of Argentine poet Alicia Partnoy illustrates what I mean. Partnoy was seized on January 12, 1977 and incarcerated by Argentine military forces without due process. Though she was never formally charged, her "crime" was participation in the Peronist Youth Movement as a university student, a movement critical of the military government; as a feminist, a political liberal, and a dissenter, she worked with other students, notably Christian advocates of liberation theology, handing out leaflets calling for governmental reform. Both she and her husband were kidnapped by the army. Her daughter, nine months old at the time, was cared for by Partnoy's parents, though Partnoy herself had no way of knowing this until she was transferred three and one-half months later from a hidden concentration camp called *La Escuelita* (the Little School) to a prison where, after two more months, she was finally allowed visits from her family. While a prisoner at the Little School, she and those imprisoned with her were regularly tortured, deprived of adequate food, shelter, and medical care, and repeatedly placed in fear for their lives. Of her incarceration she writes:

> Lunch was at 1:00 P.M.; we went without food for eighteen consecutive hours daily. We were constantly hungry. I lost 20 pounds, going down to 95 pounds (I am 5 ft. 5 in.). Added to the meager food, the lack of sugar or fruits, was the constant state of stress that made our bodies

consume calories rapidly. We ate our meals blindfolded, sitting on the bed, plate in lap. When we had soup or watery stew, the blows were constant because the guards insisted that we keep our plates straight. When we were thirsty, we asked for water, receiving only threats or blows in response. For talking we were punished with blows from a billy jack, punches, or removal of our mattresses. The atmosphere of violence was constant. The guards put guns to our heads or mouths and pretended to pull the trigger (Partnoy 1985, 15).

Partnoy is one of the few who survived disappearance; she has no idea why she was released two years later on condition of exile, when others (estimates run as high as thirty thousand) were executed instead. Under President Carter's human rights policy she was allowed to enter the United States where she remains, teaching and writing in Washington, D.C., when she is not speaking throughout the country for Amnesty International. She is also active in the Sanctuary movement and has translated and edited essays by Latin American women politically and religiously active in various liberation movements (Partnoy 1987). She has testified before the Commission on Human Rights, as well as before the Argentine Commission for the Investigation of Disappearances. Of these activities she writes, "As a survivor, I felt it was my duty to help those suffering injustice" (Partnoy 1985, 17).[2]

In 1986 Partnoy published *The Little School: Tales of Disappearance and Survival in Argentina*, a series of prose poems that bear witness to life in the concentration camp where she was first held. These vignettes capture the struggle toward life in the midst of extreme brutality, all the more cruel for its complete absurdity. Her words are spare, chilling, and vivid; yet in a manner reminiscent of biblical narrative, especially the parable, she seizes upon the extraordinariness, humor, and wonder of the commonplace, revealed with surprise, discovered buried in the struggle to survive. One of the most moving passages is titled simply "Bread." A scathing critique of the alignment of religious clergy with the military in the name of a God from whom bread must be begged, this passage also describes how bread becomes a way of establishing community among prisoners:

Bread is also a means of communicating, a way of telling the person next to me: "I'm here. I care for you. I want to share the only possession I have. . . ." When tedium mixes with hunger, and four claws of anxiety pierce the pits of our stomachs, eating a piece of bread, fiber by fiber, is our great relief. When we feel our isolation growing, the world we seek vanishing in the shadows, to give a brother some bread is a reminder that true values are still alive. . . . Under the pillow is the lunch bread. It is then time to wait until our hands are bound, and afterwards to lie down and slowly eat that piece of bread that reminds us that our present is the result of our fight—so that bread, our daily bread, the very same bread that has been taken away from our people, will be given back because it is our right, no pleas to God needed, forever and ever. Amen (Partnoy 1985, 84-86).

Partnoy's life and her poetry illustrate the incarnation I seek to depict. An iconoclastic groan, her voice transfigures pain in hope for a future liberation. Centered by life in the face of death, she shares her only possession, a small piece of bread. Bread, passed on in the midst of extreme cruelty, re-members the communicants by reminding them that true values, grounded in the common struggle for bread for all, are still alive. This bread, shared among many, most of whom are now dead, for one brief moment buys back the bodies of the prisoners from the control of the guards, for its redistribution by the prisoners themselves contradicts the guards' claims to define, to measure, and to devalue the prisoners' needs. Both the bread and the act it reflects repair and nurture broken lives in the midst of a suffering for which there is neither compensation nor justification for the victims.

The meaning Partnoy gives to the absurdity of such violations is to give voice to them so that we cannot turn away from our own complicity, through our silence, if not through our overt actions. If we do not engage in the struggle, however small our role, receiving communion is at best an act of hypocrisy and at worst collusion with the agents of violence. That Partnoy is ethnically Jewish and considers herself an atheist further clarifies the relation of Christian faith to other faiths, political as well as religious. Human participation in the process of making up and making real from the pain of our own sentience a better world is not in any way restricted to people or to a faith called Christian. The redemption of the body in all its historical particularity as a liberation of all creation, not the name of one's faith, is the issue. That Partnoy is a woman has a different significance for Christians however.

The ethical dimensions of the redemption of the body are gynocentric, or woman-centered. Unless a specifically female human face appears as necessarily characteristic of the oppressed with whom we seek solidarity in protest, then Christians have misunderstood the full depth of the oppression that requires redress; the redemption of the body, whether the human body or the planet Earth, cannot be made real. In the first place, the human oppressed, regardless of age, class, race, ethnicity, or creed, are peopled predominantly by women against whom violence is directed specifically because they are female human beings. From abortion, infanticide, and neglect of females because they are not sons, to dowry death, genital mutilation, forced pregnancy, and beating of adult women, viewed as property of their actual or potential husbands, violence against women comprises at present the greatest violation of human rights throughout the earth.[3] In the second place, by virtue of the symbolic identification and devaluation of "woman" with "nature," correlative with the symbolic identification and elevation of "man" with "spirit," this violence extends to environmental abuse and annihilation as well.

THE AMBIGUOUS PAST: SEARCHING FOR RESOURCES IN OUR INHERITED TRADITIONS

The story told above illustrates the kind of incarnation post-patriarchal Christians surely want to affirm. Understood in this way, incarnation is an ongoing process of being redeemed; indeed, we cannot talk about incarnation without also talking about redemption. The question arises, however: Is this way of putting it continuous with traditional understandings of incarnation and redemption? Let us look at those traditions, first by turning to Paul. Here we find perspectives that are both valuable and problematic for a post-patriarchal Christianity. A post-patriarchal Christian faith needs to remember the entire Christian past as much as possible, including those aspects of the past which heretofore have been neglected and forgotten. I mean specifically the past experiences of women and other marginalized people, people of other religions, other animals and the earth, as they have been victimized by patriarchal Christianity. A post-patriarchal Christianity will seek to draw upon only those aspects of the past that "promote the full humanity of women" (Ruether, 19) and the well-being of the oppressed.

Paul's Groaning Creation

In Romans 8 Paul writes of all creation, including the human creature, groaning together in travail. Those who have the first fruits of the Holy Spirit groan as they await adoption as children of God and the redemption of their bodies (Romans 8:23).[4] The image Paul sustains throughout Romans 8:18-25 is one of the cosmos in bondage as it struggles in labor and delivery, its freedom from bondage dependent upon the redemption of human flesh. For Paul it is in this hope that we are saved. Modern New Testament scholars and theologians consider this passage as both an extension backward to the implications of human exile from Eden in Genesis 3 and a projection forward that universalizes the messianic hope to include the cosmos (Kasemann, 233; Sanday and Headlam, 207-8; for a somewhat less universalizing interpretation see Barrett 1957, 167). Earlier theologians, often directly in response to this passage, likewise connected backward to Genesis and forward apocalyptically to new creation. For example, Martin Luther and Jonathan Edwards both interpreted the passage to implicate all nature in human sin. For them, the Fall, initiated by human disobedience, resulted not only in the corruption of human existence, but in a bondage to corruption of the rest of creation as well (Edwards, 344-45).[5] Edwards further connected the bondage of creation to the incarnation of Jesus as Christ; according to him the incarnation marked the beginning of the redemption of all creation, a redemption that would be completed with the coming kingdom of God on earth (Edwards, 345). This extension of human redemption to the restoration of the created order reflects an extension of divine justice beyond relations among humans and human/divine relations to human relations with nature. Its logic connects nature through the human body to the incarnation.

This dimension of Paul's thought is eminently valuable in the development of a post-patriarchal Christian theology. Reconstructing the significance of the redemption of the body in the context of a groaning creation holds promise for contemporary Christians concerned with what God requires in response to issues of gender, social and economic injustice, ecological devastation, and conflicting claims and values in a politically and religiously diverse world. Placed at the center of soteriology (the logic or structure of salvation), the redemption of the body promises an angle of vision different from that by which we customarily view sin and grace as expressed in doctrines of creation and redemption. Here we have a soteriology that addresses the context in which contemporary Christians find themselves, one which takes seriously the creatureliness we as imagining beings share with other life.

Paul's View of the Body

In addition to speaking of the whole of creation groaning in travail, Paul also speaks of the redemption of the body. It is here that a post-patriarchal Christian faith, interested in the healing of creation, and in the healing of the body as symbol of creation, as a wondrous reality in its own right, and as center of creative process, will have problems. In principle, Paul's discussion here, too, might be a resource for a post-patriarchal reconstruction of the doctrine of redemption. In fact, it is in some ways resourceful and in others extremely problematic.

Paul's reference to the redemption of the body occurs in the context of a wider discussion in Romans 8 of life in the Spirit as a child of God. Paul casts his discussion in terms of the opposition between the law of sin and death and the law of the Spirit. Whether Paul assumes a spirit-matter dualism is subject to debate. My conclusion is that in certain qualified respects he does, that bodies are "stuff" driven by spirits or energies. The issue would then be for Paul which spirit or power or energy is enlivening or driving any given body, there being good and evil spirits or powers or energies. Hence he distinguishes between psychological and spiritual bodies such that the new or resurrected human person will possess a body driven not by the logic of his or her soul or ego, but by the logic of the Spirit of God, a logic that would guarantee the body's imperishability. This dualism is a conceptual one, transcended by the dualism of good and evil. It is not the case that matter is by definition bad and spirit good. Furthermore, while body and spirit stand conceptually in dualistic relation to one another, they also appear to require one another. New creation requires the redemption of the body in order to complete itself (see Kasemann, 237-38).

Specific reference to the redemption of the body occurs in a passage that connects suffering to hope and in which Paul uses a language that is organic as well as juridical:

> I consider that the sufferings of this present time are not worth comparing with the glory that is to be revealed to us. For the creation waits with eager longing the revealing of the sons of God; for the creation was subjected to futility, not of its own will but by the will of him who subjected it in hope; because the creation itself will be set free from its bondage to decay and obtain the glorious liberty of the children of God. We know that the whole creation has been groaning together in travail until now; and not only the creation, but we ourselves, who have the first fruits of the spirit, groan inwardly as we wait for adoption as sons, the redemption of our bodies. For in this hope we are saved. Now hope that is seen is not hope. For who hopes for what he sees? But if we hope for what we do not see, we wait for it with patience (verses 18-25).

This whole passage is wonderfully rife with ambiguity: the ambiguity of *ktisis*, here translated as "creation" although it can also mean "creature"; the waiting of *ktisis* with eager longing for *apokalypsis* (revelation); the attribution of the bondage of *ktisis* to divine *fiat*; the personification of *ktisis* as a woman in labor (groaning in travail); Paul's connection of *ktisis* to the believer as a child of God by adoption, an adoption itself dependent on bodily redemption; and the liberation of all or every *ktisis* through this redemption of the bodies of the adopted.

The context here is sufficiently vague that either "creation" (all artifacts taken as a whole) or "creature" for *ktisis* would retain smoothness, though the over-all meaning could shift, depending on how broadly or narrowly one defines "creature." When *ktisis* is translated "creation," the passage conveys a sense of cosmic liberation involved in human salvation. Christ becomes, as Ernst Kasemann points out, cosmocrater (Kasemann, 234). Furthermore, a suffering cosmos itself struggles to give birth, to labor toward divine glory, a glory that in some sense frees all sentient existence. Translated as "creature," *ktisis* could refer either to any and all sentient beings (in which case the implications for the liberation of the cosmos remain essentially the same), or it could refer more narrowly to the human non-believer who even in his or her non-belief benefits from the redemption of the body promised to the children of God. This second, more restrictive sense of "creature" parallels smoothly earlier chapters (chapters 1-3) in which Paul insists that knowledge of God from nature makes Gentiles as accountable for sin as Jews to whom God has revealed God's law. Nevertheless, there exist compelling reasons for extending "creature" beyond the human realm to refer to sentience in general, in which case, whether translated as "creation" or "creature," *ktisis* links creation, as artifact and ultimately as activity, with redemption.

But again, what does "body" mean for Paul? Whatever else it may have meant, in its condition of finitude, the human body appears to mean created of biodegradable "stuff" animated by forces external, even altogether alien, to it. It further appears to serve as locus or occasion, though not the cause, of pain and temptation, a reality constantly subjected by the human mind or will to violation, whether as agent or victim (see for examples, Rom 1:28-31 and 2 Cor 6:4-5). Nevertheless, even in its condition of finitude, for believers the body's status becomes that of member of Christ and temple of the Holy Spirit (1 Cor 6:15 and 19). In light of the Holy Spirit within, a gift of God, believers no longer belong to themselves, and the body serves as instrument for divine glory (1 Cor 6:20). Thus, the body is both biodegradable stuff and, if redeemed, a sacred vessel.

What then is a "redeemed" body? It is a state of affairs in which there is no more pain, no more temptation, therefore no more sin. The process of redemption begins in the believer's earthly existence, though it does not exempt one from continued suffering, and though it will not be fulfilled until the apocalypse, the revelation by God of the adopted. Furthermore, the beginning of this redemption lies in understanding present suffering, whether physical affliction or temptation to sin, as instrumental to accomplishing future glory. Paul seems to imagine the redeemed body in its completion as "stuff" no longer biodegradable, because properly and thoroughly animated by the Spirit of God (2 Cor 5:1-5).

Although this view of the body and of the role of suffering may be unsatisfactory to contemporary Christians for a variety of reasons, it does link the body with the rest of creation: a connection which a post-patriarchal Christianity can appreciate. For Paul nevertheless sympathetically extends this suffering for future glory (initiated from his perspective by human disobedience), as well as release from this suffering, to all sentient existence.

All the same, the view is unsatisfactory. We find ourselves twenty centuries later with a very different understanding of matter and therefore of body. In light of Einstein, body becomes a highly concentrated locus of energy, a complex of temporal-spatial relations always occurring relative to a perceiver, a locus that manifests principles immanent within itself rather than dead "stuff," governed by principles or forces alien to it.[6] Yet, like Paul, we are no less vulnerable to pain and death, the fear of death, and the denial of death. Like Paul, if we are true to our faith, we yearn for an existence centered by life rather than death, a life in which the body is no longer the locus for human violation, a life in which we are no longer driven to sin by pain and its avoidance, a life in which all creation is reconciled. The differences that separate us from Paul lie not in the problem, but in its resolution. The redemption we seek is of a body constituted by time as well as space since we cannot consider space without time or vice-versa.

We seek redemption of our bodies within a historical context, within the world. Given the relationship of space and time in our understanding, resurrection as Paul seems to imagine it, as bodily escape from the flux of a world in which suffering is real, becomes fantastic, a science fiction rather than a reality. Liberation of the body from violation, though perceived differently by us some twenty centuries later, nevertheless continues to provide the acid test for a hope that saves.

The redemption of the body for our times makes hope for a historical deliverance from bodily violation—ranging from starvation, incest, and political torture, to strip mining and deforestation—a condition for claiming life in the Spirit. This hope calls for a creation on our part, a creation now understood in its classical sense as creative activity, in addition to its other connotations of artifact. As creatures of faith by grace, we are called to labor or travail together for a very material justice for all creatures, most especially those with little or no voice to raise in their own behalf. This hope constitutes a groaning creativity, for the evidence of the damage we have done to the environment and to one another indicates that it may already be too late to prevent the destruction of most of planetary life. It is a saving hope, nevertheless, for it sustains us to continue to seek to make up and make real in the flesh the justice God requires. It is our share in the continuation of the incarnation.

Contemporary Distance from Nicea and Chalcedon

The establishment of the doctrine of the incarnation as official church teaching occurred several centuries after the death of Paul. Formally expressed in the Chalcedonian confession, the doctrine seems alien to both biblical and contemporary faith. It poses conceptual and practical difficulties for Christian relations with people of other faiths as well as individual Christians. To Jew and Muslim alike the claim that God became and in some sense remains human is idolatrous; to a Buddhist the claim is irrelevant; to a Hindu it might conceivably be meaningful so long as one recognized that such an occurrence is not unique, nor does it require that there be only one deity. To those who do not identify themselves in explicitly religious terms the claim that God entered history as a human being may appear to be nonsense. One need only ask Christians, whether conservative or liberal, what the doctrine means to get a wide range of interpretations, some of which are in direct opposition to one another. Indeed, many Christians might respond in ways similar to their counterparts of other faiths. If we press Christians who espouse the doctrine in some form for further explanation, we often get the response that in the last analysis it is a paradox or a mystery, not subject to the authority of reason.

History indicates quite the contrary. Formal expression of the doctrine of the incarnation emerges chronologically subsequent to the doctrine of the Trinity. The Nicene Creed established the doctrine of the Trinity, the teaching that God is Father, Son, and Holy Spirit—one substance, three persons—in a language that left unspecified how Christ as the second person of a triune deity was also human as well. The Chalcedonian confession responds by making very precise, technical distinctions in regard to how Jesus the Christ is both human and divine. Both the Nicene Creed and the Chalcedonian formula represent valiant attempts to reason christologically in faith.[7] The councils sought especially to establish "right teaching" on God and Christ by negating views that did not preserve the triunity of God and both the full humanity and divinity of Christ. This christological reasoning occurred in the midst of extreme and sometimes violent controversy and largely in response to the diverse, sometimes conflicting, views of the significance of Jesus contained within various writings including the gospels and the epistles that finally themselves became canon. What was at stake for those embroiled in these controversies was nothing less than human salvation itself.[8] What resulted from Nicea and especially from Chalcedon is less mystery and paradox than a precise philosophical language that presupposes a metaphysical worldview to which Christians today have little or no access.

For example, the Nicene Creed states of Jesus that he is "the only begotten Son of God, begotten of the Father before all the worlds, God of God, Light of Light, Very God of Very God, begotten, not made, being of one substance with the Father by whom all things were made; who for us men, and for our salvation, came down from heaven, and was incarnate by the Holy Spirit of the Virgin Mary, and was made man." The Chalcedonian formula later adds that Jesus is one person and one reality or subsistence (*hypostasis*), of two natures, truly God and truly human, "the same perfect in Godhead and the same perfect in manhood . . . consubstantial with the Father in Godhead and the same consubstantial with us in manhood, like us in all things except sin," who for us and our salvation is human as well as divine. He is "made known" to us in these two natures (human and divine) "without confusion, without change, without division, without separation, the difference of the natures being by no means removed because of the union, but the property of each nature being preserved and coalescing" in this one person.[9]

Interpreted in its worst light, the language in both texts is static; it is as if one possessed a limited supply of active verbs and spoke or wrote almost solely in nouns and past participles frozen into adjectives. What does "very" add to "Very God of Very God"? Why is Jesus "begotten" instead of "made"? Does "one substance" mean that Jesus is made out of the same "stuff"?[10] As noted before, the Chalcedonian formula, intended by its authors to set straight any matters left unresolved by Nicea, depends on very precise technical distinctions, for example, *prosopon* (person), *hypostasis* (subsistence or reality), and *physis* (nature). What is the significance of such precision? Why only one person and only one subsistence? Why not only one nature? What is at stake in maintaining that the two natures are without confusion, change, division, and separation? By what authority do the theologians presume to speak here?[11] The insistence on deity is so emphatic and so exaggerated that one is left with a vision of Jesus as a giant supernatural male with divine plasma coursing through his veins.[12] To use a slightly different analogy, Jesus as Christ becomes a reality who assumed a sinless humanity the way a person takes a vow of poverty, such that even provided that the person keeps the vow, it simply is not the same thing as being poor without choice.[13] How does this save us humans and from what? Are not these formulations themselves subject to one of the very heresies the authors sought to avoid, namely, the assertion that Jesus only appeared to be human and was in fact first, last, and always deity, therefore ultimately escaping all the characteristics, definitive of the human condition? Carried to its logical conclusion, human salvation in these terms would lie in escaping one's humanity altogether.[14]

Confronted by the issues of our own twentieth-century context, the language becomes altogether an affront. Translated from Greek into English, all sense of the inclusiveness of humanity is lost as the masculinity of English pronouns and nouns abrasively connects maleness to deity in ways that only further exacerbate the sexism of the early fathers. From this perspective Jesus' share in substance with God the Father is a deification of maleness standing in direct opposition to the prohibition against graven images (see, for example, Deut 4:15-19 and 5:8). Furthermore, the very presuppositions of the Father/Son relation absolutely defy modern biology, indeed assume a biology in which women, viewed as constitutionally defective human males, play no role beyond incubator in the generation of new life (Ross, 11-13; Aristotle *On the Generation of Animals*, Bk I, chaps. 21-22; Borreson). Not only would it take serious education in early church history to try to apprehend what the authors meant to their own times, but were lay Christians to undertake becoming so educated, the significance of what the authors meant for our times would require additional time and effort not normally available to those outside the seminary and the academy. Finally, apart from the peculiarities of contemporary times and provided one made the effort to explore the possible relevance of this language for our own times, it is difficult to imagine how this language would have made sense to most of the earliest followers of Jesus, with the possible exception of the Johannine community. One does not have to be a New Testament scholar to realize from reading the synoptic gospels and Pauline letters that the earliest christologies were on the whole not incarnational in the sense expressed in these fourth- and fifth-century documents.

So, then, what value does the doctrine of the incarnation hold for contemporary Christians interested in a post-patriarchal Christianity? Here we need to shift focus from the content of the creedal statements to their purpose and function. When we do, a different picture emerges, a moving picture, so to speak. And we need to turn, I believe, to earlier, pre-Nicean and pre-Chalcedonian images in the New Testament.

Resources from the New Testament

Whereas the councils focused on the status of the figure of Jesus, the Christian scripture narratives tend by contrast to exhibit more concern with the revelatory significance of Jesus' acts, of his relations with others, of his teachings, and of the events of his life.[15] And on the whole, the chief significance seems to lie with how these reveal divine activity at work in everyday human social and natural existence, at work making real God's realm on earth. From this perspective Jesus in relation to others presents the occasion by which God's justice, mercy, and will are revealed and therefore made available even to "the least of these." Even the Gospel of John, the text most akin in spirit to the later documents, focuses more on Jesus as a way to right human/divine relations rather than the immediate object of worship (for example, John 14:6 and subsequent passages on friendship).

John Knox argues that the earliest followers of Jesus held adoptionist, kenotic, or docetic christologies (Knox 1967, 1-18). In Romans 1:3-4, for example, Paul proclaims Jesus the Son of God "who was descended from David according to the flesh and *designated* Son of God in power according to the Spirit of holiness by his resurrection from the dead, Jesus Christ our Lord" (emphasis mine). Paul continues the motif of adoption in Romans 8 as the object of hope for which those who accept Jesus wait, groaning inwardly along with the rest of creation. By contrast, Philippians 2:5-11 exhibits a classic instance of *kenosis* (self-emptying); that is, Jesus "who though he was in the form (image) of God did not count equality with God a thing to be grasped (grabbed onto), but emptied himself, taking the form (image) of a servant, being born in the likeness of men."[16] In response to Jesus' *kenosis* and to his taking on humility through obedience even unto death on the cross, God exalts him and bestows lordship upon him. As Knox points out, *kenosis*, unlike adoption, entails explicit reference to Jesus' pre-existence, though both christologies hold in common Jesus' full humanity and God's centrality in bestowing lordship upon Jesus. The assumption that Jesus is genuinely human distinguishes these christologies in turn from docetism, the belief that Jesus only appeared to be human, a view later rejected as heresy. Of the four gospels, the Gospel of John shows the greatest tendencies in this direction. For example, by comparison to the synoptic gospels, especially Luke in which Jesus is constantly portrayed as eating and drinking, the Jesus of John eats *explicitly* only after the resurrection (John 21:12-15). Even so, on the whole the author of John insists that Jesus is human, perhaps directly in response to tendencies toward docetism in the Johannine community (see Scroggs 57, 69, 80, 83-84; Barrett 1955, 38-39, 140-41; on the Johannine community, see Brown).

If we follow Knox's reasoning to its logical conclusion, the doctrine of the incarnation reflects an unhappy compromise that seeks to hold in tension Jesus' humanity with divine kenotic activity revealing itself through Jesus' relations with others, his teaching and healing, his crucifixion, and his resurrection. According to the compromise, on the one hand, Jesus must undergo the full limitations of the human condition in order for human salvation to occur. On the other hand, because sin is a condition of the will rather than simply an assortment of right or wrong acts that human beings by their own efforts seek to commit or to avoid, Jesus' humanity cannot save us by itself. Salvation from this perspective requires divine intervention. The salvation of humans thus calls for Jesus as fully human to incarnate in his relations with others the divine power necessary to overcome this sinful condition.[17]

This tension could be sustained without reference to Jesus' substantive nature, I think, if the incarnation were understood as ongoing divine creativity characterized as self-emptying imagination, continually making relations, things, and events up from the flesh, making these real in the flesh, and repairing broken relations and things by making them differently — creativity from the inside out rather than the top down, so to speak. Note, however, that this view of creativity places the human imagination and the reality of sentient life in a more reciprocal relation than the view expressed in the prologue to the Gospel of John (John 1:1-14), which grants priority to the Word over the flesh. It further requires that imagination as structuring activity is not altogether alien in kind from flesh. It does so because the principles governing both are not only immanent within each, but also interrelated. By *imagination* I mean creative activity that gives structure to what we experience; and by *flesh* I mean sensory and sensual. As I understand them, imagination and sentient life are not cut off from one another; rather, imagination is itself a creative way of being sentient. It is a creative dimension of flesh. Yet the imagination also instantiates the divine and enfleshes the divine. In other words, imagination is itself a way of being sentient, an extension of the kind of life and creativity we discern in other creatures and in the Earth itself; and, at the same time, it is a way of focusing on, valuing, and participating in creativity itself.

In addition, incarnation viewed in this manner is fundamentally metaphorical and destabilizing in character. As we see in the way Jesus incarnated divinity in his life and death, imaginative activities that disclose the divine turn the tables on established thinking, showing that what we take as "appropriate social arrangements" so often oppress the poor, and that what we take as "progress" so often despoils creation.[18] Viewed in this light, the incarnation reveals the nature of divine creativity itself; namely, that the process that makes things be what they are and the process that liberates, delivers, heals, restores, and reconciles are one and the same. Creator and Redeemer are one.

Jesus as Mediator Not Idol

From this perspective the doctrine of the incarnation has relevance to contemporary Christians to the extent to which the human body and the material-historical order hold central focus. Reconstructed such that the full implications of sentience are clear, the doctrine provides the foundation for a sacramental theology that transfigures pain and death without circumventing them, even while celebrating life—a theology that recognizes and addresses human injustice perpetrated through the abuse and exploitation of all creaturely flesh. Precisely because the central claim of the incarnation links our imagination with all sentient existence, both human and nonhuman, the doctrine of the incarnation invites Christians, as creatures of grace, to participate in making up, making real, and making differently a new and hopefully better creation. Reconstructed in this manner, the doctrine of the incarnation legitimates hope for the redemption of our bodies in the midst of suffering, a redemption that requires from us all, in concert, a groaning creativity.

In other words, an alternative view of the incarnation, one perhaps more attuned to both biblical and twentieth-century sensibilities, claims that Jesus saves us by directing our attention through the events of his life, death, and resurrection, as narrated in scripture, to God at work throughout creation, upholding nature and acting through human activity in history, to restore and reconcile all life, including especially life usually considered the least noteworthy. Interpreted in this manner incarnation is always going on, but Jesus in relation to others remains pivotal as the specific revelatory source by which those who call their faith Christian come to recognize, and by grace, quite literally to re-member divine activity at work throughout nature and history.[19] Jesus thus retains epistemological and soteriological centrality for Christian faith without reference to his ontological status, in this respect relieving him of the burden of idolatry. How do Christians come to faith in God? By apprehending, which includes recognition and remembering, life through Jesus who according to scripture manifests in his humanity such faith even unto death itself. In this way Jesus as image or lens serves as mediator for human/divine relations.[20] How can Christians hold such faith? By grace—the power of divine love—emptied out or extended through Jesus' existence, a grace that even death cannot conquer.

SALVATION AND RESURRECTION

Many Christians know from scripture and experience that Christian attitudes toward the human body and toward nature in general have been and continue to be ambivalent at best.[21] This ambivalence finds its most dramatic expression in Christian responses to the body of Jesus, expressed in the doctrine of the incarnation. I have suggested that this doctrine as formulated at Nicea and Chalcedon is remote from the gospel accounts of a Jesus accused of gluttony and drunkenness, a Jesus who occupied himself with rubbing up against the "unclean." Furthermore, the Hellenistic metaphysics of substance presupposed by the doctrine strikes one with twentieth-century scientific and philosophical sensibilities as altogether alien.

I have examined the doctrine of the incarnation because of the ambivalence toward embodiment that it expresses, because it formally connects creation and redemption in Christian teaching, and because this doctrine still holds as orthodox teaching for the Western churches. I have proposed that the doctrine of the incarnation is a soteriological claim, that is, a claim about how we are saved. I have maintained that it is best understood as a claim stated in metaphorical language about a process, namely divine creativity, rather than a human person somehow infused with divine plasma. Taken at face value, I suggested, the doctrine represents a failed attempt to reject as heresy the denial of the human nature of Jesus. This failure leaves the doctrine open to charges of idolatry and nonsense. Nevertheless, the teaching reflects metaphorical imagination at work making up, making real, attempting to make sense, and further making value that remains central to Christian faith to this day. In short, the doctrine of the incarnation plays a major role in the making of Christian faith and therefore the making of Christians. It is appropriately re-envisioned, not discarded, in a post-patriarchal context. As re-envisioned, and lived in a sacramental way, it can be saving. Let me draw these comments to a close by noting what salvation, and an attendant notion of resurrection, might mean in a post-patriarchal context.

Salvation in a Post-Patriarchal Perspective

Salvation presupposes a prior condition of jeopardy. This jeopardy in Christian vocabulary is the sinfulness of the human condition. While it is beyond the scope of this essay to develop a full-blown doctrine of sin, let me suggest that sin includes minimally the following features. According to tradition, sin is a perversion or distortion of human nature that was initially divinely intended for goodness. We are born into sin in the sense that we are born incomplete, falling short even at birth from that wholeness, that completeness, for which we were intended. Sin in this view is inevitable and inescapable.

The consequences of our original incompleteness are compounded by our necessary relationship with culture. Not only do we human beings enter the world incomplete, we enter an unfinished world, our humanity continually in the process of being modified or created through culture, even as we continually recreate or modify culture. This process of reciprocal modification makes inevitable and inescapable our complicity in the present culture of which we are a part. The incompleteness, the sinfulness, with which we were born is magnified by the incompleteness, the sinfulness, of our culture. We take on the sins of the societies into which we were born and with which we interact. This is the case irrespective of whether we have individually played a direct role in the injustice that characterizes it; inasmuch as we benefit from the overt sinfulness of others, we take on their sins.

Yet, our very imaginations allow us to realize that our sinfulness is not necessary. That we can imagine a different culture, one free of injustice (perhaps we now must so imagine, if we are to avoid planetary destruction), implies that an unjust culture and the sin it presupposes are not necessary. That injustice is unnecessary makes us corporately as well as individually accountable for sin, regardless of its inescapability. This accountability, when coupled with the inevitability and inescapability of sin, only further alienates us within culture, in response to one another, and in relation to nature.[22] In light of this alienation from who we were intended to be, an alienation made even worse by our accountability for cultural sins, there is a need for imaginative activity, for incarnation. The very act of imagining alternatives to the status quo, in solidarity with the human oppressed and the rest of creation, is an instance of the kind of incarnation I recommend for post-patriarchal Christian communities. It has a healing power in relation to the sinful structures of society and our lives. It is an antidote to alienation. It is what a post-patriarchal Christian can mean by salvation. Salvation is the healing that comes in prophetically imagining new and hopeful futures.

A Post-Patriarchal Understanding of Resurrection

In contrast to hope-filled ambiance of post-patriarchal imagination, which is loyal to the earth and committed to the flourishing of life, patriarchal Christian imagination has traditionally fastened upon death as the chief metaphor for the human condition or situation for reasons that are both historical and psychological. The historical grounds lie in part in Christian interpretation of the creation stories in Genesis, in which death as chief consequence and symbol for human sin figures heavily. Death being unavoidable, the tradition has held, its finality is nevertheless overcome by the resurrected Christ, a resurrection promised to his followers. The social psychology that lies behind making death the ultimate metaphor for sin is vastly more complicated than its history. It is difficult to determine the extent to which Christian views of the relation between sin and death reflect or shape human negativity toward death. Common sense, supported by literature from sources outside Christian traditions (for example, the life of Siddartha Gotama, the Buddha), indicates that for people of certain temperaments across cultural traditions death poses the ultimate injustice, ironically all the more so if life has been good, and now even more so when generalized to include the death of the planet. At the very least death confronts human consciousness with the possible meaninglessness of finite existence.[23] Living with this consciousness of meaninglessness on a sustained basis creates a variety of possible responses, ranging from emotional paralysis to suicide; living in denial of the reality of death drives one to abuse self and others in order to sustain illusions of living forever. In either case death serves metaphorically as a bondage that perpetuates sin as well as epitomizes it.

For the earliest followers of Jesus his resurrection meant that the finality of death was overcome.[24] Because the resurrection presupposed the crucifixion, it meant that one might live in hope for the future while in the midst of suffering, centered by life in spite of death. It did not mean that one could avoid suffering and death. The earliest followers of Jesus expressed this apprehension of the resurrection as an individual bodily resurrection. What they meant by *body* is at best ambiguous, as I have already pointed out. Paul, for example, writes of believers that each is individually a member of the body of Christ (for example, 1 Cor 14:27). One implication of this is that the resurrection is to some extent realized through the Spirit in the earthly community as the remembering body of Christ (see Knox 1958; and Brock). In 1 Corinthians 15-16, where Paul directly addresses the resurrection of the dead, he describes the resurrected body as an individual spiritual body (*soma pneumatikon*) which he contrasts with a psychological body (*soma psychikon*, mistranslated in the Oxford Annotated Bible as "physical body").[25] Whatever Paul may have meant by the resurrection of the dead when he writes in 16:53 of putting on an imperishable, immortal nature, he seems to be rejecting here not only the continuation of one's physical corporeality, but possibly the continuation of what we call personality as well.

Today, for many Christians, belief in the resurrection has become another form of denial of the full reality of embodiment. This denial manifests itself in some quarters in terms of biology and in others in terms of psychology. Whereas some Christians hold to what they claim to be a literal view, by which they often mean a biological resuscitation, for many Christians, a literal, individual, bodily resurrection is incomprehensible. Instead these latter Christians are more likely to interpret the resurrection in terms of a survival in some sense of one's personality. In either case, just as the doctrine of the incarnation can be interpreted to support docetism in ways that lead to idolatry, so the creedal claim to resurrection, taken literally or as a metaphor for the survival of individual human personality in some form, likewise disguises yet another attempt to circumvent the full implications of human embodiment, in this instance in ways that reveal a tendency to spiritual narcissism. In either case death becomes a necessary but merely temporary inconvenience on the way to eternal self-perpetuation. Furthermore, both fundamentalist and modern views run the risk of denying that the God who redeems is also the God who creates; they do so by denying the full material reality of creation, as this creation involves coming to be and passing away in continual change. Whatever the resurrection may have meant or continues to mean to Christians, the survival of an individual ego for all time, especially when made the driving force of human agency, reflects a response to death by way of its denial. Concern for survival beyond our own death means ironically that we continue to live in bondage to death.

Given these inadequacies in conventional understandings of resurrection, what might a post-patriarchal understanding look like? A post-patriarchal Christianity will recognize that resurrection, whatever else it means, appropriately means living as a creature no longer bound by death as the central and driving force of this life, either by way of despair or denial. This is not discontinuous with certain strands of the tradition. Christian attitudes that seek to circumvent material reality, especially as this involves death, stand in antithesis to a *crucified*, risen Christ. Correcting such misguided attitudes requires the redemption of the body as central to salvation. This should be the heart of a post-patriarchal way of thinking about resurrection. Resurrection is the individual and communal body redeemed, and thus recognized as integral to existence and as a locus of divine creative activity. It involves imagining alternative historical futures for bodily existence and all that is associated with it, not in opposition to it. It involves affirming the flesh and all who live in the flesh. The healing that comes through this affirmation, this imagining, this way of participating in divine creativity, will be the true meaning of resurrection.

CONCLUSION

In the early history of Christian traditions Valentinian was declared a heretic for claiming that, although Jesus ate and drank, he never defecated. Speaking metaphorically, the insistence that Jesus, like the rest of us, underwent biological elimination of his "waste" products indicates a possible willingness on the part of Christians to struggle with the full implications of embodiment and the wastage that human violence perpetuates. In regard to the doctrine of the incarnation, Christians stand at a juncture. On the one hand, centered by the redemption of the body, the incarnation has the potential to become, as Rubem Alves so aptly wrote, "the mother of the future" (Alves, 59-60). On the other hand, it may continue to perform in the Christian imagination a role long ago declared heretical, namely, the refusal to confront the ambiguities of material existence as symbolized by the humanity of Jesus the Christ. In either case, unless and until we take seriously our dependence upon the body and blood of others—our mothers, those whose labor produces the goods we use to survive and to enhance our lives, the plant and animal life we consume, and our earth itself—there can be for humans no salvation. Whether we come to such struggles through the sacraments of baptism and holy communion or by some other media, the question remains the same: Are we driven by death to perpetuate injustice or centered in hope by life, a gift that binds us to all sentience? If centered by life, then we welcome life in other creatures, whether like us or different. Another, more ancient poet, attempting to be God's mouthpiece, a calling to which I have no claim, captures the gift far better than I:

> Cry aloud, spare not,
> lift up your voice like a trumpet;
> declare to my people their transgression,
> to the house of Jacob their sins.
> Yet they seek me daily,
> and delight to know my ways,
> as if they were a nation that did righteousness
> and did not forsake the ordinance of their God;
> "Why have we fasted and thou seest it not?
> Why have we humbled ourselves and thou takest no
>   knowledge of it?"
> Behold, in the day of your fast you seek your own
>   pleasure,
> and oppress all your workers.
> Behold you fast only to quarrel and fight
> and to hit with wicked fist.
> Fasting like yours this day
> will not make your voice to be heard on high.
> Is such the fast that I choose,
> a day for one to humble oneself?
> Is it to bow down one's head like a rush,
> and to spread sack cloth and ashes beneath one?
> Will you call this a fast, and a day acceptable to the
>   Lord?
> Is not this the fast that I choose:
> to loose the bonds of wickedness,
> to undo the thongs of the yoke,
> to let the oppressed go free,
> and to break every yoke?
> Is it not to share your bread with the hungry,
> and bring the homeless poor into your house;
> when you see the naked, to cover the naked,
> and not to hide yourself from your own flesh?
> Then shall your light break forth like the dawn,
> and your healing shall spring up speedily;
> your righteousness shall go before you,
> the glory of the Lord shall be your rear guard.
> Then shall you call and the Lord will answer;
> you shall cry and God will say,
> Here I am (Is 58:1-9, my adaptation[26]).

NOTES

1. For the classic argument for this inverse relation from a feminist perspective see de Beauvoir; for the most recent analysis of the body as battleground for power see Scarry.

2. For readers unaware of the present situation in Argentina, the military leaders brought to trial and convicted of kidnapping, torture, and murder of the disappeared ones were granted amnesty by President Alfonsin in the late 1980s as part of his efforts to gain support from the military in the face of economic disaster and rising demands among workers and students.

3. For a brief comprehensive overview of violence against women on a global scale, see Heise.

4. Unless otherwise noted, all quotations from scripture come from *The Oxford Annotated Bible with Apocrypha*, Revised Standard Version, ed. Herbert G. May and Bruce M. Metzger (New York: Oxford University Press, 1977).

5. For an excellent historical treatment of Christian theological responses to nature, see Williams.

6. For an excellent discussion of the problem posed by the different ways we conceptualize nature and related concepts and their significance for religious faith and theological method, see R. R. Niebuhr 1957, 105-28.

7. Drawing upon speech-act theory, one could argue that the purpose of these documents, especially the Nicene Creed, is performative rather than descriptive and rational. In other words, the documents establish the realities of which they speak by limiting what constitutes orthodoxy or "right teaching." To stand and say the Nicene Creed each Sunday cultivates certain attitudes in the believer, for which rational assent is only the tip of the iceberg. This performative role only makes theological analysis and critique more important, however. For a discussion of the distinction between descriptive and prescriptive language in relation to religious experience, see Proudfoot. For a discussion of the relevance of speech-act theory to biblical criticism, see *Speech Act Theory and Biblical Criticism, Semeia* 41 (1988). The entire issue is devoted to this topic.

8. That the conflicts were at times resolved by criteria other than solely logical, theological, or ethical criteria and that these disputes were at times motivated by the desire for political and economic power on the part of the disputants does not detract from this precision. As witnessed by the gospels, Acts, and the Pauline epistles, such desires have characterized the followers of Jesus from the calling of the disciples to the present.

9. For the Nicene Creed, see *The Book of Confessions*, part 1 of *The Constitution: Presbyterian Church (USA)* (New York: The Office of the General Assembly, 1983) 1.1-1.3. For the Chacedonian confession, see J. N. D. Kelly, 339-40.

10. To the Hellenized mind *substance* meant the opposite of what it has come to mean now. In contrast to a contemporary popular association of substance with matter or "stuff," substance was that which underlies whatever is and all that is, such that it is what it is and not something else. In short, substance was a sort of dynamic principle by which accidents such as quality, quantity, relation, and so forth might cohere in particular configurations. See Aristotle's *Categoriae* (Aristotle, 7-37).

11. There really are serious answers to all these questions, serious in the context in which they were originally raised. The problem is that both the questions and

the answers are so heavily dependent upon historical context that their relevance to the present is at best obscure.

12. This association of divinity with masculinity is no exaggeration, nor is it restricted to feminist critique. See John Paul II; see also Bouyer.

13. For this analogy I am grateful to Dawson Tunnell, a Presbyterian minister who took a christology course I taught for the Synod of the Sun, held at Trinity University in June 1989.

14. For an excellent treatment of the problems posed to contemporary Christians by the doctrine of the incarnation, see Knox 1967.

15. Lest we oversimplify, there are obvious exceptions, for example: Philippians 2:5-11 (note however that God exalts Jesus and names him and does both for divine glory, that is, even here the emphasis is on divine activity); Hebrews 2:9-18 (note also the equal emphasis given to Jesus' humanity and God's activity); and, of course, John 1:1-14 (one of the most ambiguous passages in the Christian scriptures).

16. The words in parentheses reflect a more accurate translation of the text, one that renders the nature of Jesus more ambiguous and could connect backward to Genesis 1:26-28, the creation of humans in the image of God. For commentary on this text, see Scroggs, 44-45. On Jesus' pre-existence, see Dunn 114-23, 179-83. Pauline authorship of this text is disputed.

17. As Knox so aptly states the situation: "How could Christ have saved us if he was not a human being like ourselves? How could a human being like ourselves have saved us?" These questions could be asked . . . because the original recognition of an act of God in Christ was followed by so intense a preoccupation with the nature of Christ himself as that the original, and only adequate, explanation of the salvation actually found in him was obscured. The more appropriate questions would have been: "Who could have saved us but God himself? How could even he have saved us except through a human being like ourselves?" These questions . . . pose no logical dilemma" (Knox 1967, 91-92).

18. For discussions of the significance of metaphor to theological thinking, see McFague 1982 and 1987, 29-57; and Morton 31-39, 122-75. For a discussion of metaphorical thinking as constitutive of human cognition see MacCormac. For a discussion of the relation between imagination and sensation in the construction of worldviews, see Scarry.

19. For a discussion of the role of recognition in Christian faith, see Richard R. Niebuhr 1967, 79-100. For a discussion of the significance of memory for the life of the church and its interpretation of scripture, see Knox 1958 and R. R. Niebuhr 1957, 62-71, 89-102, 136-61.

20. For discussion of Jesus as image or lens for human-divine relations, see McFague 1982; H. Richard Niebuhr 1967; Niebuhr's "Metaphors and Morals" and "Responsibility and Christ," in Niebuhr 1963, 149-60, 161-78.

21. For two recent treatments of this ambivalence see Clark (with respect to patristics) and Ross (with respect to contemporary attitudes).

22. This does not imply that human incompleteness or culture are in themselves evil. Rather, sin is thoroughly and pre-eminently a social condition, for which individual acts of irresponsibility and violence are only the tip of the iceberg.

23. See Tillich's *The Courage to Be* as a classic theological treatment of finitude and meaninglessness.

24. For the very best critical discussion of resurrection, the difficulties it poses

for contemporary consciousness, and the difficulties its rejection poses to Christian faith, see R. R. Niebuhr 1957.

25. I am indebted to William O. Walker, Jr., Dean of Humanities and the Arts at Trinity University, for pointing this out to me. A scholar of Paul, Bill has been most generous with his time spent with me, discussing the Pauline epistles and particularly Romans 8:18-25. He suggested a number of sources for me to pursue and motivated me to return to the Greek text and muddle through selective passages. He has further suggested that Paul might have meant by *soma pneumatikon* a communal rather than an individual body. I did not always follow his suggestions as much as I should have, nor does my amateurishness reflect on him. I did, however, learn much and benefit greatly from our discussions.

26. I have replaced masculine pronouns with reference to both the deity and humanity with "God" and cognates of "one" respectively in this text to indicate the inclusivity I find essential to its meaning.

WORKS CITED

Alves, Rubem. *A Theology of Human Hope*. New York: World Publishing Co., 1969.

Aristotle. *The Basic Works of Aristotle*. Ed. Richard McKeon. New York: Random House, 1941.

Barrett, C. K. *The Gospel According to St. John*. Philadelphia: The Westminster Press, 1955.

———. *The Epistle to the Romans*. New York: Harper and Row, 1957.

Borreson, Kari. *Subordination and Equivalence: The Nature and Role of Woman in Augustine and Thomas Aquinas*. Washington, D.C.: University Press of America, 1981.

Bouyer, Louis. *Women in the Church*. San Francisco: Ignatius Press, 1985.

Brock, Rita. *Journeys By Heart*. New York: Crossroad, 1989.

Brown, Raymond E. *The Community of the Beloved Disciple*. New York: Paulist Press, 1979.

Christ, Carol P. "Why Women Need the Goddess: Phenomenological, Psychological, and Political Reflections." In *Womanspirit Rising: A Feminist Reader in Religion*. Ed. Carol P. Christ and Judith Plaskow. New York: Harper and Row, 1978.

Clark, Elizabeth A. "Foucault, The Fathers, and Sex." *Journal of the American Academy of Religion* LVI/4:619-41.

Daly, Mary. *Beyond God the Father: Toward a Philosophy of Women's Liberation*. Boston: Beacon Press, 1972.

———. *Gyn/ecology: The Metaethics of Radical Feminism*. Boston: Beacon Press, 1978.

De Beauvoir, Simone. *The Second Sex*. Trans. and ed. H. M. Parshley. New York: Random House, 1974.

Dunn, D. G. *Christology in the Making: A New Testament Inquiry into the Origins of the Doctrine of the Incarnation*. Philadelphia: The Westminster Press, 1980.

Edwards, Jonathan. "An Humble Attempt to Promote Prayer, Explicit Agreement and Visible Union of God's People in Extraordinary Prayer." In *Apocalyptic Writings: Notes on the Apocalypse, An Humble Attempt*. Vol. 5 of The Works of Jonathan Edwards. Ed. Stephen J. Stein. New Haven: Yale University Press, 1977.

Fiorenza, Elisabeth Schüssler, "Feminist Spirituality, Christian Identity, and Catholic Vision." In *Womanspirit Rising: A Feminist Reader in Religion*. Ed. Carol P. Christ and Judith Plaskow. New York: Harper and Row, 1978.

Heise, Lori. "The Global War Against Women." Excerpted from *World Watch* (March/April 1989). In *Utne Reader* 36 (November/December 1989):40-45.

John Paul II. *"Mulieris Dignitatem*: On the Dignity and Vocation of Women." *Origins* 18/17(October 6, 1988).

Kasemann, Ernst. *Commentary on Romans*. Grand Rapids, Michigan: William B. Eerdmans, 1980.

Kelly, J.N.D. *Early Christian Doctrines*. Vol. 3. New York: Harper and Row, 1958.

Knox, John. *Jesus: Lord and Christ*. New York: Harper and Row, 1958.

———. *The Humanity and Divinity of Christ*. New York: Cambridge University Press, 1967.

MacCormac, Earl R. *A Cognitive Theory of Metaphor*. Cambridge: MIT Press, 1985.

McFague, Sallie. *Metaphorical Theology: Models of God in Religious Language*. Philadelphia: Fortress Press, 1982.

———. *Models of God: Theology for an Ecological, Nuclear Age*. Philadelphia: Fortress Press, 1987.

McKim, Donald K. *Theological Turning Points: Major Issues in Christian Thought*. Atlanta: John Knox Press, 1988.

Morton, Nelle. *The Journey Is Home*. Boston: Beacon Press, 1985.

Niebuhr, H. Richard. *The Responsible Self: An Essay in Christian Moral Philosophy*. New York: Harper and Row, 1963.

———. *The Meaning of Revelation*. New York: Macmillan, 1967.

Niebuhr, Richard R. *Resurrection and Historical Reason: A Study in Theological Method*. New York: Charles Scribner's Sons, 1957.

———. "Archegos: An Essay on the Relation between the Biblical Jesus Christ and the Present-Day Reader." In *Christian History and Interpretation: Studies Presented to John Knox*. Ed. W. R. Farmer, C. F. D. Moule, and R. R. Niebuhr. Cambridge, England: Cambridge University Press, 1967.

Partnoy, Alicia. *The Little School: Tales of Disappearance and Survival in Argentina*. Pittsburgh: Cleis Press, 1985.

———. *You Can't Drown the Fire: Latin American Women Writing in Exile*. Pittsburgh: Cleis Press, 1987.

Proudfoot, Wayne. *Religious Experience*. Berkeley: University of California Press, 1985.

Ross, Susan A. " 'Then Honor God in Your Body' (1 Cor. 6:20): Feminist and Sacramental Theology on the Body." *Horizons* 16/1:7-27.

Ruether, Rosemary. *Sexism and God-Talk*. Boston: Beacon Press, 1983.

Sanday, W., and A. C. Headlam. *The Epistle to the Romans, The International Critical Commentary*. Eds. Charles Augustine Briggs, Samuel Rolles Driver, and Alfred Plumer. New York: Charles Scribner's Sons, 1902.

Scarry, Elaine. *The Body in Pain: The Making and Unmaking of the World*. London: Oxford University Press, 1985.

Scroggs, Robin. *Christology in John and Paul*. Philadelphia: Fortress Press, 1988.

Tillich, Paul. *The Courage to Be*. New Haven: Yale University Press, 1952.

Trible, Phyllis. "Eve and Adam: Genesis 2:3 Reread." In *Womanspirit Rising: A Feminist Reader in Religion*. Ed. Carol P. Christ and Judith Plaskow. New York: Harper and Row, 1978. 74-83.

Williams, George Hunston. "Christian Attitudes Toward Nature." *Christian Scholar's Review* 2 (1971).

7

Images of the Feminine in Apache Religious Tradition

INES TALAMANTEZ

In contrast to the view of many authors in this volume, many of whom deem their own inherited traditions patriarchal, I believe the Apache not to be. Unlike many other cultures in which authority and leadership roles are specifically considered male, Apache culture often places women in positions of authority in group leadership as well as in religious ceremonial roles. Apache religious traditions consider women in a very special place within the culture as it seeks to establish balance and harmony. Women influence appropriate behavior by their own everyday examples as workers, compassionate mothers, wives, and as political and religious leaders. Apache history, when studied carefully, provides from a woman's point of view an excellent American paradigm that demonstrates feminine ideals to which others can aspire. Hence, Apache traditions do not so much require reconstruction; rather, others who are not Apache would do well to adopt some of these traditions.

'Isanaklesh, the Apache deity, is a leading religious authority for most women. She exemplifies compassion, balance, knowledge, harmony, power, *diye*, ultimate spiritual strength. Apache women and men can come to her whenever necessary for their own well-being and special needs as well as for the needs of the community, because she is seen as the perfect example of virtue and strength for the culture. It is clear that oral tradition through-out Apache history has provided the framework for male and female iden-tity. Women in this tradition have always had influence and have worked toward a balanced sense of power within the culture.

This is true even today, especially as we observe how young girls are trained from birth into integrating their social, physical, and spiritual devel-opment as they grow toward adolescence and their initiation ceremony. In this ceremony the young girls are provided with the necessary cultural knowledge and marked as carriers of the wisdom of the religious traditions that will see them into the world of wisdom and a wise old age. They are instructed as to why living their lives according to Apache religious ethics is so important for the survival of the culture. They are recognized as potentially strong and powerful women capable of handling both political and religious authority. They are instructed to recognize *'Isanaklesh*, and through ritual transformation, themselves, as the feminine aspect of wisdom and divinity.[1]

As we work to reconstruct the roles of women and religion in the diversity of the world's cultures, it is necessary not to forget American paradigms such as the one provided in the following pages. In examining my tradition, I suggest that an emphasis on ritual and ceremony that empowers girls and assists them into positions of leadership will be critical in a post-patriarchal age. Furthermore, the society and family that surrounds and sustains these girls and the women they become must take seriously the nurturance that an emphasis on ritual and ceremony requires. It must take seriously those ceremonies and rites of passage that mark true turning points in the lives of girls and women. It must recognize them as serious focal points for the entire culture. Any post-patriarchal tradition must incorporate ceremony that specifically links girls and women to the knowledge and use of power that will be required of them when they assume responsible roles of leadership and authority and when they finally pass on the culture to subsequent generations of women. It must link them to the divine.

POWER AND THE ROLES OF WOMEN

In what follows I draw heavily upon the Mescalero tradition, the tradition of those Apache who live on the Mescalero Apache Reservation in New Mexico. In elaborate, explicit detail the Mescalero Sun Clan creation myth relates that from the very beginning of time the earth already existed and was in a process of continual change, change which was seen and continues to be seen as the manifestation of the cyclical powers of nature. Myths and stories up to this very day account for the experiences that the ancestors had with the animals, plants, sun, sky, moon, and stars. The understanding of the physical world, however, involved more than just the information acquired by the senses. From the very beginning, we are told, there was an awareness of the inner forms of the animals and plants and other elements of nature—sources of power understood as *diye*, the power responsible for objects being alive or having life, as well as the supernatural force that allows ritual transformation to occur in people engaged in ritual or ceremonial activity. Concerns with enduring and surviving as a people have given an urgency to the attention the Mescalero focus on the girls of the tribe as they enter womanhood.

Mescalero women understand power and are judged according to the way they conform to traditional social standards and the ethics of the tribe, for their behavior bears directly on the well-being of the community and the appropriate use of power.

Women usually have control of the household food supply and have primary roles in the inheritance of property. Mothers with adult children are especially powerful and are accorded respect by children who feel for them a strong and life-long bond. The hope is that a woman will complete the circle of life in beauty and balance by taking care of herself in all aspects: mental, physical, and spiritual, and by obeying ceremonial traditions and the laws of nature. Special ceremonies are performed to ensure that young girls will mature safely, adjust to life easily, become secure and self-confident women in order to propagate the traditions of their culture.

The life cycle of Apache women, then, is thought of as movement on a path or trail, *'intine*, protected by a complex of ceremonies from the time a girl child comes into being, *guuli*, through babyhood, *'elchine*, through puberty or the age when she can have children, *guzhaa gulaa'e dadziiya*. This later phase of life receives great attention because it is the time when "you become aware of all your senses and you begin to notice with care all the things around you, especially nature."[2] This significant time in a young girl's life is ritually marked and blessed with the ceremony called *'Isanaklesh Gotal*, the girl's initiation into womanhood.

If a pubescent girl's ceremony is successful, it is believed that she will reach adulthood, *'isdzaa dziili*, as a physically, spiritually, and intellectually capable mature woman. It is these capacities that carry her on the path of life into the many growing seasons that are required for reaching old age, *sa*. If a woman lives her life according to Apache ethics, ritual traditions, and social values, and if she has been additionally blessed from birth with all the appropriate ceremonies for protection, she is said to have reached the spiritual and physical status of old person, *saane*, by following the footsteps of her ancestors, *'i kek'jagal*.

The importance of living right on this journey, on the path of beauty and harmony, is symbolically and repeatedly reinforced in songs, stories, myths, and ceremonies. A woman's appropriate actions throughout the life cycle make her acceptable to the people. It is impossible to know the beliefs, feelings, and perceptions shared by women with respect to the life cycle, but it is clear that they all know what is acceptable behavior and what is unacceptable. From a very early age children are persistently corrected in terms of appropriate behavior. It is not what they know they should do, but what they actually do that matters.

The female child is protected and guided through the performance of traditional rituals that mark each significant stage of development. All these ceremonies carried out to avoid undesired injury or harm to the young child are in a very remarkable sense collapsed into one ceremony, which is held for the pubescent girl at menarche or soon thereafter.

Such an emphasis on female nurturance and protection through ritual has become a quite foreign idea to many religious thinkers and cultural leaders in modern society. Ritual often is seen as unnecessary and empty. But Apache tradition has always sensed and valued the presence of divine power in all things, and it asserts the presence of power in ritual to transform. In Apache tradition women have lived as mothers and wives, but they have also assumed positions of responsibility, handling property and holding authority to make decisions about many societal needs.

To do these things correctly, to behave correctly, requires great power; it requires that women achieve real transformation through ceremony into beings who are creative and strong enough to bear the culture and carry it forward. A realization that ritual can transform will be requisite for any religious thinking that truly intends to advance the status of women and to uphold women as authoritative leaders in a world where women and men can strive to reach their full potential as human beings.

CEREMONIES FOR THE PATH OF LIFE

Arranging for the appropriate ceremony is the parents' responsibility. Traditionally, at the birth of a child, the baby is bathed, rubbed, and then blessed with pollen by the midwife or another woman who knows the ritual procedure. A post is erected to mark the birth and the umbilical cord is buried near the home if the baby was a girl. The baby with a blanket under her is lifted up in front of the woman's head as she prays and offers pollen blessings and slowly turns from east to south to west to north, the directions in which the sun travels. This blessing, it is believed, assures the child of protection against the dangers of illness during infancy. Some of this is still done today.

The same attendant sometimes also performs the cradleboard ceremony, *bizane ts'al*, within a few days after the child's birth.[3] The person performing the ceremony will usually also make the cradleboard. All the materials for the cradleboard are collected and gathered with care and accompanied by prayers in order to assure a healthy and long life for the baby. For a girl, the canopy that shields the child's head is decorated with symbols of the moon. The back piece of buckskin is pierced so that Life Giver will look in on the child with favor. The cradle is often decorated with beadwork, pieces of turquoise, and a tiny pollen bag. The child's face is marked with pollen below her eyes and pollen blessings are offered to east, south, west, and north. The cradle is also lifted to the four directions. Then, three times, it is lifted to the east, and the fourth time, the baby girl is placed in the cradleboard and carefully wrapped and strapped in place to ensure she will continue to live safely as she occupies her cradleboard.

Even at birth, then, the connection of the infant to nature and divine power is celebrated and made apparent. From the beginning of her life, the girl is seen to be in harmony with nature. The girl's femaleness and her connection to feminine wisdom and power is recognized and upheld. Her family and her culture celebrate the girl, her power, and her harmony, and affirm a need to protect the girl and to ensure that she will be guided along a traditional path toward a long, fruitful life.

Such careful, ceremonial attention to the details of the girl's life is critical, and should be critical for any post-patriarchal vision, since such an emphasis throughout the life of the female is important to her continuous maturation and her eventual growth into womanhood. It is important to her eventual assumption of *'Isanaklesh*'s power.

In my tradition the ceremonies look something like the following, and I suggest that other traditions would do well to pattern themselves similarly.

Several weeks after a girl's birth, it is the custom to pierce the girl's ears. This is done so that she will have keen hearing and will therefore respond quickly. Responsiveness and critical ability are important, then, from the beginning.

Since life is thought of as a path, there is also a ceremony for putting on a child's first moccasins and taking the first steps along the path. For a girl, the ceremony should be performed by a woman who has *'Isanaklesh*'s power. Early in the morning, ideally during a new moon, the ceremonialist marks those who are present with a pollen blessing. At sunrise she takes the child and with prayers and blessings lifts her four times to the east, four times to the south, four times to the west, and four times to the north, and then lowers her.

The ceremonialist makes pollen footprints on a clean white buckskin. Then the child is helped as she walks through the pollen footprints in the early dawn. Prayers are said for each footstep the child takes. The child is now ready to take her first four steps alone, as blessings are spoken for a good long life on the trail of pollen. The child walks through the pollen footprints four times, each time returning to the buckskin. Finally, she circles the buckskin four times in the ceremonial circuit from east to south to west to north as four more prayers are offered. Everyone present then blesses the girl with pollen. The moccasins are blessed with pollen and lifted to the four directions. Next pollen is placed on the right foot, the right moccasin is put on, and then the same is done for the left moccasin and the left foot.

The first hair-cutting ceremony occurs in the springtime.[4] The child is marked with pollen four times, and pollen is sent to the four directions with the proper prayers for the growth and long life of the child. The hair is divided into sections, and next to the section to be cut, a small bunch of grama grass is placed with the hair. The two are then cut together. This is continued until all sections of hair are cut. This ceremony is usually repeated for four consecutive growing seasons. The hair is placed in a tree that is in full bloom, and prayers are offered so that the little girl's life will be fruitful.

Other ritual activities also occur to focus attention on the child's advancement along the path toward maturity and to ensure her well-being. Around the age of one year, she is introduced to her first solid foods. This too requires a special ceremony. The child is presented with her first four Apache foods: yucca, mesquite, mescal, and sumac or chokecherry.

If the child was given a name at birth, this too was done with a ceremony, *ka'agujila*. This name, however, can later be changed and made to suit the character of the little girl.

From a girl's birth on, she is touched by ritual. Ritual, through its repetition, aims to teach the young a sense of being cared for and made safe from harm. The idea of protecting the *persona* of the child from birth through adolescence by the appropriate rituals forms the theoretical basis of many of the ideas about child-rearing. The child is not considered ready to be responsible for her own behavior. But even though children are given almost complete freedom, they are constantly taught through ritual practices what will be expected of them when they reach puberty or the onset of the age of responsibility. By participation in this array of ritual activity, the parents are also repeatedly reminded of their own personal, spiritual, and social responsibilities, and are reminded of the importance of balance and harmony in life. They are reminded of the importance and potential power of the female child. Their child shares in the good of the people.

The ceremonies reflect the historical and cultural heritage, but at the same time they often incorporate new ideas influenced by the fact that today Apaches live in a complex world. Slight changes in ceremonial procedure often point to a new aesthetic sense of changes in tribal religious, psychological, or social perspectives. The ceremonial practitioners depend on their power and understanding of the ritual structure to accomplish the desired results and to realize their own ideas about ceremonial efficacy.

In her study of Navajo religion Gladys Reichard states that "during the period from babyhood to adolescence there is little difference in the ritualistic treatment of male and female children. At adolescence, however, there is a definite change" (Reichard, 38). This distinction is also in part true for Mescalero childhood ceremonies. Usually the ceremonial differences for boys and girls are related only to the idea that girls' lives should be patterned after *'Isanaklesh*. The boys tend to follow the exemplary model of Child of the Water, the male culture hero. Young boys are taught about hunting, for example, through rigorous physical activity where they learn how to care for and protect themselves. Even today they are taught at a young age how to hold, clean, and load a rifle as well as how to hone and use an axe. By helping older male kin, they learn to fend for themselves. This experience, along with their school experiences, prepares them for the years ahead. In earlier times boys were also trained in the skills of trading, and when necessary, they learned through experience how to prepare for warfare. Gradually, through ritual experience which accompanies all of these life tasks, a boy acquires the necessary power and skills required for assuming the position of being responsible for himself within his family and clan group. Later, if he marries, he must prove that he is reliable to both his wife and her family. If he can be relied upon, he is referred to as *haasti' dziili*, one who has become a man and is following the footsteps of his male ancestors.

Because of the importance of women in Apache culture, the proper raising and caring for a daughter evokes even more concern. Mothers tend to be more watchful of daughters than of sons. Mothers and female kin teach through example. Slowly the little girl learns to participate in the duties of women. She is instructed in being aware, obedient, and polite, and in her use of language. She is expected to care for younger brothers and sisters and to help with the daily household chores. Very early she learns the difference between the work of women and the work of men.

The girl is instructed by the women on a variety of activities such as learning to keep her body clean and healthy, to recognize important medicinal and food plants, and to prepare them for drying and storage. Girls learn to shop, cook, and sew as well as to accompany female kin on gathering parties when the piñon is ripe. They help to collect pollen, white clay, red clay, and yucca, which are often saved for their ceremony or given to another girl preparing for her feast.

I should note here that, though the roles of men and women are different and though women assume the responsibilities of motherhood, the ceremonies about which I speak are designed to lead females into positions of real responsibility and authority in the tribe. Though some "female" duties in Apache tradition are those of patriarchal traditions, many are not. The ceremonies that mark the path of life for a girl do not merely enculturate her into a position of subservience. While she does indeed learn ways of behavior that in other traditions are the duties of women, she also learns of her own great importance and of leadership roles other than those of a subservient housewife. As she grows older, the girl's tasks often become more varied and demanding.

Girls are encouraged to learn about traditional female behavior even though today they are also socialized into the behavior pattern of the dominant culture as they attend school. Young girls are encouraged to obey their teachers at school and to excel in their school work. Some parents encourage them to think of having a career as well as a family. They emphasize the importance of physical fitness for survival. Childhood is a time when a girl hears and learns from the elaborate Apache mythological traditions why it is so important to be prepared for life and its difficulties. The values of the society are once again repeated in the oral tradition which relates Apache origins, stories that are both sacred and profane, songs in a variety of genres, and the complexities of the ceremonial system.

These rites are often explained to a girl by her mother or grandmother. They relate the supernatural experiences of the women of the tribe so that she learns that she too is capable of this type of encounter, and how it should be sought. If she is fortunate when she is older, her grandmother might even pass on to her a specific rite. Respect for the age and wisdom of her grandmother is required. She learns about the importance of a wise old age and long life by hearing it referred to over and over again in conversations, myths, stories and ceremonial songs. The young girl's maternal aunt and her *K'is 'ilndi Naaghan*, her older sisters and female cousins, also take responsibility for teaching, guiding, and protecting her whenever necessary. This bond is present today in a variety of social situations, but it is especially apparent during *'Isanaklesh Gotal*. It is in this ceremony that the full relation of the girl with divine power is asserted and established.

'ISANAKLESH GOTAL

I suggest that other traditions can benefit from the Apache example of preparing young girls for a ceremonial time that links them with divine power. Without such life-long preparation even post-patriarchal versions of the various traditions will fail to truly empower women. Such preparation of young Apache girls in these ceremonies must begin spiritually and psychologically much before their menarche. It is the women of the tribe primarily who carry this responsibility. The symbols that are used to influence the young girls vary considerably in their function, but their overall purpose is to convince the adolescents that they will undergo good and positive changes if they participate fully in the ceremony. Today some of the girls require more convincing, but many others have been told from a very young age about the importance of the ceremony for a good, healthy life, and many from birth are influenced by female kin so that they in a sense begin to anticipate their ceremony. Whenever a ceremony is held, pre-pubescent girls will often gather at the tipi to observe the initiate primarily as a way of knowing what to expect when their ceremony occurs. Many times I have heard mothers or other female kin say to these little girls, "Go up toward the front of the Big Tipi where you can see and hear everything better."

At this young age the girls are thought of as soft and moldable, implying that they are still capable of being conditioned and influenced by female kin. It is easier to convince some girls to participate than others. Some need to be awakened to their female identity; others, on the other hand, need to be calmed down and taught to be more feminine. Within the ritual design of the ceremony, two concepts are at work: one is awakening the initiate to the world around her and to her abilities, and the other is to carefully calm down the unrestrained nature of adolescence. Both concepts, as well as the symbols necessary to strengthen the concept of self that is central to the transformative process, are nurtured and encouraged in the young girl's everyday activities. These are the symbols that are engaged over and over again in the multiplicity of ceremonies concerned with the life cycle of individuals as they face the critical periods of transition in their lives.

Preparation for the ceremony begins early in the life of a young girl. She is slowly and carefully made ready, then suddenly uprooted from her special privileged childhood in a family where female kin watch over her from the time of her birth. Menarche signals a physiological marker that the young girl immediately recognizes. Suddenly her life changes. Her first menstruation is usually celebrated by family and kin. She is sung over by a Singer who will emphasize to her the importance of this intimate celebration, the gift of the goddess 'Isanaklesh to a young, changing woman. Nearly all girls had this private rite of 'Isanaklesh Gotal in traditional times. An Apache elder, *saane*, recalled for me her feast, which took place in 1912, along with that of two other girls:

> When I became a woman, my parents conducted a feast for me, but there was no dance and no Big Tipi. An old woman made "medicine" for me. I ran four times, so I would be strong, just as they do in the Big Tipi Ceremony. My buckskin dress was not finished yet; it took my aunt and grandmother two years to make that dress. In that traditional ceremony, 'Isanaklesh ran a mile and the ceremony used to take eight days. In the morning, about 4:30 or 5:00, they took me out and prayed songs for me as the sun came up, and painted me with pollen to represent the sun's rays. The sponsor said, "I want this maiden to get old like me with all the good luck." That meant things like good health, good crops, long life, and fertility. The Singer prayed over me. No Mexican word, no American word, just Apache words were used.[5]

Even today some families prefer to hold private celebrations for their daughters rather than participate in the public ceremony held each year on whatever weekend comes closest to July 4. In the July rite, which attracts a large number of tourists, there are usually four to six girls who participate. *Na Ih Es*, a similar Apache ceremony, is held at Cibecue two or three times a year (Basso, 125-26). Some Apache are no longer believers in the effectiveness of *Na Ih Es*, as it is called there. Others, however, strongly believe that it will assure the pubescent girl, among other things, a long life and prosperity. Some use the expense of the ceremony as a reason for not holding it as often. For still others the influence of Christianity on most Apache reservations explains why some girls do not have their ceremonies. The decision to have 'Isanaklesh Gotal is usually made long before a girl's menses, which occurs around the age of eleven or twelve years. In the opinions of most of the people with whom I have consulted, the majority of families want the ceremony for their daughters, though often the grandmothers may want it when the parents do not. Some people no longer believe in the power of the Singer due to their commitments to Christian religions on the Reservation. Among Catholics, however, the church encourages the girls to participate in the ceremony and the priests often attend the feast. Most grandmothers had the ceremony and strongly urge this for their granddaughters. Because of the status of older women, the wishes of a grandmother are taken seriously. Great efforts are made to encourage the sharing of expenses with kin so that the decision to have a ceremony is not based solely on economic reasons. The family also receives support from non-kin who are concerned with the well-being of the young girl.

Today, as in traditional times, a young girl's first menstruation, as I said earlier, is usually celebrated with a small private feast to honor the occasion. It still includes pollen blessings, songs, and a dinner for select relatives and friends. This family gathering precedes *'Isanaklesh Gotal* and begins to prepare the young girl for being placed at the center of the more elaborate ceremony. Young girls today are often reluctant to agree to participate in a ceremony. Their shyness and fear of being the center of attention make them hesitant to cooperate with their family's urging. But in a traditional family, a girl's participation is expected and she is prepared for this event long in advance of reaching her menarche. Once she makes up her own mind and accepts her role as an initiate, the specific preparation begins. Her female kin, who view the ceremony as a joyous occasion, now put forth every effort to make this feast a very special and solemn ceremony.

They begin to gather the necessary objects that will be placed in the ceremonial basket. Expeditions are planned to the countryside in order to collect the golden yellow cattail pollen, white and red earth clays, and the black, shiny galena. The initiate is required to participate in the gathering. She accompanies the women in her family and sometimes close friends, and is instructed in the method of selecting and gathering the needed materials.

Extended kin and friends are requested to assist in the preparation of these materials. I usually have been asked to bring pollen, abalone shells, and baskets for a feast. Thus the preparation assumes a female bond of solidarity as all unite to give support to the initiate and her immediate family in planning for her successful ceremony.

Work on the girl's ceremonial dress and the special wrap for her private tipi starts at this time as well. Often the girl's grandmother or another female relative is the one who designs and completes these special garments. Finances must be managed so that the family can have enough resources to purchase the large amounts of food needed for all the guests who will come to the ceremony. Relatives gladly contribute as much as they can to assist the family with this financial burden, knowing that the favor will be reciprocated when they need such assistance.

The family must also select a Sponsor, who will assume the responsibility of preparing their daughter for the ceremony. This woman will play an important role in the immediate preparation, in the actual ceremonial process, and throughout the girl's life. Once selected, the family engages in appropriate gift exchanges with the Sponsor. In this way the ritual relationship is established and affirmed.

The Sponsor, *nade 'klehen* (the one who introduces the girl to woman-hood), is a keeper of Apache tradition. She assumes the role of mother to the initiate; she represents the right hand, the guiding hand. The *nade 'klehen* is the one whom the girl falls back on, the one who sat down with her prior to her ceremony and told her everything that she would need to know. She is the one who will mold and massage the young girl's body; she is the one who makes her run.

The Sponsor knows the proper ways to collect, gather, and prepare food; where, how and when to gather traditional Apache medicines; what to do at the time of the first snowfall; how to prepare for the stillness of winter; and most of all, how to prepare the initiates for their ceremonies. Through ceremony the Sponsor assures the people that Apache tradition will continue from one female generation to the next.

The family selects the Sponsor they want for their daughter. It is believed that only those women who have had the feast should be *nade 'klehen*, because only in this way can they have the necessary knowledge.[6] She is well versed in traditional ways and is respected in the community. The family arrives very early in the morning at the house of the woman whom they have chosen. The morning star is still bright in the sky. Timing is important, as the morning star is to be the ruler of the initiate's future. The family brings pollen to the woman and makes the request of her to be *nade 'klehen* for their daughter. A woman must never refuse such a request unless there is a very good reason to do so.

The Sponsor begins to instruct the young girl as soon as the family has selected and engaged her. The instruction centers on this basic message to the initiate: "So far your life has been simple and easy. You have had very little responsibility. Now I need to prepare you for what to expect as a woman." The basic instruction also includes how the girl deals with her first menstruation and her subsequent monthly periods. The Sponsor teaches her about hygiene, pregnancy, family planning, and childbirth. She differentiates among the girl's future roles: wife, mother, member of the Apache tribe, and Apache woman.

She deals with the problems and advantages of living in two cultures, the mainstream culture and the Apache way, and how to respect both. In addition, the Sponsor emphasizes the girl's responsibilities as a member of both cultures. She relates all her instruction to the actual upcoming ceremony. For example, it is through the experience of being cared for by the Sponsor that she will learn the value of caring for others. In having the sensation of being cared for by others, she learns and experiences the good feelings such care generates. She then will extend such caring for others in the future. The Sponsor emphasizes the importance of learning her language and of education in the ways of the Apache culture and through the American society's educational system. Both types of education are important in order to be a successful woman and member of the tribe.

The instruction also includes certain restrictions and taboos. The young girl learns the taboos related to food, water, fire, rainbows, bears, and snakes. During the ceremony she is instructed on specific restrictions. She must not smile or act in a lazy or tired manner, or display a negative attitude. She must not scratch herself directly but use the designated scratch stick for such purposes during the length of the ceremony. She cannot drink water directly but must use the drinking tube when she wants water. She is told to be careful with words and how she acts among the people. If she follows this advice, she will never be put in a position of shame. "You don't play around with your language or your life."[7]

The Sponsor reviews the entire ceremony with the initiate so that the girl will be well-prepared and know what is happening and what it means. She explains how she will be washed, bathed, and fed; about the songs and dances; how she will be blessed and the manner in which she must bless others; her part in starting the ceremonial fire; and some of the symbolism that is used throughout the ceremony.

The girl learns the importance of generosity through the example of her family, who must provide large quantities of food for the guests. The family must not run short of food during the ceremony. If they should do so, the girl's life will be one of want.

A family decides on the most appropriate Singer to conduct the ceremony for their daughter. They choose one as soon as possible after the girl's menarche. They approach the Singer, the *gutaal*, and ask: "We are here requesting your help to sing for our daughter." If he decides they are the "right family," meaning they are people who follow the Apache traditional ways, he agrees. The family then offers the Singer feathers, cigarettes, shells, and pollen as a sign to affirm the agreement. The Singer then prays that he will be in a good frame of mind for the ceremony in order for it to work right for all concerned. He prays for a clear mind and the strength to perform the rituals according to sacred tradition. The Singer is responsible for assuring that all involved carry out their specific ritual roles in a sacred manner and according to tradition.[8] The family of the initiate, along with their extended kin, assist in the preparation of the ceremonial grounds for the feast. These collective activities foster a strong sense of cooperation and serve to strengthen kinship ties. The men gather *tules* (cattails) for a ground covering, poles for the tipi, and the special prayer sticks the Singer uses during the ceremony. The women have earlier collected the four rocks for the fire pit that will burn throughout the ceremony in the sacred tipi. The Singer and his assistant in charge of the ceremonial grounds mark the sacred area, bless the rocks, and place them where the tipi will be erected.

The family members erect the special cooking arbors where the women will prepare the food. They then bring the supplies to the ceremonial grounds where the women begin to prepare them and plan how best to serve throughout the ceremony. The Singer, if requested, appoints a head cook to oversee food preparations and to see that food is distributed correctly to all those involved.

The camp is then prepared for the initiate's tipi and the tipis of the family members. Early in the afternoon of the day before the first day of the ceremony, the *nade 'klehen* and the initiate usually go off to collect yucca, mountain mahogany, the branches of greens that go into the ceremonial basket, and a small purple flower. The flower will be used to keep the initiate's dress smelling sweet like flowers while it is in storage. One *nade 'klehen* did not know the name for the flower, but she described it as follows: "When you take your dress out of storage years after your feast and shake it, you will smell the flower." Roots of soapweed and yucca are also gathered. The initiate is told that the long wiry roots are used for red dyes for the basket and the devil's claw is used for the black dye.

Late in the afternoon, in the initiate's private tipi the *nade 'klehen* cuts the long central branches of the yucca to prepare pieces about one foot long for starting the ceremonial fire. The initiate will later have to light the fire. The initiate assists the *nade 'klehen* with shaving the yucca branches. All the shavings from the yucca are saved for the fire in the sacred tipi, where they will be used to keep the fire going for the four days. While she is engaged in this activity, the initiate is often instructed in other traditional ways. For example, she is told that whenever she handles deer, she must cut toward her so that the deer will always be plentiful. Deer have important cosmological significance to the Apache, and when the initiate dances in the ceremonial tipi, she will dance on a deer hide.

During the ceremony, the girl is re-created on the earth as *'Isanaklesh*; in this way, her thoughts and her breath become the thoughts and breath and power of the deity. The strength of all Apaches comes from *'Isanaklesh*. The prayers ask that it be that way always, and not just for one day.

In order to prepare the initiate for the right frame of mind, she is moved into a private tipi on the ceremonial grounds. With this isolation and detachment from her regular interaction with community and friends, her specific ritual instruction begins. She is taught the use of the ritual equipment and procedures: the drinking tube, the scratching stick, how to prepare the pieces of wood for starting the fire, and the use of the local plants she has collected with her sponsor, as well as those that were collected by other kin.

In this protected environment the initiate is cleansed and purified of her childhood ways. A void is temporarily created—a state of liminality, nothingness, *tabula rasa*—in which her mind is prepared for the transformation to come. On the first morning of her ceremony her hair will be washed; she will be ritually bathed, and dressed carefully in her ceremonial attire.

On the first and last mornings of the ceremony, the Singer comes to bless her and feed her traditional Apache foods. The Sponsor sees to her meals at all other times during the ceremony. This total attention by others teaches her the way that Apaches value the idea of caring for others.

The initiate is prepared for another reality through all these activities. The ceremony in which she is about to participate contrasts markedly with her everyday life. She now lives in a separate tipi. She is primarily cared for by her Sponsor rather than her family. She is attired in ceremonial clothing that is in sharp contrast to her daily attire and something she will not wear again except in other ceremonies in the future. She must follow restrictions that are imposed only for the duration of the ceremony. All these ritual preparations allow her to move into another reality, that of ceremony. This move requires her willingness to step out of the ordinary and familiar and into the unknown.

THE CULTURE BEARER

She has been selected as a "culture bearer." Everything begins anew for her as she enters a role requiring new responsibilities. The ceremony moves her toward maintaining ethnicity and therefore the culture. As soon as she is blessed, she enters the new role. Although she often is reluctant to become the center of attention, her fears, anxiety, and excitement are somewhat allayed by the special caring she receives from her Sponsor and Singer, as well as her family. It is her Sponsor who "fixes" her and "molds" her into a good Apache woman through her words of wisdom and traditional knowledge. It is her Singer who sings her into womanhood and reassures her that just as everything in nature comes alive every growing season, so too they want life to be continually renewed for her as she travels through her seasons.

Note the importance of family in the ceremonies of a female's life. The family assists her in preparation for her most important times; it nurtures and supports her and assists in the preparation of the ceremonies themselves. It encourages her to take on the power of *'Isanaklesh* and—through ceremony—recognizes that power in her. In the traditional ceremony, too, the tribe, the *public*, recognizes this power. Both men and women participate in helping her along the path and in recognizing her central importance to the people. Such nurturance, support, and recognition of the power of the female and of each woman is critical for the instantiation and full envisionment of *any* post-patriarchal religion.

The ceremonies and specific ritual that surround a girl as she travels on her path into womanhood are geared to instill in her the traditional values of her people and emphasize her own value as a human and a *woman*, a woman who indeed carries within her the capacity to become the bearer of the culture. They point to her interconnectedness with nature and with others, and therefore encourage compassion and caring, self-control or balance and power. In *'Isanaklesh Gotal*, the girl experiences a ceremonial transformation that provides a source of real empowerment for her daily life, an empowerment that can and should be vital to her own personal growth and involvement and to her culture.

As I noted at the beginning of this chapter, *'Isanaklesh* is an authority to whom both men and women can come for their own personal as well as societal needs. Through a successful *'Isanaklesh Gotal*, the girl begins to mature into precisely such an authority. The strength of *all* Apaches comes from *'Isanaklesh*. Through her initiation ceremony, and in the subsequent transformation into a respected and wise woman of her culture, the female in Apache tradition undergoes transformation into something so strong and vital that she, too, becomes a source of strength for the men and women around her. Similar ritualistic transformation and empowerment can and should become valuable resources for post-patriarchal religion and life. Care and attention for girls becoming women, becoming the bearers of culture — as this care and attention is exemplified by the family that takes responsibility for the proper arrangements of the traditional ceremonies that occur throughout a girl's life — can serve as productive, powerful roots for a society after patriarchy, for a society that values women and encourages their roles as powerful leaders, as powerful human beings who see within themselves the feminine aspects of wisdom and divinity.

NOTES

1. Yet in order to get the complete picture one has to look at the history of the Apache women who were forced to relocate and were denied knowledge of their culture, language, and religious traditions. A necessary comparative study focused on the dynamics and consequences of assimilation and religious conversion would provide some very important perspectives on this historical reality.

2. Willetto Antonio, leader of the Sun Clan, on the Mescalero Apache Reservation, September 1985. Personal communication.

3. According to Willetto Antonio, this is announced as "they are going to put her in a *ts'al*."

4. Meredith Begaye, a medicine woman, waits until everything is growing and budding forth with life.

5. This elder woman referred to the ceremony as the "Big Tipi Ceremony." When I verified this information with the medicine woman, she said that the proper Apache name for the ceremony is *'Isanaklesh Gotal*.

6. According to an Apache elder, only a woman who has been an initiate and experienced the ceremony can be a sponsor. This allows her to adequately prepare a young girl. She recalled: "These were the things that were said to me during my feast and I try to stay with them."

7. Meredith Begaye, September 1985.

8. For Willetto Antonio, this is especially important. Since he has been confined to a wheelchair because of a spinal cord injury, he has more difficulty maneuvering in the tipi during the ceremony. He knows how important it is to do everything correctly if the ceremony is to be effective for the young initiate.

WORKS CITED

Basso, Keith H. *The Gift of Changing Woman*. Bulletin of American Ethnology. No. 196. Washington, D.C.: U. S. Government Printing Office, 1966.

Reichard, Gladys A. *Navajo Religion: A Study of Symbolism*. Princeton: Princeton University Press, 1950.

8

The Spiritual, Political Journey of a Feminist Freethinker

EMILY CULPEPPER

The spiritual/political path presented here is in many respects a highly individual one. Yet it traces the outlines of a life philosophy shared by a great many contemporary women who are difficult to document or describe collectively. This difficulty arises precisely because we do not join or name ourselves after any specific religious tradition. An increasing number of women have decided against channeling our energies into the reconstruction of any religion. We choose instead to create more eccentric pathways that aid us and encourage others to deviate as widely as possible from patriarchal centers of meaning. The old androcentric faiths may sometimes provide fragments of inspiration, but we do not judge them to be trustworthy means for moving beyond patriarchy. We are women who may have grown up in a religion and left it, tried several, or never been part of an organized religious tradition. What we have in common is a depth perception of our life path as a feminist journey. The transformative feminist insight that "the personal is political" has also become for us "the personal is political is spiritual."

The ways we describe our spiritual/political beliefs vary widely, and we are delighted that they do so. Most such journeyers would probably not be uncomfortable with the name I have chosen in the title of this essay—feminist freethinker. As you will see, I might easily have chosen other names, such as witch, amazon, pagan, oddwoman, "Nag-gnostic"[1] ... all of these name parts of myself. But I have begun with "freethinker" because this term most widely names my frame of reference and that of the large, loose-knit tribe of folks whom I hope to represent or at least partially evoke. Feminist freethinker serves well enough, for it is a positive phrase that sets one's imagination going and raises questions. It is an open-ended name, yet strong.

An early clue to the strength of this name occurred many years ago. I had participated in a conversation for a feminist film, and the filmmaker wanted an identification to run on the bottom of the screen when I appeared. It was one of those many moments when my usual preference for at least a paragraph, rather than a quickly recognizable label, just would not do. "Feminist freethinker," I proposed. "I like it," she said, "but it's just too, too . . . radical, too unconventional." Exactly. And what a colossal comment on the restrictions of our society. I believe that "to think freely is ontologically, organically the first free act" (Culpepper 1984, 5). It is this commitment to be-ing free, and to be-ing a catalyst for freethinking and acting in others that most characterizes the disparate grass-roots "traditions" I represent. A freethinker, according to the *Oxford English Dictionary*, is "One who refuses to submit his reason to the control of authority in matters of religious belief." Feminist freethinkers add to this definition our exuberant biophilia, with its iconoclastic, pluralistic openness to inner guides wherever we may find them. My story here stands for all those women who slip through the categories of religious classification, who pledge faithful allegiance to no institution, and who are a growing cognitive minority.

CONTRADICTIONS OF (WHITE SOUTHERN) CHRISTIANITY

My own story begins in the deep South, in a Protestant church whose activities were a major part of my family's life. From childhood through high school (the fifties and early sixties), I was a highly involved Christian who earnestly believed in the Christian message as I understood it. What happened? My church's support for segregation pained and infuriated me. "Red and Yellow, Black and White, all are precious in his sight. Jesus loves the little children of the world." I have clear memories of singing this song in my all-white kindergarten Sunday school class and being upset. I believed and loved that message and the interracial pictures showing one child of each color gathered laughing at Jesus' knees. (I did not then notice how white-anglo-saxon-protestant were the features of this Jesus.) My church wanted these "other" children to stay safely out in the mission field or to be included after the second coming. They were not welcome in my church, nor were my questions about this state of affairs. I was, however, blessed to have a family that valued freethinking, and especially a mother who was not afraid to tell me that the segregation of our church and our society was wrong and would one day change.

I remember going with Mama one Sunday to the "colored" congregation across town, one to which my church occasionally donated money, since it was in our denomination. The "colored members of our brotherhood," as they were referred to by my minister, had extended an invitation for some representative of our church to worship with them—for reasons I was too young to comprehend. But I comprehended quite clearly and happily that it was my mother who would go. I was fascinated and bothered by this development. It seemed like a step in the right direction. Yet, young as I was, I knew that there would be no reciprocal invitation from my church. This worship service was louder and livelier; I was having a good time. The offering plate went by and I put in my usual nickel. The preacher had been commenting and giving thanks for each offering that went into the plate, but I had been more intent on the singing and clapping all around me. Suddenly I was acutely aware of his booming voice saying "and the little white girl gives five cents." I flushed with self-consciousness and confusion. Was it not enough? That thought had never occurred to me. I was proud of the fact that I gave one-fifth of my twenty-five cent allowance to the church, and I already understood that this amount was more than a tithe. Was it an acknowledgment that I was a faithful giver? And the thought began to surface that perhaps because I was white, my gift had a different meaning here. But what was it? This moment stayed in my mind as a sort of riddle. I knew it was enormously important, that it revealed something about race and the church, but it was all much more complex than I understood.

I sought earnestly to balance these experiences with the faith message that I loved like a best friend, that God is love and that Jesus came to teach us that we should all love each other. It wasn't just the failure of the people in my church to love across the racial divide that troubled me—we all sin, I knew—but their insistence that there was no failure, no sin in this segregation of the heart. They saw no need for change, indeed, saw any suggestion of desegregation as the sin. By the time I was in junior high school, I had developed my response. I just knew they were wrong and I would do my part to help them realize that belief in racial inferiority and segregation were not Christian. I became a youth leader, playing the piano for my Sunday school class and picking hymns about brotherhood, planning Sunday school lessons on race and brotherhood, praying obvious prayers about racial harmony at monthly Wednesday night supper prayer meetings. By now I had learned that there were integrated churches and that some white Christians were even activists for integration. I found readings about the Black church, and I was beginning to hear about Martin Luther King.

As far as I could tell, my attempts in church were only making people uncomfortable. But still my anger fueled my hope. A movement was coming and I wanted to be a part of it. I didn't understand then that in my own small ways, I was already joining it. I thought I had to go to Atlanta and join a sit-in or freedom ride—activities far from Macon, Georgia—and it was very frustrating that I was too young. I wanted to get out there and fight for what I believed in, for what I believed the church was really all about. As I volunteered to help my high school prepare for the desegregation that would finally come the year after I graduated, I realized acutely that I did not know how to reach out to "colored people" in my own town. Contemporary reports from South Africa remind me of the homegrown version of American apartheid with which I grew up. The only break in the color line was also a traditional part of it, my relationship with Essie, who worked for my family after my mother returned to work outside the home when I entered first grade. Something was very right yet also very wrong and increasingly awkward in this relationship. Begun in a laden context, it has carried and transcended the ambiguities of our lives over the years. I hungered for my church to help me with the bewildering divisions and contradictions that hurt and angered me, and it did not. Religious racism clearly legitimated the segregated schools, buses, drinking fountains, and picture shows that seemed so smugly entrenched. I knew I could not continue to live with the hypocrisy of white worship.

I have spent some time on these memories, because they were an early cauldron that changed and shaped me. Most feminist freethinkers have their own stories of growing awareness about the continual hypocrisies of established religions old or new. For a long time I believed that legitimation of oppression was the exception in Christian history, a distortion and departure from the "true church." My faith was redefined, reconstructed, many times in an attempt to hold onto it. It worked for a while to believe that even if the message of love and freedom had been carried only by a minority of Christians, it was still the true flame, and I would still carry it. Perhaps, I decided, this liberating message had only existed in the very beginning, with moments of flaring up despite all, in the long march through many oppressive centuries. But gradually disappointments deepened into disillusionment and widened the rift of estrangement. The church seemed more often to limit than to free.

LEAVING THE PROCRUSTEAN CHRISTIAN BED

The last gasp was somewhere in the late sixties. Like many Christians I attempted to remain connected with the faith of my childhood by reconstructing it in ever more existential ways. The intellectual discoveries of college made this a stimulating option and a renewed source of hope. I had for some time left any literal belief in a Christian heaven and hell, Jesus by the right hand of the Father, souls all singing in heavenly afterlife. They were all metaphors, of course, and the real message was the incarnation of divinity in all of us here and now. Studying "Death of God Theology" with Tom Altizer at the peak of its notoriety helped me identify as Christian for a while longer. (Friends back home, of course, thought the opposite, never understanding that my interest in a Nietzschean Christian atheism was an attempt to stay Christian.) But when my father died suddenly, this intellectually sophisticated Christianity did not soothe the horror I felt. Christian doctrines of salvation and life after death seemed elitist and obfuscating at best and a manipulative, cruelly false promise at worst. I had been coexisting uneasily with a recognition that Christianity was a complex tissue of truths and lies. But now I saw that I could no longer accept the whole package. Turmoil over the Vietnam war was another life-shaping event for me as for many of my generation. While I organized prayer vigils, speak outs, and conferences with a small band of Southern protesters, I was, sadly, no longer surprised that Christians militantly supporting the war far outnumbered those opposing it. As hypocrisies piled on contradictions, the discrepancies became too great. A new pattern had begun to shape in my mind and heart. Something in my deepest intuition told me that the basic symbols of Christianity were all too easily compatible with life-denying attitudes and oppressive social structures. I did not fully understand that bedrock intuition then; I did not even want to have it. But to keep my sense of spiritual honesty and sanity, I knew I could no longer call myself Christian.

Often I was asked, and still am, if I do not miss the community of the church. This question raises bittersweet memories. The community that the church promised was sweet, and I will never deny some tangible moments of its fragile existence. Sunday night hymn singing echoes still in my inner ear. These less formal services often attracted the more plain-spoken, down-to-earth members of our congregation, people who simply and unselfconsciously opened their throats to pour out feelings that ran deep, beyond the words that were sung. Taking turns with my brother to kneel at our family Christmas altar evoked special feelings as we read Bible passages from Matthew and Luke leading up to the wonder of a newborn baby God. And, yes, I rejoiced at joining the church (an adolescent rite of passage in our "brotherhood"), immersing in the waters of baptism and taking the every-Sunday little wafer and cup of grape juice that stood for such big and wonderful mysteries. When I was older, I rejoiced at finally finding Christians who did speak and work from a fierce vision of justice and love combined. I do not now abandon those parts of my life. But the bitterness of the church's constant betrayal broke through the sweetness and severed its connection to the doctrines and institutions where I first encountered such fullness and connectedness of be-ing. Nelle Morton has pointed out the dangers of religious nostalgia (Morton, 150). To turn these memories into nostalgic quicksand, drawing me back into complicity with a tradition I no longer believe, would be the ultimate betrayal, not only of myself but also of the biophilic force present in those moments.

I embarked on a wide-ranging spiritual journey. I was not looking for a new religion to join, but for insights from any religion or philosophy that resonated with my love of life and passion for justice. It was a tremendous relief that I no longer struggled to fit a procrustean Christian bed. I began, instead, learning to pattern the crazy quilt of spiritual paradoxes that I am composing still. I discovered that "mystic" and "eclectic" (reactions I frequently encountered) were considered put-downs, though my response was "Yes! Yes!"

The community I found was diverse and never all in one place. Certainly the political communities of the Civil Rights/Black Power movement, the Anti-Vietnam War/Peace movement, and the hippie/freak movement were major sustenance. A freedom in loving and a love of freedom were the sparks of recognition that warmed and incited me whenever and wherever I met them. Like many freethinkers, I found enlivening ideas and insights in the riches of many world religions, especially since I did not feel a need to fit into the whole of any doctrine. Fragments from Upanishads, vision quest tales from Native America, Sufi dancing, mind-altering mystical adventures, evanescent glimpses of the "something" that had flowed onto a canvas or into a sculpture or a blues/rock/jazz note . . . these experiences were teaching me that the whole world was a sacred text. I had a lifetime to learn to read.

FEMINIST FANTASTIC COHERENCE

Then the women's liberation movement broke open new worlds. A "fantastic coherence" (Morton, 127) began to emerge in my eclectic crazy quilt of spiritual paradoxes. Consciousness-raising felt like a process on which I was already embarked, but which now took a quantum leap, developing means to become more focused and self-critically aware. Feminism has given me a language (as it has for so many) that more fully than any other names and struggles with the spiritual/political issues that animate my living. It also has brought a deeper centering, as it is finally a movement/ philosophy that does not place women second. In a patriarchal world that daily devalues and destroys women, feminist validation of women's Selves functions as an axis that shifts universes of meaning and possibility. Consciousness of women's Selves emerging radically reorients our vision and makes relative the constructions of patriarchy. This creative process is a primary ground of meaning, a continually unfolding "first moment" for the construction of theology/thealogy/philosophy.[2] It is for this reason that many feminists see the women's revolution as a political and spiritual movement.

Feminist analysis and activism clarified for me the deep underlying androcentrism of Christianity, not only in its practices but in its core symbolism. Even beyond the problems presented by a male god and male savior, there remains the central foundational Christian faith claim—one incarnation of the divine into humanity at one specific point in history. Belief in a unique penetration of divinity into humanity was no longer just implausible, it was offensive. This concept of one anointed-from-on-high messiah sent to enter/save the world is inescapably hierarchical. And salvation requiring bloody sacrifice is necrophilic and sadomasochistic. These faith events are inextricably bound up with any use of the name *Christian.* Otherwise, why choose this name? With these insights, I understood in a fuller, more conscious way that difficult bedrock intuition I had had to face earlier: the basic symbols of Christianity are all too easily compatible with life-denying attitudes and oppressive social structure. Feminism brought to light the subliminal structures producing the contradictions, hypocrisies, and betrayals I had had to leave. I comprehended in an ever deeper way why reform and reconstruction of Christianity would never be enough.

This new clarity was exhilarating, but it was also unsettling. A feminist perspective points up vast global patterns of patriarchy, the interconnections of its structures in personal, political, religious, and secular forms. Early in the seventies Mary Daly wrote of "the courage to see" what feminism involves (Daly 1973, 4-6). Courage is a necessary part of this path. It can be frightening and overwhelming at times to feel the necessity to move beyond the boundaries of so many centuries of meaning. But it feels even more frightening to shrink from the task, trying to re-define all the old religious meanings so that they are said to mean something else entirely. Let these religions have their place in history. It is a massive one. But let us not cling to them because of their longevity or through some sleight of heart that neutralizes the witness of centuries of pain.

Religious reconstruction can be a form of denial, glossing over parts of patriarchal patterns that we need to face. I do not at all doubt that at many times, in certain contexts, for particular people, even the most oppressive of patriarchal religions have sometimes been transcended by making a humane use of them.[3] Such events are to be honored. Certainly they make my view of religion more complex and add to my wonder and respect for the human spirit's capacity to work in amazing ways with available tools. But such precious positive moments of liberation in patriarchal religions are not enough to validate continued commitment or erase their harmful deep structures.

That women especially hold onto identifying with and reforming world religious traditions is not surprising to those who reject this approach. It has become a commonplace to observe that men have constructed religions and women believe in them. Religion has been one of the major channels for the life of the heart and has often been a source of meaning beneath and beyond daily difficulties. For these reasons many women have found religion a "place" to try and be, in a world that says women have no place. But organized religion is no longer a place for me and for increasing numbers of women. The price is too high and the integrity of our newly emerging vision too vivid. We are going many different ways, yet there is a sense of being on a shared journey. We are the spinning voyagers Mary Daly writes about, time travelers seeking the temple of our familiar, as Alice Walker puts it. And as Nelle Morton so eloquently expressed in her title, for us "The Journey Is Home."

So what does this spiritual/political path feel like: How does one live as a feminist freethinker? What values? What rituals? What meaning do we grant our past? What are our sources of guidance, comfort, strength when we face the horrors that confront us in human existence? What sources of joy? Of community? In many ways the answers will be highly individual from one freethinker to another. Yet there are some common values and strategies which I can best point to by telling more of the stories that have become pieces of this quilt. I have chosen this quilt metaphor because it arises from an image of women's creativity, fashioning from whatever scraps of material available something new and useful and beautiful. It may not sound as grand as a systematic theology or an analytic philosophy, but it can meet real human needs in a direct way. I do not want to romanticize this metaphor. While many women found sustenance (both solitary and communal) in their quiltmaking, many women did not like it and suffered from the requirement that they do so. Nor do I myself take any literal stitches in fabric to make quilts. There is in this metaphor some irony and ambivalence, and a sharp knowledge that one's form of creativity and comfort must be chosen with a free heart. When our work is chosen, it can be luminous, with meanings beyond the particulars. This is the power Alice Walker sees in her mother's garden, a work this overworked woman chose before and after her hard days in the fields, a work so free in spirit that it transformed Walker's childhood, such that she can write, "even my memories of poverty are seen through a screen of blooms" (Walker, 241). Like most feminist freethinkers, I choose to stitch together wildly diverse stories. We select ones that carry ideas and feelings that touch a deep nerve of spiritual honesty and power. We swap stories as we meet, sharing the threads of meaning that help us weave our worlds into existence.

GODDESSES HEALING THE HE-GODS

There are many goddesses in my quilt, but I am not a goddess worshipper. Belief in "the Goddess" is not my religion. Too often Goddess Religion succumbs to the inertia of monotheism and fails to leave behind patriarchal patterns of thought. Elsewhere I have offered a "sympathetic critique" of the "thealogy" of the Goddess/the Mother (Culpepper 1987), and I do not want to repeat that here. I want to focus instead on the nonaffiliated approach, which is perhaps the most widespread of all. Many of us find an expanding personal pantheon of goddesses and other mythic images to be a great psychic counterweight to the father gods of patriarchy. Goddess images for the sacred in ourselves heal wounds inflicted by the dogma that women are second-best to god's image and servants in a man's world. Carol Christ has rightly pointed out that in times of crisis and transition, when we do not have new images for our sense of ultimate reality and power, we revert to old images, including ones we long ago rejected (Christ, 73). And, I would add, in times of intense joy and celebration this reversion to old images can pull at us if we have not explored more satisfying forms of naming our changing realities.

Goddesses and other mythic images can open up new avenues for self-exploration. Such images are some of the emerging figures of thought in a major change of consciousness, a new symbolic transformation. Feminist freethinkers find many diverse psychic companions in our journey. Gorgons have guided me in plumbing the depths of my rage and releasing my fighting spirit, so numbed in gynocidal society and spirituality (Culpepper 1986). Such an Amazon Epiphany is not abstract or escapist romanticizing when an attacker is there at the door. Mermaids have reminded me of early unnamed moments of woman-identified sensuality (Culpepper 1984). As our inner guides increase, we often discover and reclaim earlier moments of insight. This remembering brings a multidimensional harmony into our lives that helps us face the fragmentations of contemporary life.

Perhaps the earliest intuition I had of a goddess occurred when I was about twelve or thirteen, before I would have applied this name to my experience. The passionate and inquisitive thinking that usually accompanied my church-going intensified as I prepared to join the church. I paid close attention to the sermons and loved to ask the preacher questions about them. One Sunday, as he preached on the Second Coming, it dawned on me with a great certainty that the Second Coming of Christ would just have to be female. It would only be fair! I felt that a great mystery had been revealed to me which was tremendously exciting. And didn't Dr. Sherman always say that any true experience of Jesus was a "tr-r-remend-jous" feeling? It was so obvious: God loved us all; we were all made in God's image; Christ came to save us all and represent the new humanity; Christ came first as the man Jesus; therefore (it took my breath away!) the Second Coming would have to be a woman, to include everyone. I even dared to wonder if I might become the mother of this woman messiah, if I were good enough—probably not possible, but . . . ?

These personal thoughts were more speculative and I kept them to myself. But I eagerly blurted out my discovery about the Second Coming to Dr. Sherman as I filed past in the line to shake his hand after the sermon. I do not honestly remember his exact response, except that it was another of many experiences in which he shook his head and tried to make me realize that this was impossible. I do remember something about Christ having a sword for a tongue in the Second Coming (which sounded disgusting) and that he *would* be Jesus and he *would* be male.

By this age I had become familiar with Dr. Sherman's less than enthusiastic response to my budding theological reflections. But I was undaunted. My parents usually consoled me with their own familiar response: Dr. Sherman was old-fashioned, there are some things that are God's mysteries, and who knows . . . perhaps it could be so, perhaps not, and it was good to be thinking about what God meant to us. I was a long way from imaging a goddess or goddess-in-me, but I never let go in some way of this early intuition. Years later in graduate school when I learned about Mother Ann Lee and the Shaker belief in a female Second Coming, Sophia of the mystics, and the Father/Mother of Christian Science, I felt a particular satisfaction and recognition stretching back to childhood.

In college I met Kali, Hindu goddess of creation and destruction. By this time I was in the midst of leaving Christianity and Kali's combination of nurture and violence was fascinating. Theodicy had become a very troubling theological problem in my life. Kali spoke to my need for trying to face the contradictions of goodness and suffering, life and loss. I had no illusion that I was necessarily understanding Kali as a Hindu devotee would. I was riveted by how she spoke to me, in those wild paintings in which her teeth gleamed and she danced ecstatically, wearing her necklace of babies' skulls. She was representing something I needed to contemplate, pointing in a direction I needed to go. I did not decide to "worship" her; instead I named my black cat for her. This incarnation of Kali became my wise companion for eighteen years, teaching me much (as witches' familiars do) about the mysteries of living and dying. Her principal message has always been never to forget that any concept/experience I have of the wonder of creation must include my knowledge of destruction. I must live in the paradox. Not in the sense of a stalemate, but as a thought-provoking catalyst for integrity in my quest. My cat taught me that the fearful symmetries of nature so inspiring to me included her flashing beauty, her sweet friendliness and playfulness, and her appetite for hunting and killing. She conjures for me the voice in the Upanishads chanting one of the basic mantras, "I am food, I am food, I am food. I am the food-eater, I am the food-eater, I am the food-eater" (*Taittiriya Upanishad* III. 10.5). Our age needs to experience such mystical connection with the processes of living, beyond dualism.[4]

WITCHCRAFT ACTIVISM

From my practice of living with a goddess incarnation/meditation, I was more than ready for the playful, creative approach of Wicca, as the women's movement began to spread and expand on its ideas. Feminist witchcraft has become one important vehicle for spiritual/political liberation (see Starhawk). Many women are inspired by its spontaneous creativity in rituals, refusal to solidify into fixed book or creed or hierarchy, and insistence on honoring the memory of those consumed by inquisitions past and present. The twin pillars of feminist paganism resonated with my own ethical guidelines. In Wicca oral tradition the goddess says: "All acts of love and pleasure are my rituals"; and, "Do as you will and harm none." I did not decide that this wonderful new source of political spirituality was my religion. Rather, it introduced me to a particularly rich resource and to more companions/conspirators on my journey. I was already a witch, having discovered with many sisters that radical activist identity in early women's movement organizing. In *Sisterhood Is Powerful* we read:

WITCH is an all-women Everything. It's theatre, revolution, magic, terror, joy, garlic flowers, spells. . . . Witches have always been women who dared to be: groovy, courageous, aggressive, intelligent, nonconformist, explorative, curious, independent, sexually liberated, revolutionary. .... You are a Witch by saying aloud, "I am a Witch" three times, and thinking about that. You are a Witch by being female, untamed, angry, joyous, and immortal (Morgan, 540).

Being a witch has always meant to me, not joining a faith, but developing an identity that channels anger and ecstasy into creativity. Being a witch means believing in magic as part of politics; it's part of dancing in the revolution, as Emma Goldman would put it. Being a witch means understanding ourselves to be on the boundaries and beyond of patriarchal realities. Being a witch unleashes gynergy and calls forth daring, health, and fun in others. Of course, many say it cannot be a practical way to live. Unconventional and often predictable—yes. But impractical—no. Unless it is impractical to want a clean environment, an end to injustice, a community of love. Being a witch means discovering whatever disciplines in one's life help craft the long, hard work of social change while refusing to succumb to self-martyrdom and burn-out. Knowing we are in it for the long haul is something that the pain of growing up with racial segregation taught me. Knowing we are in it for the long haul has also impressed upon me the vital necessity of expanding our opportunities and capacities for joy now.

My identity as a semi-anarchist witch highlights some of the underlying outlines of the freethinking sensibility I represent. Many of us share a belief that patriarchal society is in part kept in place by its sheer mass of over-organization. Institutions and ideologies become deadly serious and maintain a hold on people, including many feminists, far beyond reason or health. Patriarchy is an ideology of hierarchy and perpetuates itself in us by inculcating a worship of structure for the sake of structure. Structure for its own sake is dominance, dominance of form over organic meaning. Patriarchy addicts us to a need to maintain connection with the structures of the past, *whatever the cost.* A witch, a freethinker, an amazon does not reject all structures. But we see structure as a framework, a channel, a skeleton for organic social entities. Patriarchal society is grotesquely imbalanced in the direction of maintaining structure/beliefs/institutions long past their useful life. I believe that patriarchy biases our consciousness of the need to change in favor of always reforming rather than transforming. Anarchists have often suggested that when in doubt, vote out the incumbent. Freethinkers understand the wisdom in this advice.

There is an irony here. Just this irreverence about standard structures means that freethinkers are often individuals who start projects, groups, organizations, networks, movements. Certainly this has been true in my own life. We are not overawed by what embarking on a new organization might involve. We are often impatient with waiting for existing, long-standing institutions to address unmet needs. We know a bad track record when we see it. We are committed to conjuring up, by example, by invention, by desire, by scotch tape and baling wire, what we need for liberation and love. Coexisting with our sense of being in it for the long haul is our par-

adoxical sense of urgency on the edge of nuclear nightmare. We are icon-
oclasts wanting to bring about new worlds by both sudden and gradual
enlightenment.

IRREVERENT AND ILLEGITIMATE

To the surprise of many of my friends, I do have my own favorite patriarch, Hui Neng, the Sixth Patriarch of Zen Buddhism (Fung and Fung).
This delightful fellow imparts several important messages to me. As a child
I was often positively regarded for achieving in school. Therefore I can be
bedeviled sometimes by spooky, inner voices making me doubt whether I
am on the right track for continued approval. These voices seductively
insinuate that the right track, however unusual, will shine forth as somehow
smart/clever enough to gain credibility/success/praise. (Such voices are a
form of that old prod in the oppressed reminding us to smile and shuffle.)
Enter Hui Neng, an illiterate commoner who achieved sudden enlightenment when hearing the chanting of the Diamond Sutra. He upset the ox
and the applecart of Zen by receiving the mantle of leadership (from the
Fifth Patriarch) instead of the number one, long-studying best student and
head monk in the monastery. Hui Neng's own Sutra begins with him
recounting the story of his unlikely succession to an assemblage of earnest,
obedient students who, we hope, awoke to the irony of the event.

Hui Neng reminds me of far more than the dangers of getting lost in
unquestioning diligence, however. His story transmits a belief in enlightenment as awakening to one's self-nature, the wisdom of ordinary people
when unobscured by prejudices and false hierarchies. This radically egalitarian and compassionate insight does not merely inspire me. It challenges
me to question especially the distinctions and divisions that I myself set up,
my most favorite icons. Hui Neng does his own dance in my mind's eye to
convey his messages. The image comes from a pen-and-ink drawing showing
Hui Neng, with a raffish look of bliss, ecstatically ripping up pages of the
sacred Sutras in a fit of *satori*. The Sutra that hinders *satori* is no Sutra.
The Buddha that closes off enlightenment is no Buddha. The feminism that
closes off a zest for liberation is no feminism. The feminist theory that
disdains the grass-roots common wisdom of women is no feminist theory.

My spiritual/political journey includes working as an activist on the
boundaries of academia. I am often disturbed by new icons of feminist
theory becoming rigid within disciplines as reform additions. More than
once I have been advised that my attention to grass-roots women's thinking
is only "popular," a second-class sister in a rarefied atmosphere of "real"
critical theory. For example, rather than writing lyrically here about radical
witches with their guerrilla approach to undermining patriarchy by irreverence and anarchistic invention, I should be more intellectually respect-
able. I could/should translate this subject into detached prose about
deconstruction, preferably with voluminous erudite footnotes to whatever

favorite fashionable fathers of thought are the latest legitimators of feminist discourse.

Freethinkers/witches/les guerilleres move through many terrains and are happy to form coalitions with amazon allies wherever we find them, whether immersed in Foucault, Derrida, and Lacan, or Anzaldua, Parker, and Grahn. The women's movement needs many women with many tools, and no one of us can know each and every source that inspires another. I have no interest in narrow canons or trashing any woman for working with what moves her. This diversity is one of our principal strengths. However, when feminist scholarship forgets her mother, the women's movement, or becomes embarrassed by her, the old patriarchal story of Athena begins to be replicated. Zeus—the father god—swallowed Athena's mother Metis (Wisdom, remember?), and Athena began to know only her birth from Zeus' brain, believed she sprang full-grown in his armor, and declared, "No mother bore me." When the body of feminist work becomes skewed toward seminal thinkers who provide legitimacy, we must look to realign the balance. *Legitimacy is a primary patriarchal construct.* It makes bastards of our independent offspring, judging them to be "something that is spurious, irregular, inferior, or of questionable origin." It makes independent mothers and sisters into bitches, judging us "lewd or immoral . . . malicious, spiteful and domineering." These are Webster's common definitions. Are they so hard or frightening for us to remember? We ignore these pressures and patterns at our peril. The growing imbalance in what counts as feminist theory distorts our thinking, stifles creativity, and functions to marginalize even further those women who are already under-represented (Culpepper 1988). I believe women and feminism are strong enough to raise such hard questions with each other.

SHAMANS FOR A FUTURE AGE

By my stories you can see that a feminist freethinker has many *personas:* witness to demanding contradictions in living; catalyst for sticky questions; iconoclast and icon maker; tickler of fancies; celebrator of the overflowing wonder of existence; reminder of forgotten folk; agitator for justice; poser of paradoxes; conjurer of dreams. Freethinkers claim no monopoly on these qualities. The more we encounter them in others the happier we are. But we do feel deeply impelled in our life path by an affinity for performing these functions, wherever we find ourselves. We seem to have a third eye out for the imbalances in any orientation.

I have come to conclude that over-all we fulfill a shamanistic function, an occupation woefully under-represented in an increasingly mechanized, commodified, bureaucratized patriarchy. Judy Grahn has eloquently demonstrated the shamanistic function and "ceremonial office" that lesbian/gay peoples have always held in every society.[5] Her imaginative tracings of these patterns across centuries and cultures aided my understanding that the feminist freethinkers' journey is an analogous and overlapping phenomenon. This perspective helps explain why, as adamant as freethinkers often are in our actions, we do not intend for everyone to act in an identical way. We suffer from a palpable sensation that patriarchy acts to shrink universes of meaning into a pitifully limited, homogenized, proscribed set of opinions. We are drawn by the voices in the wind and the rhythms in the rocks to provoke multi-verses of meanings among us. We listen for the odd thought, the left-hand path, the counter tones that challenge any complacency, including our own. A mystic sense of organic necessity urges us on and sustains us. These are not altruistic acts undertaken from some sense of noble moral superiority. Bluntly put, we feel concretely and cosmically safer the more difference and diversity human beings are able to celebrate with each other. Nothing makes us sadder than for someone to say, "How courageous you are, I could never do that."[6] Contagious freedom is our intention.

The diverse patches in my expanding crazy quilt of spiritual paradoxes are gathered from the stories and events and people who have inspired in me just this contagious, free, biophilic bonding. They are markers and teachers on the journey. They help me tell my story in the hopes that it will help you tell yours. This quilt is a collection of shamans and visions that refuse easy systematization. Like the Native American weavers who always place one flaw in a design so the spirit will not be captured, these tricksters resist conforming to one creed. As such, my quilt is also a model of spiritual coalition. Bernice Reagon often reminds audiences at Sweet Honey in the Rock concerts that real coalitions—bonding across and despite differences—are not easy. By definition, coalitions challenge us, as we find some points of common cause while other priorities and cherished beliefs may be in conflict. If it is always comfortable, Reagon cautions, it is not coalition, but preaching to the choir. A healthy sense of shamanistic diversity can help us stitch together the coalitions we need to do effective political work. It enables me simultaneously to insist on the need for women to separate from men, to commit the patriarchal heresy of putting women first, and to assert occasional kindred bondings with communities other than my own.

IRREGULAR RITES FOR PROTEST AND CELEBRATION

Let us examine a few more patches to convey a more tangible sense of how my path has been unfolding. Some rituals that run through my life may help reveal the rites of a nonreligious, political feminist spirituality. Look at this wildly multicolored, glittering collection of pieces. They are the residue that warms me from my participation in the National March on Washington for Lesbian and Gay Rights. More than a protest march, it was an enormous tribal gathering, a cultural crossroads for so many of us who cross over the bars of the prisons of gender and demand to be free.

Women and men from the extremely outrageous to the adamantly assimilated assembled our collective presences in a great semi-chaotic festival of
our right to love. I met Ahdamah, a lithe bearded fairy of a man, wearing
a gathered skirt of brown and green camouflage-print fabric. Intrigued by
his band of brothers all wearing these skirts over their blue jeans, I asked
for an explanation. Unexpected tears welled up when I heard, "We want
to reclaim the colors of the mother earth from the desecration of the military's use of them to hide violence and promote war." A shaman if I ever
met one. For most of the hundreds of thousands of us there, that event
was a powerful ceremony, giving us strength to go back to our scattered
locations and renew our diverse ways of working for social and personal
change. It was a dazzling coalition, bringing together and making visible to
each other a network wider than our individual daily connections.

As I feasted on the sight of so many of us, I heard echoing in my mind
shouts and songs from another, earlier time. I had been here two decades
ago on my twenty-first birthday, that traditional American rite of passage,
for a most untraditional rite—the first march on Washington to end the
war in Vietnam. The next day I visited the Vietnam War Monument and
recalled that earlier tribal outpouring, somberly noting how many more
years and deaths on both sides had occurred before the war's end. An
exhilarating sense of connection between these two events stirred within
me. I caught a fleeting glimpse of a slender silver thread of hope and
determination running through time, hovering in air. I felt again the
alchemy of rage fueling hope, laughing with the memory of how we danced
to chants by Allan Ginsberg and the Fugs as we concentrated on levitating
the Pentagon. We may not have literally levitated the Pentagon that October day in 1967, but we levitated our spirits and our resolve. I thought of
the camouflaged young men we had tried to bring home then and the
camouflage-skirted, flaming faggots I had just met. We are a patchwork
network of kindred tribes, I realized, and we are still coming into a sense
of our own power.

The movement communities that intertwine on my spiritual path would
never all agree, yet they constitute a free-lance band of visionaries who try
to live their way out from under various oppressions. Our various gatherings
also function as doorways into alternative communities for individuals just
beginning to seek out other ways of living. Over the two decades between
my visits to Washington there have emerged numerous large and small
women's gatherings—especially music festivals and conferences—that
become temporary towns in a changing sense of society. Of course, there
are many problems and shortcomings. But it has been sophisticated in the
repression of the eighties to look condescendingly at these countercultural
comings and goings. There is a history to honor here, a tradition that guides
us to continue creating forms that meet current needs.

Just as these large ever-evolving rituals nourish me, so do countless
smaller and many solitary rites. A major hallmark of feminism is the vast

renaming of our Selves that women are taking up. This process (which includes reformists and radicals) reflects a rising tide of women's consciousness that surges still despite ebbs and flows that are the organic rhythms of any life force. A splendid sense of the sacredness of our female bodies is unfolding. See this red ribbon here in the quilt? It marks my fascination with menstruation, which has led me to explore new territory with women. As we evolve our own menstrual customs, I feel myself linked with a long line of women who have—sometimes for a lifetime, sometimes only for a moment—known truths larger than patriarchal denigration. I have drawn women's symbols with my menses on pages of scripture calling us unclean and known that some ancient sisters hoped and conspired for days like these. Some rituals are invented as needed and not repeated. Some recur often, like the candle I light on my desk when I write. Its flame marks the presence of energy and elemental mystery, lighting my way into the labyrinth of my own thoughts.

There is so much grief and horror in this world that must be faced, lived with and through, that rituals cultivating the ability to savor and share bliss are a survival necessity. Last summer I was able to grow towering sunflowers that called me out to dance around them, singing stanzas from William Blake:

> Ah, Sunflower! weary of time,
> Who countest the steps of the Sun,
> Seeking after that sweet golden clime,
> Where the traveler's journey is done.
> (Kazin, 110)

Their huge, bowed, seeded heads awed me. I imagined them secretly following the moon at night, linking their sun-tracking with my own meditations on the moon's phases.

This flood of thoughts spiraled around into a familiar longing to ask my mother about her gardens, to be able to talk to her again, to have her alive again. All the paradoxes in the world do not fully address the impossibility of her being gone. She was a shaman of the extraordinary ordinary world, bringing lobster claws home from a restaurant on her visit to me in Boston to show middle Georgia Sunday school children who had never seen such a shellfish. Her God was a god in nature, like the hymn, "In the rustling grass I hear him pass, he speaks to me everywhere." Her god was love enacted in the everyday. Her motto was from Proverbs 17:22, "A merry heart doeth good like a medicine." And somehow this medicine woman understood that her feminist daughter, who could no longer go to church, nevertheless was keeping company with her in some strange faith that ran so deep it does not depend on creeds or names.

When my family sat with her as she died, a conscious natural death, and I held her hand, I had the strangest, unexpected feeling that I saw her go somewhere. This is not an event my conscious mind exactly knows how to encompass, nor do I try to make it do so. I remember knowing I would never forget it. It is paired in my heart with a moment at the end of the graveside part of her funeral. I saw my young niece and nephew break free from the receiving line and dance on top of nearby gravestones, sun glinting in their hair, sparrows alighting and chirping. The peace that came to me for a moment then and the ability to savor it in the midst of such a great loss was a skill and a free thought that I knew she had first taught me: Not to close the self to the possibility of joy.

My quilt shimmers with such moments. With them the path I follow is never ultimately lonely. They are life lines connecting me with a clan of friends and lovers, of strangers and even sometimes apparent enemies. This quilt is not perfect; it is not always secure. It does not always keep out despair, for it can slip off sometimes in the night. But it is enough. For it is a continual work, as I gather new pieces and give some away, rework some places and discover new meanings in others. In its mix of chaos and order, there is an eclectic integrity that I work to maintain.

CHRISTIANITY AS COMPOST

Since a freethinker can surely mix her metaphors, let me end by spiraling back to the beginning and tell you how my Christianity has become compost. I was "heard to speech" (in that way Nelle Morton chronicled for us) with this metaphor in a Judaism and Feminism Consultation. We were discussing the issue of connection to one's religious past. Knowing I no longer identified as Christian, one of the women asked, "But you do draw on it in some ways still, don't you? Would you speak of it as your roots?" I paused, searching for words. That phrase has never felt quite right to me. From the root springs the tree; they are a continuous growth. The ecology of my spiritual life is more complex than that, with moments of radical discontinuity and continuity. "Compost," I heard myself say. And again, with an increasing sense of satisfaction that at last I had found the apt metaphor, "Compost. My Christianity has become compost." It has decayed and died, becoming a mix of animate and inanimate, stinking rot and released nutrients. Humus. Fertilizer. The part of organic life cycles with which everyone gets uncomfortable and skips over in the rush to rhapsodize growth and progress and blossoms and fruition and rebirth. But in between is the dark, rich mysterious stage, when life decomposes into soil. It is a sacred time—like the dark no-moon new-moon in my meditations, that liminal stage and dangerous essential passage between the last slender waning crescent and the first shred of a shining waxing new one. Compost. A pile of organic substance transforming into a ground, a matrix into which we must mix other elements for the next seeds to sprout. Other vital forces must wet and warm the matrix. And additional deaths, so inevitable in changing/ living, will need to feed this ground. Humus. It is from this that we are named human, to acknowledge our connection to the earth, the place where we stand in the vast living universe. If our traditions and symbols are truly part of living, then they are organic and will have rhythms of living and dying.

My current path is one that must acknowledge such mysteries mixed with certainties, without enshrining and codifying them, or setting up authorities to administer them. Does my "tradition" exist "after patriarchy," engaged as this pathway is in simultaneously ignoring, resisting, dismantling, burying, and transforming it? In a linear historical way, "after patriarchy" is something I will not see in my lifetime. But I live now in some moments that know the ultimate voidness of patriarchy. Moments in which we have withdrawn from patriarchy into another creation so profoundly that it has no substance. There are traditions, I think, that do not survive this transformation out of their patriarchal bodies and remain intact as we have known them. But perhaps they become compost too, and does it matter if their old names are no longer all that is on our lips? *Tradition* comes from a Latin root meaning to "hand over." If we hand over our traditions to feminist freethinking, at least what will survive will be stories that spark liberation and can be shared with each other as we meet on the road.

NOTES

1. Mary Daly has created the words *Nag-gnostic* and *Nag-gnosticism. Nag-gnosticism* is "the philosophy of those who Sense with certainty the reality of transcendental knowledge and at the same time never cease to Nag our Selves and Others with recurrent awareness of questions and uncertainties; the philosophy of those who overcome the pseudodichotomy between transcendence and immanence, between otherworldliness and worldliness" (Daly 1987, 83).

2. In *An Essay on Theological Method,* Gordon Kaufman describes the "moments" of constructive theology. For Kaufman, the first moment is cosmological, emphasizing God's relationship to the world. But he acknowledges that another approach might be one in which "the first moment would be an analysis or interpretation of the self" (Kaufman, 67, n.18).

3. Since my own journey has been away from Christianity, let me acknowledge two examples of such transcendence within that tradition. Branches of Afro-American Christianity have at times directly catalyzed personal and political liberation and challenges to racism. Rita Brock cites the effect Christianity sometimes has had in challenging male dominance when Christianity moves into other cultural contexts, such as Asia.

4. As Radhakrishnan comments on this chant:

This is a song of joy. The manifold diversity of life is attuned to a single harmony. A lyrical and rapturous embrace of the universe is the result. The liberated soul filled with delight *recognizes its oneness with the subject and the object,* the foodeater and the food *and the principle which unites them* (Radhakrishnan, 562, emphasis added).

5. As Grahn points out:

It is easy, especially for white people, to imitate and romanticize this by borrowing heavily from what they have read about other cultures while totally ignoring the ritual history of their own Euro-American culture. In our society, as in any, the "shamanic" office is a charged, potent, awe-inspiring, and even fear-inspiring person who takes true risks by crossing over into other worlds (Grahn, 44).

6. I have had extended conversations about ways to meet this dilemma with many feminist freethinkers, particularly Linda Barufaldi, Mary Daly, Janet Lake, and Beverly Smith.

WORKS CITED

Brock, Rita Nakashima. *Journeys by Heart: A Christology of Erotic Power.* New York: Crossroad, 1988.

Christ, Carol. "Why Women Need the Goddess: Phenomenological, Psychological, and Political Reflections." *The Politics of Women's Spirituality: Essays on the Rise of Spiritual Power within the Feminist Movement.* Ed. Charlene Spretnak. Garden City, New York: Anchor Press, 1982.

Culpepper, Emily Erwin. "Mermaids: A Symbol for Female Identified Psychic Self-Reflection." *Woman of Power: A Magazine of Feminism, Spirituality, and Politics* 1 (1984):42-45.

———. "Simone de Beauvoir and the Revolt of the Symbols." *Trivia: A Journal of Ideas* 6 (1984-85):6-32.

———. "Ancient Gorgons: A Face for Contemporary Women's Rage." *Woman of Power* 3 (1986):22-24, 40.

———. "Contemporary Goddess Thealogy: A Sympathetic Critique." *Shaping New Vision: Gender and Values in American Culture.* Vol. 2, The Harvard Women's Studies in Religion Series. Ed. Clarissa Atkinson, Margaret Miles, and Constance Buchanan. Ann Arbor: University of Michigan Press, 1987.

———. "New Tools for Theology: Writings by Women of Color." *Journal of Feminist Studies in Religion* 4, 2 (1988): 39-50.

Daly, Mary. *Beyond God the Father: Toward a Philosophy of Women's Liberation* (1973). Boston: Beacon Press, 1985.

———. *Webster's First New Intergalactic Wickedary of the English Language.* With Jane Caputi. Boston: Beacon Press, 1987.

Fung, Paul F., and George D. Fung, trans. *The Sutra of the Sixth Patriarch on the Pristine Orthodox Dharma.* San Francisco: Buddha's Universal Church, 1964.

Grahn, Judy. *Another Mother Tongue: Gay Words, Gay Worlds.* Boston: Beacon Press, 1984.

Kaufman, Gordon. *An Essay on Theological Method.* American Academy of Religion Studies in Religion. Ed. Stephen D. Crites. Missoula, Montana: Scholars Press, 1975.

Kazin, Alfred, ed. *The Portable Blake.* New York: The Viking Press, 1946.

Morgan, Robin, ed. "New York Coven Statement." *Sisterhood Is Powerful.* New York: Vintage Books, 1970.

Morton, Nelle. *The Journey Is Home.* Boston: Beacon Press, 1985.
Radhakrishnan, S. *The Principal Upanishads.* New York: Humanities Press, 1953.
Starhawk. *The Spiral Dance: A Rebirth of the Ancient Religion of the Great Goddess.* San Francisco: Harper and Row, 1979.
Walker, Alice. "In Search of Our Mothers' Gardens" (1974). In *In Search of Our Mothers' Gardens: Womanist Prose.* New York: Harcourt Brace Jovanovich, 1983.

Contributors

Paula M. Cooey is Associate Professor of Religion at Trinity University. She received her Ph.D. in the Study of Religion from Harvard University and her M.T.S. in Theology from Harvard Divinity School. She is co-editor with Sharon Farmer and Mary Ellen Ross of the book *Embodied Love: Sensuality and Relationship as Feminist Values* and author of *Nature and Divine Destiny in the Works of Jonathan Edwards: A Systematic Analysis,* as well as numerous articles on feminism, women, and theology. She is a Director of the Southwest Commission on Religious Studies, 1990 President for the Southwest Regional American Academy of Religion, and member of the Editorial Review Board for the *Journal of Feminist Studies in Religion.*

Emily Culpepper represents a large number of women who do not participate in organized religions, but whose feminism is deeply spiritual and political, reclaiming elements from various traditions. She received her M.Div. from Harvard University in 1974, and the Th.D. from the same institution in 1983. Her publications include numerous articles and book chapters on feminism and spirituality, and she is currently completing a book tentatively titled *Revolt of the Symbols: Feminist Thealogy and Philosophy.*

William R. Eakin is Consultant for the Marshall T. Steel Center in the Study of Religion and Philosophy. He received M.A. degrees in philosophy from Baylor University and the University of California at Davis. He was a Dialogue Group Leader with the Liberation Theology Dialogue Group of the 1987 meeting of the Buddhist-Christian Society and 1989 President of the Arkansas Philological Association. His publications include the introductory essay for the book *Thomas Reid's Lectures on Natural Theology (1780)* and numerous articles and book chapters in epistemology, literature, and spirituality. He is co-editor with Jay McDaniel and Charles Birch of *Liberating Life: Contemporary Approaches to Ecological Theology* (Orbis Books).

Rita M. Gross is Associate Professor in the Department of Philosophy and Religious Studies at the University of Wisconsin-Eau Claire and has served as a Faculty Visiting Professor at Kansai University of Foreign

Studies, Hirakata City, Japan, and a Visiting Faculty Member at Nairopa Institute in Boulder, Colorado. A Buddhist, she has been active as a lecturer and panelist and has written extensively on Buddhism and feminism. She is author of the book *Worldviews: An Introductory Text in World Religions,* editor of *Beyond Androcentrism: New Essays on Women and Religion,* and co-editor with Nancy A. Falk of *Unspoken Worlds: Women's Religious Lives in Non-Western Cultures.* Her work *Buddhism and Feminism: Toward Their Mutual Transformation* is in progress.

Lina Gupta is Assistant Professor and Lecturer with the Department of Asian Studies at California State University in Long Beach and Northridge. She received the Ph.D. in Asian and Comparative Philosophy from Claremont Graduate School and her Master of Arts in Philosophy from the University of Calcutta, India. She has participated in numerous conferences on women in religion, Asian and comparative philosophy, and Advaita Vedanta. Her publications include articles on Samskara, Buddhism, and Sikhism.

Riffat Hassan is Professor and Chairperson of the Religious Studies Program at the University of Louisville, Kentucky. She writes on women and Islam from a tradition which she describes as rigidly patriarchal even to the present time. "So far as I know," says Hassan, "I am the only Muslim woman 'theologian' who has been involved in a systematic theological exploration of women-related issues in the Islamic tradition."

Jay B. McDaniel is Director of the Marshall T. Steel Center for the Study of Religion and Philosophy at Hendrix College (Arkansas) and Associate Professor of Religion at that college. He received the Ph.D. from Claremont Graduate School, specializing in the dialogue between Christianity and Buddhism. His articles have appeared in numerous publications, and he is author of the books *Of God and Pelicans* and *Earth, Sky, Gods, and Mortals.* He is also co-editor of *Liberating Life: Contemporary Approaches to Ecological Theology.*

Judith Plaskow is Associate Professor of Religious Studies at Manhattan College. Co-founder and co-editor of the *Journal of Feminist Studies in Religion,* Dr. Plaskow has authored numerous articles on Jewish feminism, theology, and spirituality. She is author of the book *Sex, Sin, and Grace: Women's Experience and the Theologies of Reinhold Niebuhr and Paul Tillich,* co-editor with Carol P. Christ of *Womanspirit Rising: A Feminist Reader in Religion,* and editor of *Women and Religion: 1972.*

Ines Talamantez, Associate Professor of Religious Studies at the University of California, Santa Barbara, is a scholar of Native American religions and philosophies and is herself of Mescalero Apache and Sioux descent.

She received the Ph.D. in Comparative Literature and Ethnopoetics from the University of California, San Diego, and has lectured widely on women and female rites of passage in various Native American traditions. Her published works include *K'ehgosone: Native American Ritual Texts, Tse'ghi: Navajo Night Chant,* and *The Goddess Within, 'Isanaklesh Gotal: Introducing Apache Girls to the World of Spiritual and Cultural Values* (in press).

Delores S. Williams, received her Ph.D. from Union Theological Seminary in New York and has taught at Drew University in Madison, N.J., at Fisk University in Nashville, Tennessee, and at Harvard University. She is currently Associate Professor of Theology and Culture at Union Theological Seminary. Her many articles on womanist theology have appeared in *The Feminist Journal of Religious Studies, Christian Century, Christianity and Crisis,* and *Sojourners.*